Amin Saikal is Director of the Centre for Arab and Islamic Studies (the Middle East and Central Asia), Professor of Political Science and Public Policy Fellow at the Australian National University. He has been a visiting fellow at Princeton University and the University of Cambridge, as well as at Sussex University's Institute of Development Studies. He has also been a Rockefeller Foundation Fellow in International Relations. He is an elected Fellow of the Academy of Social Sciences in Australia, and was awarded the Order of Australia (AM) in 2006 for services to the international community, and to education through the development of the Centre for Arab and Islamic Studies, and as an author and advisor. He is the author of a number of works on the Middle East, Central Asia and Russia, including *Islam and the West: Conflict or Cooperation?* (2003); *The Rise and Fall of the Shah: Iran from Autocracy to Religious Rule* (2009); and *Modern Afghanistan: A History of Struggle and Survival* (I.B.Tauris, 2012). He has published numerous book chapters and journal articles as well as providing op-ed pieces in major international dailies, including the *International Herald Tribune*, the *New York Times*, the *Wall Street Journal*, the *Guardian* and the *Globe and Mail*.

ZONE OF CRISIS

AFGHANISTAN, PAKISTAN, IRAN AND IRAQ

AMIN SAIKAL

I.B. TAURIS

LONDON · NEW YORK

Published in 2014 by I.B.Tauris & Co Ltd
6 Salem Road, London W2 4BU
175 Fifth Avenue, New York NY 10010
www.ibtauris.com

Distributed in the United States and Canada Exclusively by Palgrave Macmillan
175 Fifth Avenue, New York NY 10010

ISBN: 978 1 78076 319 4
eISBN: 978 0 85773 512 6

A full CIP record for this book is available from the British Library
A full CIP record is available from the Library of Congress

Library of Congress Catalog Card Number: available

Typeset in Minion Pro by Free Range Book Design & Production Limited

Printed and bound in Sweden by ScandBook AB

CONTENTS

PREFACE

The area comprising Afghanistan, Pakistan, Iran and Iraq has historically been a zone of conflict, major power rivalry and foreign interventions. These variables have interacted effectively with overlapping internal circumstances of the states in the zone to make the region highly volatile in the context of changing regional and international situations.

The idea for this book came to me two years ago as part of my research focus on these four countries. The considerations that motivated me to take on the task of writing about them in one volume was that whilst a great deal of both scholarly and popular material in the form of books, chapters, journal articles, reports and feature articles have been published about each of the states, there has been little or no attempt to study them within a zone where their landscapes have been shaped by as many common factors as those that have set them apart from one another in various distinct ways.

The book does not aim to provide a theoretical discourse. It essentially seeks to furnish an analysis of the factors that have played a key role in determining their past and present, and that are likely to influence their future development within an integrated geostrategic zone. Nor does it attempt to provide a detailed account of all the complex dimensions of life in each country. The main objective is to provide a snapshot of the most salient features that underpin the operation of state and society in each of the constituent states and across their geographical zone to inform those – in both the public and private sectors – who are engaged in policymaking, journalism, education, and for those seeking general knowledge.

In writing this book, I am deeply indebted to a number of individuals, institutions and sources of funding. First and foremost, I owe much gratitude to two hard-working and extremely able research assistants:

Jonathan Cheng and Stephanie Wright. Without their compilation, editing and footnoting skills, I would have found it difficult to complete this book and present it in its current form. I cannot praise them enough, and I am especially grateful to Stephanie for her brilliance and dedication. I am also grateful to Aly Zaman for reading the Pakistan chapter, and to Dr Grigol Ubiria for doing a final check of the manuscript. In the course of completing this book, I have been privileged to be able to gain much insight into the situation in each of the countries and across the region from a number of scholars, analysts, policymakers and political figures who have been directly involved in the affairs of the states that the book addresses. They are too numerous to name, and the ones who should be named hold positions that could make them vulnerable to unwarranted pressure in one form or another. However, they all know who they are.

Further, I remain thankful to the Australian National University (ANU) and its Centre for Arab and Islamic Studies (the Middle East and Central Asia) – CAIS – which I have headed as the foundation director since 1994, for having provided me with valuable support in my research and other academic preoccupations over the years. In recent times, no particular individual has been as supportive as the university's Vice-Chancellor, Professor Ian Young. I must also thank two of our former professional staff in CAIS – Mrs Carol Laslett and Ms Leila Kouatly – who until recently assisted me selflessly in many administrative responsibilities that enabled me to have the necessary time to devote to this book and a number of other concurrent research efforts. I am also grateful to the Australian Research Council for its Discovery Grant that helped fund this and several other research projects.

Last but by no means least, I owe an enormous debt of gratitude to my wife, Mary-Louise Hickey, for being such a wonderful companion every step of the way and in every aspect of my life, including reading a draft of this book as a very accomplished editor. Without her love, support and patience, as well as those of my three daughters, Rahima, Samra and Amina, I would have been a lonely scholar in the wilderness.

Amin Saikal
December 2013

ABBREVIATIONS

AAC	Assembly of Assertive Clerics
AIOC	Anglo-Iranian Oil Company
ANA	Afghan National Army
ANDS	Afghanistan National Development Strategy
ANP	Afghan National Police
CENTO	Central Treaty Organisation
CIA	Central Intelligence Agency
CPA	Coalition Provisional Authority
CSP	Civil Service of Pakistan
ECC	Electoral Complaints Commission
EU	European Union
FATA	Federally Administered Tribal Areas
GCC	Gulf Cooperation Council
GDP	Gross domestic product
IAEA	International Atomic Energy Agency
IEC	Independent Election Committee
INA	Iraqi National Accord
INC	Iraqi National Congress
IRG	Iranian Revolutionary Guard
IRP	Islamic Republican Party
ISAF	International Security Assistance Force
ISCI	Islamic Supreme Council of Iraq
ISI	Inter-Services Intelligence (Pakistan)
KDP	Kurdistan Democratic Party
KRG	Kurdistan Regional Government
LeT	*Lashkar-e-Taiba*
LGO	Local Government Ordinance
MP	Member of Parliament

NATO   North Atlantic Treaty Organisation
NGO   Non-governmental organisation
NIOC   National Iranian Oil Company
NPT   Nuclear Non-Proliferation Treaty
NWFP   North-West Frontier Province
OIC   Organisation of Islamic Cooperation
OPEC   Organisation of Petroleum Exporting Countries
PDPA   People's Democratic Party of Afghanistan
PDS   Public Distribution System
PKK   Kurdistan Workers' Party
PML–N   Pakistan Muslim League (under Nawaz Sharif)
PML–Q   Pakistan Muslim League (Quaid-e Azam Group)
PPP   Pakistan People's Party
PUK   Patriotic Union of Kurdistan
SCIRI   Supreme Council for Islamic Revolution in Iraq
SGSR   Secretary-General's Special Representative (Afghanistan)
TTP   *Tehrik-i-Taliban Pakistan*
UAE   United Arab Emirates
UN   United Nations
UNAMA   United Nations Assistance Mission in Afghanistan
UNAMI   United Nations Assistance Mission for Iraq
UNDP   United Nations Development Programme
UNODC   United Nations Office on Drugs and Crime
WMD   Weapons of mass destruction

The Afghanistan, Pakistan, Iran and Iraq zone

INTRODUCTION

A Mosaic Region: Past and Present

Situated at the crossroads of Asia and Europe, and at the intersection of Central, South and West Asia, Afghanistan, Pakistan, Iran and Iraq form a strategic landmass that has historically been the site of both internal turmoil and violence, and outside invasions and interferences in one form or another. At times, deep in the past, the peoples inhabiting these modern-day states either ruled their own great empires or were part of one another's domains. The region comprising the territories of modern Afghanistan, Pakistan, Iran and Iraq stretched from the Indus River to the Caucasus, and from the shores of the Persian Gulf* to the northernmost border of Uzbekistan and Tajikistan at the Oxus River, and was the birthplace of many great empires and ancient civilisations that rose and fell long before the advent of Islam in the early seventh century. The Median Confederation (725–550 BC) was conquered by the armies of the Persian King Cyrus the Great, founder of the Achaemenid Empire (550–330 BC), an empire which was in turn destroyed by Alexander the Great, whose death resulted in the formation of the Seleucid Empire and soon after its replacement by the Parthian Empire (250 BC–AD 225). The last of the great pre-Islamic empires, that of the Sassanids, came to power in the wake of dynastic power struggles among the Parthians. The Sassanids ruled for four centuries until their ultimate defeat by the invading Arab-Islamic armies in AD 651.

The cultural heritage of the region was further enriched and, some might argue, undermined by cross-cutting invasions and influences

---

* Notwithstanding the Iranian–Arab controversy, the term 'Persian Gulf' is used throughout this book because of its common historical and contemporary usage.

throughout history. The influx of Hellenic culture and ideas and the introduction of East Asian philosophies (such as Buddhism, which first arrived in Afghanistan in 305 BC, and was subsequently expanded to the west of the country by Mongol armies), followed by the spread of Arab and Islamic influences, and finally the invasion by the Turkic forces of Timur the Lame of today's Iran, Afghanistan and Pakistan in the fourteenth century and Iraq in the next century, were all critical in shaping the evolving cultural and intellectual landscape of the region. The area itself has also been a wellspring of religions and thought, giving rise to Zoroastrianism, the oldest monotheistic faith from the sixth century BC, before the latter's eclipse by Islam in the early seventh century AD. It is no surprise, therefore, that the region today remains defined by its intrinsically mosaic character. Afghanistan, for example, formerly an important link in the Silk Road trading network, is known today as the 'Central Asian roundabout'.

Major Power Rivalry and Foreign Interference

In modern times, the region's constituent states have been repeatedly invaded or intervened in by major powers such as Tsarist and Soviet Russia, Great Britain and the United States, with each seeking, often in competition with one another, to redirect the domestic and foreign policy objectives and priorities of the constituent states in accordance with their individual geopolitical and ideological preferences. Ultimately, none of these powers have been able to achieve their goals entirely to their satisfaction, and all have, at times, bowed out of the arena in one way or another, at high costs to themselves and to the subjected peoples. This proved to be the case first with the British, whose many decades of colonial domination and interference ultimately bore little fruit. The same proved true for Tsarist and Soviet Russia, whose empires collapsed and ambitions shrank during the Anglo-Russian rivalry from the mid-nineteenth century to the Second World War and, subsequently, during the course of the US–Soviet superpower competition that lasted from shortly after the Second World War to the disintegration of the Soviet Union in 1991. As for the United States, since its rise to global hegemony from the end of the Second World War, its efforts in taming Afghanistan, Pakistan, Iran and Iraq at different times and in different manners, according to its preferences and in defiance of other powers, seem to have been equally unrewarding. It is still unclear as to what extent China's emergence as a global and regional power, with its growing need for natural resources and concomitant quest for strategic influence, will impact on the countries that are the focus of this book.

Divided Societies and Historical Legacies

Shaped by different legacies, the modern states of Afghanistan, Pakistan, Iran and Iraq nevertheless retain many similar characteristics as a result of their common historical heritage and experiences. All four are defined by the mosaic composition of their societies, which are made up of various ethnic, tribal, linguistic, sectarian and cultural units. Their territorial boundaries have often been shaped by Western influence, with the result that their social entities or micro-societies frequently straddle national lines and retain cross-border ties with neighbouring populations. Tribal, clan, family and sectarian divisions remain prominent, especially along the Afghanistan–Pakistan border, and in both countries the ethnic cleavage continues to spill over into the political realm.

Two case studies, discussed later in this book, illuminate the on-going importance of cross-border ties in these states today. Pashtun nationalism is one important phenomenon that has the potential to disrupt and even cause the fragmentation of both Pakistan and Afghanistan. Iranian influence among Iraq's Shi'a population is another highly important example elaborated here, with a focus on the historical interplay between the Iraqi and Iranian Shi'as. Both phenomena provide insight into the perennial challenges faced by all four states and societies as a result of invested cross-interests and the continuing involvement of outside actors.

Internal divisions and sectarian rivalries form a common theme across the region, but it is Afghanistan and Pakistan that are truly the lands of minorities. Ethnic Pashtuns form the largest (but not majority) cluster in Afghanistan, followed by significant Tajik, Hazara, Turkmen, Uzbek and Nooristani minorities. The Punjabis form the largest ethnic group in Pakistan, followed by Sindhi, Pashtun, Baluchi and Seraiki minorities. The ethnic composition of Iraq and Iran is somewhat less complex, made up of clear Arab and Persian majorities respectively. Nevertheless, the presence of Kurdish minorities in both countries, Turkmen in Iraq, and Azeris, Baluchis and Arabs in Iran, complicate the ethnic landscape.

Sectarian Divisions

Religious cleavages, the most prominent of which is the Shi'a–Sunni division among the Muslim community, further fragment the populations of all four states. The schism dates from a dispute over the leadership (*khalifa*) of the Muslim community (*ummah*) following the death of Prophet Muhammad in AD 632. Those who supported the Prophet's cousin and son-in-law, Ali ibn Talib, as the rightful leader (caliph), became known as the *Shi'atu 'Ali* ('the party of 'Ali'; later, the Shi'a). The Shi'as held that only 'Ali and his direct descendants (*imams*) could be the rightful leaders of the *ummah*. The majority, on the other hand, who favoured the succession of the Prophet's societal leadership by his four companions in the order of seniority, with 'Ali coming last, rejected the notion of birthright and insisted that the caliph be elected by the *ummah* itself. Those who held this opinion became known as the 'people of the tradition' (*sunna*), or Sunnis.

Although the instigating cause of the Sunni–Shi'a division was more political than doctrinal, real differences in religious and political outlooks have, over time, become deeply ingrained in the two sectarian communities. Addressing these differences is somewhat complicated by the fact that both sects encompass a large number of sub-groups and traditions: Shi'a Islam includes three dominant branches, each with their own legal school (Twelver, Zaidi and Ismaili), and the Sunni world is similarly divided into four dominant schools of thought (Hanafi, Hanbali, Maliki and Shafi'i). Despite the complexity and nuances within both sects, a number of important differences between Shi'a and Sunni Islam may be broadly identified. In Shi'a Islam, the emphasis on the lineage of 'Ali and, in Twelver Islam, the doctrine of the Occultation (which holds that the last *imam*, or Mahdi, was born and disappeared (869–941), and that his authority is to be exercised *in absentia* by clerics), has contributed to the evolution of religious hierarchy and the institutionalisation of clerical authority. Shi'a clerics, particularly those who have attained a high rank, are believed to be divinely guided and inspired, and their rulings (*fatwas*) are considered binding. This is not the case in Sunni Islam, which lacks an established clergy and where the rulings of religious scholars (*ulama*) are largely recognised as fallible and non-binding. Lacking the strict hierarchy of the Shi'a religious establishment, Sunni Islam has produced a substantial number of breakaway leaders whose authority derives less from religious education than from personal charisma and popular appeal.

Today, the Sunni–Shi'a split is the most prominent source of tension in the Muslim world. The minority sect, whether Shi'a or Sunni, is often ill-treated, discriminated against, or repressed by the majority sect. In some cases, however, the reverse has been true, as in Iraq under Saddam Hussein's Sunni leadership. Iraq and Iran are unusual in the fact that they are the only countries in the world, along with Bahrain and the highly secularised, former Soviet Republic of Azerbaijan, with a Shi'a majority population. With some 15 per cent of the global Muslim population belonging to the Shi'a sect, Iraq's and Iran's Shi'a communities represent around 60 and 90 per cent of their countries' populations respectively. The remainder of Iraq's and Iran's populations are overwhelmingly Sunni, although very small minorities of non-Muslims are present in both. Afghanistan and Pakistan, on the other hand, are predominantly Sunni states, with majorities of around 80 and 85 per cent respectively, and the remainder predominantly Shi'a in each case.

A Misunderstood Past

Modern-day tensions and divisions, therefore, have a long history in the region. Yet despite the critical importance of historical legacies in understanding present-day Afghanistan, Pakistan, Iran and Iraq, the past has often been overlooked or misunderstood by outsiders, with frequently serious consequences. An improved understanding of the region among foreign policymakers is imperative to enhancing prospects for stability and mutually beneficial international relations. Indeed, deleterious foreign influence and involvement pervades the histories of all four states, and remains prominent today.

We can see this first in the case of Afghanistan, which, since its consolidation as a modern state from 1747, has been perennially subjected to invasions and interference by foreign powers, although in the early decades of its existence it too had invaded neighbouring territories. Afghanistan is the only country to have been invaded by each of the three great powers of their times: Great Britain, the Soviet Union and the United States. This raises the question: what is it about Afghanistan that has made it so much the focus of regional and world players, and for so long? Throughout the nineteenth century and into the twentieth, Great Britain and Russia competed for influence in the country. During the Cold War, Afghanistan was subjected to geostrategic competition between the two superpowers at the time, the United States and the USSR, with the latter gaining the upper hand, given Afghanistan's geographical proximity to it. Since 2001, it has been the United States and its North Atlantic Treaty Organisation (NATO) and non-NATO allies that have struggled to shape the Afghan political and strategic landscapes. This has been accompanied by a number of regional players also competing for influence in the war-weary country for often conflicting geopolitical interests.

The involvement of so many external players has helped to ensure that the Afghan state has remained weak, and Afghanistan's historical legacy of local strongmen remains a critical feature of its political landscape. Pakistan's support of the *Mujahideen* commander Gulbuddin Hekmatyar, and later the Taliban and their affiliates (including the Hekmatyar group), provides a recent and ongoing example of this. The persistent power vacuum in the wake of the US-led invasion of 2001 gave rise to a new generation of 'strongmen' of various shades and capacities competing for control of Afghan lands.

Founded in 1947 and a by-product of Indian independence from Britain, modern-day Pakistan is, in effect, an accident of history. Pakistan was the paradoxical product of the efforts of the All India Muslim League, which had pushed its agenda in anticipation of concessions within the framework of a united India. Since the unexpected partition, Pakistan has found itself at odds with its larger and more powerful neighbour, India, particularly over the contested territories of Jammu and Kashmir. Pakistan's strategic imperative with regard to India has defined its history since its emergence as a state.

For most of Pakistan's history, the military and Inter-Services Intelligence (ISI) have consistently played a central role in holding the country together and influencing its politics, while civilian governments have remained corrupt, self-centred and nepotistic. Whenever civilian leaders have come to power through what has transpired as quasi-democratic phases, they have found themselves largely at the mercy of the military and ISI, and have done whatever possible to expand their political and financial largesse and patronage, despite incurring the public's resentment. The export of Sunni extremism has also become an entrenched feature of Pakistani politics since the military rule of General Zia ul-Haq (1977–88), and has been used both against India and in support of perceived Pakistani interests in Afghanistan, although Islamabad has always been in a state of denial about this. The May 2013 democratically elected government of Prime Minister Nawaz Sharif may change the equation, but serious doubts linger about its chances of success.

Modern Iraq, a country shaped very much by British colonialist designs in the 1920s, has undergone a reversal of some of its most persistent trends since the US-led invasion of 2003. Historically a rich and relatively strong modernising state under the long years of Saddam Hussein's dictatorial leadership, especially in the 1970s and 1980s, the political power vacuum in post-invasion Iraq strengthened various societal groups at the expense of the state. After his toppling, however, the backlash against his brutal regime became tragically apparent. The Kurds and the Shi'a Arab majority, marginalised and persecuted under Saddam Hussein's Sunni-centred Arab Ba'athist regime, emerged as powerful players in Iraqi politics, deepening sectarian divisions and impeding national unity. These sectarian groups are in turn often divided into competing factions, such as the Iranian-supported Islamic Supreme Council of Iraq (ISCI) (representing some of Iraq's middle-class Shi'as) and the Sadrists (representing some of the more marginalised and lower-class Shi'as). These divisions have become extremely entrenched in post-invasion Iraq through the spilling of blood over time. Just as Afghanistan has served as a battleground for various outside actors by proxy, Iraq has suffered from a similar fate since the 2003 invasion and occupation of the country that lasted until the end of 2011 – a withdrawal that left unfulfilled the goal of creating a stable and democratic Iraq.

Although never directly colonised, Iran has historically been fearful of foreign intervention and often subjected to direct and indirect external influence. Like Afghanistan, Iran under the Qajar dynasty (1796–1925) was caught up in the 'Great Game', in which Great Britain and Russia competed for primacy in Central and West Asia. Foreign influence dramatically re-entered the Iranian scene in 1953 in the form of a US and British-orchestrated coup, which saw the removal of the reformist Prime Minister Mohammad Mossadegh and the reinstalment on his throne of the pro-Western Mohammad Reza Shah, who had been forced to leave Iran for a stay abroad.

Following the deposition of the Shah in the 1978–79 Revolution that brought to power the Islamic regime of Ayatollah Rohullah Khomeini, with its anti-US and anti-Israeli posture, Iran's relations with the United States and many of its allies grew tense and intrinsically adversarial. The Islamic Republic of Iran's attempt at exporting its radical Shiʻa Islamism and the American hostage crisis (4 November 1979–20 January 1981) engrained a pattern of US–Iranian hostility, reflected in both US support for Iraq during the Iran–Iraq War (1980–88) and serious political debates, particularly over Iran's nuclear programme. Iran's attempts to expand its regional influence, especially in the wake of US debacles on the Iraqi, Afghan, Lebanese and Israeli–Palestinian fronts, have also strained Tehran's relations with the neighbouring oil-rich Gulf Arab states. The election of moderate Islamist Hassan Rouhani to Iran's presidency in June 2013 raised hopes about an improvement in Iran's relations with its Gulf Arab neighbours and the West, but the obstacles remained formidable.

Dysfunctional Governance and Fragmented Elites

Dysfunctional elites characterise all four states, in various guises. Factional, fragmented and self-aggrandising elites produce nepotistic, corrupt and ineffectual governance, divorced from the desires of the people they govern and incapable of meeting many of their most pressing needs. These elites nevertheless reflect the mosaic nature of their respective societies, as well as the historical imperatives that have shaped their political actions.

Regional strongmen, dominant families and political dynasties continue to underpin the personalisation rather than institutionalisation of politics in all four countries, although in varying forms and to different degrees of magnitude. Despite the introduction of an elected presidential system under US tutelage, Afghanistan remains, as noted above, dominated by local power-holders (many of them recognised as warlords). These dynamics, together with a flawed electoral system, have acted as major factors in impeding the development of a truly representative government.

As mentioned earlier, Pakistan has perpetually oscillated between military and civilian governments. The latter are invariably dominated by family dynasties of the country's landed elites – the Bhutto–Zardari family and the Sharifs provide two examples. These clans have in the past resorted to violent actions to defend their interests against rival families. Behind the scenes of civilian government, the military and various local strongmen – some of them allied with the ruling forces and others violently opposed to them – remain important political players.

Iraq's fledgling democracy, implemented after the 2003 US invasion, is dominated by newly formed parties which represent historical constituencies from Saddam Hussein's era. Bitter rivalries within sectarian groups persist in Iraq. The US-instigated policy of de-Ba'athification, which saw the removal and marginalisation of all Iraqis formerly associated with Saddam's regime, and its place within the reconciliation process, continue to pose difficult questions for Iraq. The Iraqi situation in many ways parallels that of Afghanistan. The two share a number of variables with Pakistan, ranging from elite fragmentation and Islamic extremism to adversarial social divisions.

Since 1979, Iran's political system has been dominated by a clerical cluster whose experiences have been significantly shaped in various ways and to different extents by both the Islamic Revolution and the eight-year war with Iraq (1980–88). Wary of its neighbours, and outside powers, especially the United States and Israel, Iran is internally divided between those who push for progressive reform and those who remain entrenched in conservative beliefs. Even the core ruling elite, which has dominated the levers of power from the early years of the Islamic Republic, has grown incongruous within itself, with power and authority revolving rather than deposited with a single identifiable source, although the Iranian Supreme religious and political leader is often identified as the repository.

Foreign Intervention and Influence: A Continuing Theme

External intervention, either overt or threatened, continues to impact severely on the region. The US 'war on terror' and the American push for democratisation have affected not only the invaded countries (Afghanistan and Iraq) but have also had substantial consequences for Pakistani and Iranian domestic and foreign policies. The environment within which these four countries interact has changed dramatically since the start of the century.

Invasion and occupation have introduced new political systems into Afghanistan and Iraq, but the old political culture and practices remain pervasive in shaping the political behaviour of those in power in particular, and the polity in general. The 'democratisation programme' has taken different forms in each as a result of their distinctive national features. Afghanistan has historically been defined by a strong society in relation to a weak state; the reverse was true of Iraq in a specific way under Saddam Hussein for most of his rule. Both, however, have lacked any historical experience with democracy. In addition, the issue of reconstruction remains a priority for both states.

Pakistan and Iran, in contrast, have avoided direct intervention by American and Western powers. Both states have nevertheless experienced drastic transformations in their internal and external politics as a result of foreign occupations of neighbouring states. Pakistan initially sided with the United States in the 'war on terror', promising to support its efforts to suppress extremism in exchange for substantial American aid to the country. Subsequent developments, however, saw Pakistan revert to its pre-11 September 2001 tactics while becoming increasingly disrupted as a result of often divergent and contradictory policies. In Iran, the US invasions of Iraq and Afghanistan bolstered conservative factions, and precipitated the reversal of the progressive reforms of the late 1990s and early 2000s. An emboldened Iran, with the Iraqi government playing to its tune, exudes external strength, even if the ruling faction has become internally divided, although not to the extent to lose its grip on power.

Economic Inefficiencies

Each country has further suffered from a clear disconnect between their political goals and the economic means implemented to achieve them. Bribes for votes or political support remain widespread, and corruption and nepotism pervade both the public and private sectors. Out of the 176 countries ranked by Transparency International's Corruption Perceptions Index in 2012, Iran was placed 133rd, Pakistan 139th, Iraq 169th, and Afghanistan 174th.

All four countries also lack efficient taxation frameworks. Iraq's fiscal system, relatively advanced for the region, began to fall apart following the US-led reversal of Saddam Hussein's 1990 invasion of Kuwait, and disintegrated altogether in the wake of the 2003 US invasion of Iraq. Afghanistan has always lacked any central fiscal scheme, and both Pakistan and Iran are defined by a culture of redistribution rather than taxation. The argument has been made, for example, that only 2 per cent of Pakistanis are effectively taxed. Redistribution in the form of subsidies remains the norm in Iran, where half of the population remains tax-exempt. The loss of income from systematic taxation in these countries is compensated for in two ways: by foreign aid and oil money.

The four countries are all rentier states – that is, states that derive all or most of their national revenue from the 'renting' of indigenous resources to foreign clients or are dependent on foreign aid. The common trend of dependency and unequal relations with foreign powers highlights once more the extent to which problems in the region remain connected to the broader international environment. The governments of Afghanistan and Pakistan, for example, are largely sustained through foreign aid from the international community, the United States in particular, and private donors. Poor coordination of aid often produces negative results in these countries, either by undermining the central government (Afghanistan) or by buttressing factional interests (Pakistan). In the decade following the US invasion of Afghanistan, donor fatigue gradually set in, with the international community increasingly failing to meet aid commitments. Foreign aid is likely to continue to fall, presenting a future challenge for these states.

Iraq and Iran are oil-rich, with the vast majority of their governments' income coming from oil sales. Iran's capacity to show largesse toward its citizens depends largely on oil income, which dropped precipitously as a result of EU-imposed sanctions and the decline in oil prices in 2012. Iraq, on the other hand, has experienced a rise in oil production through reconstruction efforts. Continuing regional squabbles over Iraqi oil reserves, particularly the Kurdish–Arab struggle over Kirkuk and the Basra–Baghdad dispute over the Gulf oil supply, nevertheless raise doubts over whether Iraq's oil will prove a blessing or a curse. Black gold, it must be noted, has often been responsible for a breakdown in responsiveness between a government and its citizenry.

Islamism and Secularism

The tensions between radical Islamist and neo-fundamentalist forces on the one hand, and advocates of secularism and pluralism on the other, continue to define the political dynamics of all four states. Al-Qaeda and other counter-systemic groups drive Sunni extremism in the region, raising the risk of a backlash from Shi'a populations, central governments and the international community. These forces are strongest in the Afghanistan–Pakistan region, and operate entirely independently of the civil–political arena, especially in Afghanistan. Disunited among themselves, yet united in their desire to establish an Islamic state along the lines of that envisioned by the Afghan Taliban, the more prominent of these groups today include the forces of Hekmatyar, the *Tehrik-i-Taliban Pakistan* (Pakistani Taliban), the Afghan Taliban and *Lashkar-e-Taiba*.

The ideological fault lines between radical Islamism/neo-fundamentalism and secular pluralism are equally visible within these states' political establishments. Islam continues to provide a badge of legitimacy and unity for those seeking or having obtained political power. In Pakistan, Zia ul-Haq set a precedent for the state use of Sunni Islamism and Islamist organisations. Sharif's Pakistan Muslim League–N and elements of ISI are remnants of this tradition;

the Pakistan People's Party, on the other hand, is more in tune with secular pluralism. In Iraq, the backlash against Saddam Hussein's heavily 'secular' Ba'athist state has ensured the prominence of 'Islamism' in political discourse. This has aggravated sectarian divisions among Iraq's Sunni and Shi'a communities, with the possibility of an Iranian-like system of governance often discussed by the Shi'a Islamic Supreme Council of Iraq. In Iran, where the political establishment has developed as a bastion of struggle between traditionalist (*jihadi*) and reformist (*ijtihadi*) Islamists,[1] the split between reformist and conservative clerical leaders remains pronounced.

Complicating these tensions is the ongoing struggle between authoritarian and democratic currents. The aforementioned divisions and developments often produce convoluted governments that combine elements of both authoritarianism and democracy. Chaotic contexts breed a preference for strong governments, yet make poor soil for democracy to take root. All four countries possess some form of *electoral* democracy – holding elections, guaranteeing voting rights and having a parliament and various branches of government. *Substantive* democracy – defined by improvements in human rights, separation of powers, rule of law, civil liberty, and freedom from state coercion and violence – is nevertheless lacking in all, although in varying degrees. The tendencies outlined here have all contributed to the stifling of civil society and little progress towards substantive democracy.

The Purpose

This book addresses these issues, in a broad and at times overlapping context, on a country-by-country basis. The objective is not to provide a new theoretical framework or, for that matter, a comprehensive coverage of all aspects of the state and society in each country. It is rather to focus on a number of national, regional and international dimensions that connect and divide the four states, and that have fostered domestic volatility and serious regional complications for all of them and the world community. Overall, this book seeks to provide an understanding of the political and strategic trends in each country and the region within a historical and contemporary context. It is a formidable and complex task, but one that is necessary because of the centrality of the issues involved and the global importance of the countries discussed. Events in this critical region have the potential to destabilise the entire international system and undermine the building of a new viable post-Cold War world order. An understanding of their contexts, their modern histories and the salient variables that continue to affect each and all of them, arising from within their national and regional conditions as well as external pressure and intrusions, especially those by major powers, is therefore crucial to improving prospects for peace in the area and in the world. Each of the following chapters – which deal with Afghanistan, Pakistan, Iran and Iraq respectively – also makes potential and plausible suggestions to deal with the problems confronting these four countries.

AFGHANISTAN

Turbulent and on the Brink

Introduction

After more than a decade of a US-led intervention, commencing with Operation Enduring Freedom in October 2001, Afghanistan remains in the throes of long-term structural instability and insecurity, with peace and democracy continuing to elude the country. The human sacrifices of ordinary Afghans and international forces, as well as significant amounts of foreign material investment, have proved unable to stem the tide of the Taliban-led insurgency or to neutralise Pakistan's support for it. Afghanistan faces a quagmire of political, social, economic and security quandaries. Its mosaic character has become more pronounced as a multitude of actors – states, non-governmental organisations (NGOs) and international organisations – have become involved in efforts to stabilise and rebuild the country, bringing with them a host of frequently conflicting interests.

Afghan President Hamid Karzai, who took office in December 2001 following the US intervention and the toppling of the Taliban Islamic regime in Afghanistan a few weeks earlier, came to preside over a corrupt and dysfunctional administration. He failed to make good his publicly avowed goal of laying down the institutional foundations necessary to transform Afghanistan into a stable and secure democratic state. Nor could the international community, coordinated by the United Nations Assistance Mission in Afghanistan (UNAMA) and led by the United States, claim to have made meaningful progress towards this goal. Disarray, confusion and despair have now beset most of the largely impoverished

Afghan people. A majority of them have come to live only for today, with little prospect for a better future.

Meanwhile, the United States and its North Atlantic Treaty Organisation (NATO) and non-NATO allies finally found themselves in a no-win situation. A deep sense of fatigue and declining public support for the war, combined with serious financial and economic difficulties at home, precipitously led them to rethink their approach to involvement in Afghanistan. After many years of fighting and reconstruction efforts without being able to secure a viable and effective partner in Karzai, they became increasingly preoccupied with the question of finding an exit sooner rather than later from what shaped up to be the 'Afghan trap'. US President Barack Obama, whose administration grappled with serious tensions when tackling the Afghan problem that it inherited from the Bush administration, led the way in this regard. Obama announced a revised strategy in December 2009, with a shift in emphasis from counter-terrorism to counter-insurgency, from fighting for the Afghan government to empowering its forces to handle Afghanistan security, and from defeating the Taliban-led armed opposition to reaching a political settlement. It considered this as the best way to stabilise Afghanistan as a prelude to ending America's combat involvement and to withdrawing most of its troops from the country by the end of 2014. America's allies were happy to follow suit. Thus, the US and its allies took the same path as their Soviet predecessors, who invaded and occupied Afghanistan for a decade in the 1980s, and the British invaders, who made two military expeditions into Afghanistan in the nineteenth century – all to no avail. The revised US strategy essentially meant the 'Afghanisation' of the war, despite the fact that such an approach had failed in relation to the US withdrawal from Vietnam four decades ago, as well as in relation to the Soviet retreat from Afghanistan in 1989.

What brought Afghanistan and the United States and its allies to this point? How might we explain why the situation in Afghanistan proved so intractable, both for Afghans and the international community? A number of factors may be called upon in attempting to account for the difficulties faced in post-invasion Afghanistan: the country's historical legacy, in the context of its mosaic society and geographical location; the misguided strategy of the United States and NATO; poor governance and corruption; Afghanistan's re-emergence as a 'narco-state'; and the

Taliban-led insurgency and competing neighbourly interference, with Pakistan seeking to play a determining role.

Social Divisions

Ever since the emergence of modern Afghanistan in the middle of the eighteenth century, state-building enterprises have been beleaguered by the mosaic make-up of the country. Patterns of power in the country have been moulded by the persistence of local identities and traditional social ties. This has played a central role in Afghanistan being traditionally characterised as a weak state in dynamic relations with a strong but multifaceted society. The largely uneducated, traditionally Muslim Afghan population, currently estimated to number around 30 million, is composed of various ethnic, tribal, linguistic, cultural and sectarian clusters, forming distinct micro-societies, many of which have close and extensive cross-border ties with Afghanistan's neighbours.[1] The Pashtuns, who overwhelmingly populate the southern and eastern provinces along the border with Pakistan, have historically formed the largest ethnic group and currently comprise around 42 per cent of the Afghan population.[2] The Tajiks, who constitute the next most significant ethnic minority, number around 25 to 30 per cent of the population. The remainder is composed of a number of other ethnic minorities, including Hazara, Uzbek, Turkman, Nooristani and Aimaqi. Each of these groups speaks its own multiple-dialect language, although only two tongues, Pashtu and Dari (a dialect of Persian), have achieved national prominence, with Dari traditionally forming the main medium of official communication and intellectual life.

All of these clusters are further divided along various family, clan, tribal and regional lines. The Pashtuns, for example, fall into two large and traditionally somewhat hostile groupings: the Durrani and the Ghilzai, each of which is in turn segmented into a plethora of sub-tribes. The Mohammadzai clan of the Durrani tribe dominated Afghan political and military leadership for most of the life of modern Afghanistan until the 1970s. Karzai and most of his cohort belong to the Durranis, whereas the Ghilzais have spawned most of the Taliban and their supporters. This reflects the historically more settled lifestyle of the Durranis in comparison with their migrant Ghilzai counterparts.

This urban–rural cleavage also plays out within other Afghan ethnic groups. Religious sectarian diversity further compounds the situation. While around 80 per cent of the Afghan population are followers of the Sunni sect of Islam, the remainder belong to the Shi'a sect, with different schools of thought and religious orders causing widespread variations in the practice of both branches.[3] Afghanistan is truly a land of minorities.

Afghanistan's geographically strategic location and landlocked status have added to the complexity and vulnerability of the country. Lying at the crossroads of Asia and Europe and intersecting the three important regions of Central Asia, South Asia and the Middle East, as well as linking to the Far East, Afghanistan has historically been in a zone of major power rivalry and in the past two centuries, for reasons both ideological and strategic, has been subjected to multiple invasions by powerful neighbours and major powers. From the mid-nineteenth century until early in the twentieth century, the country was of central interest to the rival powers of Great Britain and Tsarist Russia as they competed for influence from Tibet to Istanbul in what has come to be known as the 'Great Game'. Anglo-Russian rivalries in Afghanistan continued following the overthrow of the Tsarist regime and the establishment of the Bolshevik government in 1917, although this dynamic was somewhat muted in comparison with previous decades. The rise of US competition with Soviet Russia in the global climate of the Cold War brought a third international power onto the Afghan scene after the Second World War.

The US–Soviet struggle enabled Afghan dynastical rulers to play off the two superpowers to Afghanistan's advantage in the 1950s, and to a considerable extent in the 1960s, but not without consequences for the nation at large. The greatest cost of this dynamic was a growing Soviet influence in Afghanistan, which laid the foundation for the eventual Soviet invasion of the country in late December 1979. The Soviet occupation endured until the withdrawal of the last Russian troops in defeat in May 1989, which ushered in a devastating period of internal conflict that ended ultimately in the rise to power of the Taliban. Taliban rule was only brought to an end with the 11 September 2001 al-Qaeda attacks on the United States, which prompted the latter's intervention in response. US intervention was widely welcomed in Afghanistan itself, as a majority of Afghans appeared keen to be free of the draconian theocratic rule of the Taliban, and was met with almost universal support within the international community, with the United States' NATO and non-NATO allies taking the lead.

Historical Legacy

Strongmen, regional influence and foreign interference

Social and cultural divisions, cross-border ethnic and sectarian ties, geographical location, major power rivalry and local dynastic factionalism have traditionally played a critical role in keeping Afghanistan internally weak and externally vulnerable. These variables have also made the country politically volatile and strategically valuable. Lacking a strong and stable central power, modern Afghanistan has remained a land of 'strongmen' and 'local power-holders'.[4] Until the 1970s, these figures took the form of *khans* (tribal leaders), *sardars* (nobles), *pirs* and *mullahs* (local religious figures) and *malleks* (district managers). Since then, such figures have largely been replaced or supplemented by individuals popularly and collectively known as 'warlords', who have managed to build up individual power bases with defensive and distributive capabilities. Many of them have the capacity to make alliances and counter-alliances both within and outside of Afghanistan, against one another and the central government, whenever possible and desirable.

The evolution of modern Afghanistan has mostly been on a rentier or foreign aid basis and proved to be turbulent and bloody, undermining the development of self-sufficiency, national unity and institutionalised processes of state building in the country. An exceptional period of lasting peace and stability was achieved during the reign of Mohammed Nadir (1929–33) and that of his son, King Zahir Shah (1933–73). This achievement relied largely on a triangular relationship that the monarchy nurtured with the religious establishment and local power-holders, with limited state interference in the affairs of micro-societies. Critical, too, was the state's commitment to a policy of neutrality in world politics, which enabled it to somewhat minimise the deleterious effects of foreign dependency and interference that had plagued Afghanistan in the past. The approach adopted to state building was evolutionary, entailing a process of incremental change and development. As a result, the centre (Kabul) was able to forge an informal national structure within which Afghan micro-societies were carefully placed. Kabul was linked to the peripheries to the extent that the former could claim a degree of jurisdiction in areas such as defence, foreign policy, very limited taxation and military drafting, while allowing local groups the freedom to exercise self-regulation and responsibility for security at a local level.

The events of July 1973 dealt a serious blow to this harmonious and delicate arrangement. The 'palace coup' of that year, led by the King's rival cousin and brother-in-law, Mohammed Daoud, resulted in the overthrow of the monarchy and the declaration of an Afghan republic. Daoud, at once an autocrat and a nationalist moderniser, pursued a form of republicanism that involved the centralisation of power, the acceleration of social and economic change and the reduction of his regime's dependence on local pro-Soviet groups and the USSR itself, with which he had forged close ties during his premiership from 1953 to 1964. Daoud's fiercely centralising agenda entailed a radical departure from his predecessors' somewhat decentralised politics. His policy changes also included a tentative shift towards the West and some of the United States' regional friends (Iran, Saudi Arabia and Egypt in particular), with a view to settling Afghanistan's long-running border dispute with Pakistan. This alarmed Moscow, which had made hefty economic, military and, for that matter, political investment in Afghanistan since the mid-1950s, as well as Moscow's Afghan supporters, especially within the small and yet highly factionalised People's Democratic Party of Afghanistan (PDPA). The opposition of these groups to Daoud's regime opened the way for the successful PDPA coup of April 1978, and the Soviet invasion of Afghanistan 20 months later.

The PDPA takeover and Soviet occupation, lasting nearly a decade, was opposed by various Afghan Islamic resistance, or *Mujahideen*, groups. The main Sunni *Mujahideen* groups had their political leaderships based in Pakistan, whose powerful military intelligence (the Inter-Services Intelligence or ISI) had forged a close partnership with the American CIA in order to coordinate outside financial and military assistance to these groups. The conflict between the Soviet-sponsored regime and the *Mujahideen* transformed Afghanistan into a zone of national and international conflict that gave birth to a new breed of local strongmen. With support from multiple outside actors, these figures rapidly emerged as critical players not only in the defeat of the Soviets and their protégé PDPA government, but also in the shaping of Afghan politics and society in the post-Soviet era.[5]

The 1988 Geneva Accords, which paved the way for Soviet withdrawal from the country, led simultaneously to the empowerment and entrenchment of these 'strongmen'. The forces of the distinguished Afghan-Tajik *Mujahideen* commander Ahmad Shah Massoud took control of much of Kabul by 25 April 1992, opening the way for the establishment of the first *Mujahideen*-led Islamic government under at first Sibghatullah Mojaddedi on an interim basis and then President Burhanuddin Rabbani, with Massoud still dominant as the military strongman. However, other factions, especially that of Pakistan-backed Gulbuddin Hekmatyar, soon decided to fight for complete control of Kabul, resulting in a bloody inter-*Mujahideen* power struggle. Within five months, Hekmatyar's forces, later joined by the Iranian-backed Shi'a *Mujahideen* group of *Hezbi Wahdat* (Party of Unity) and the troops of the Uzbek warlord, Abdul Rashid Dostum, were besieging Kabul at the cost of thousands of lives and the destruction of half of the city.

Hekmatyar's ultimate failure to consolidate control led Pakistan to realise the futility of continuing its support for his faction. The ISI turned its eyes to the creation of a fresh force: the 'Taliban' ('religious students'), who were drawn primarily from the ranks of Ghilzai Pashtuns, trained in Pakistani Islamic schools (*madrasas*). By September 1996, the Taliban had successfully routed Hekmatyar's forces, forcing Massoud to retreat from Kabul to the north. The Taliban formed the Islamic Emirate of Afghanistan in the process, but were unable to establish full control of the entire country. Recognising the strength of the new rulers in Kabul, Dostum realigned his forces under Massoud's United Front for the Islamic Salvation of Afghanistan, or what, at Islamabad's instigation, became known as the 'Northern Alliance'. Massoud successfully consolidated his forces in the north-east, but Dostum was betrayed by one of his subordinates, Abdul Malik Pahlawan, unleashing a further wave of violence. In 1997, Abdul Malik let the Taliban into Mazar-e-Sharif, Dostum's stronghold, and captured and handed over the leading Afghan-Tajik *Mujahideen* commander in western Afghanistan, Ismail Khan. Only a year later, Abdul Malik recognised the untrustworthiness of his erstwhile allies and changed his allegiance once again.

The 'strongman' legacy of Afghanistan's history has, in conjunction with what is now recognised as a widely flawed US intervention strategy, seriously undermined processes of stabilisation and reconstruction in Afghanistan. Although Massoud was assassinated by al-Qaeda agents two days before the organisation's terrorist attacks of 11 September 2001 on the United States, his forces (the United Front) played a leading role in the US military response to al-Qaeda and its Taliban harbourers. The United States presented its intervention as a battle of good against evil, and promised to help rebuild and transform Afghanistan into a stable and secure democracy. Yet the narrow lens through which the United States viewed the Afghan situation limited the scope of its understanding and the success of its goals, and resulted in a consistent failure to grasp the true complexity of Afghanistan and its region, as was publicly confirmed a decade later by the former US Commander of NATO forces in Afghanistan, General Stanley McChrystal.[6] The United States took little account of the relevant historical information in its analysis: Afghanistan's historical peculiarities, the Soviets' bitter Afghan experience and America's own Vietnam debacle.

The United States and its Afghan allies successfully toppled the Taliban regime and drove the al-Qaeda leadership out of Afghanistan into Pakistan. The United States also managed, with the assistance of its NATO allies, the United Nations and Afghanistan's neighbours, to convene an inter-elite meeting among four Afghan anti-Taliban factions in Bonn, Germany. The Taliban, who were branded as terrorists at the same level as al-Qaeda, were not invited to participate. These discussions culminated in the Bonn Agreement, signed on 5 December 2001. It legitimised the US intervention, backed by NATO allies, and set up an interim government led by a largely unknown Pashtun and former moderate *Mujahideen* figure, Karzai, to see the transition of Afghanistan from a conflict-ridden past to a stable democratic future, under overall UN auspices, but with the United States and its allies firmly at the helm.

US-led NATO Approach

The military and reconstruction strategy pursued by the United States and its allies was not commensurate with the goals that were originally set up for Afghanistan in the Bonn Agreement. As the overwhelmingly predominant actor, the United States from the outset neglected to map out a strategy that could coherently integrate Afghanistan's security building with programmes of political and economic reconstruction and appropriate socio-cultural development. Its initial fixation on retaliation against al-Qaeda and the Taliban, lack of direction on reconstruction, ill-fated attempt to utilise civil society for its own purposes and inability or unwillingness to prompt Islamabad to restructure its Afghanistan policy substantially contributed to the persistence and further entrenchment of Afghanistan's long-standing political, social and economic difficulties.

Military strategy

The initial deployment of US troops to Afghanistan comprised just 10,000 soldiers, joined by a further 5,000 from the NATO allies, which formed the UN-sanctioned International Security Assistance Force (ISAF). Yet the two forces were tasked under separate commands and with little coordination between the two. Whereas ISAF's only task was to secure Kabul in support of the Karzai administration, the US troops, who constituted the bulk of what became known as the Coalition Forces, were largely focused on hunting down al-Qaeda and Taliban leaders and operatives. As could have been expected, this level of deployment soon proved to be inadequate in a country still reeling from 24 years of warfare and bloodshed. The shortage of troops left the field wide open for the Taliban and their supporters and a range of other sub-national actors – from local power-holders and poppy growers to drug traffickers and criminal gangs – to regroup within less than two years of the intervention.[7] Although it became clear as early as mid-2003 that more troops and resources were needed to expand ISAF's and the Coalition Forces' operations, neither the United States nor its allies were willing to meet this requirement. The US focus had already shifted away from Afghanistan to Iraq, the invasion of which in March 2003 is discussed in detail in Chapter 5. In addition, the involvement of many of its NATO partners in Afghanistan's security building and reconstruction was, from the outset, a short-term commitment, undertaken largely as a way of avoiding sending troops to the far less popular war in Iraq.

When the United States and its partners finally decided in 2004 to boost their troop deployment and expand their operations, they opted for a safe and incremental troop build-up. By the end of 2008, 40,000 soldiers (including 10,000 Americans) operated within ISAF under NATO, and 20,000 under US command. But several European members of NATO still remained totally unwilling to deploy their troops in danger zones in the south. The Dutch withdrawal from Afghanistan in August 2010 was partially attributed to angry domestic public opinion over fellow-European intransigence on this issue. Repeated NATO meetings to generate more troop deployment and better strategic coordination fell persistently short of desired results.

Faced with insufficient resources to secure Afghanistan as a whole, Washington resorted to outsourcing a number of important security functions. It continued to arm and finance, as an exigency under the circumstances, a number of private security firms and existing local power-holders – 'strongmen' – and their militias.[8] Both the security firms and armed groups operated independently of the Afghan central government, and the United States could not ensure control over them in the medium-to-long term.[9] By December 2008, private contractors, who were often neither accountable nor effective, represented 69 per cent of the US Department of Defense's workforce in the country.[10] Of the first group of 32 provincial governors appointed in 2002, at least 20 were leaders of armed groups, with most of the remainder having links to such leaders.[11] These 'strongmen' thus benefited from both state building and state weakness. Despite a faint-hearted attempt by Karzai to tame some of the 'strongmen' following the 2004 presidential election, the resurgence of the Taliban and Karzai's concern to maintain his own position reinvigorated them once more. Karzai's selection of Mohammad Qasim Fahim, former defence minister from the United Front or 'Northern Alliance', as his vice presidential running mate, in 2009, was a reflection of this trend.[12] With the Coalition military strategy almost in tatters, any entrenched 'strongman' unsupportive of the Taliban came to be seen as an acceptable ally by the United States and NATO, a development that exacerbated social divisions and political fragmentation. This fact became an important element in the United States' exit strategy under George W. Bush's Democrat successor, Barack Obama, who assumed office on 20 January 2009.

In contrast to Bush's stress on counter-*terrorism*, however, President Obama turned to what was called a population-centric counter-insurgency strategy. Materialising after months of debate, the revised strategy, which was announced in October 2009, reflected the prevailing influence of the US Commander of all NATO forces in Afghanistan, General Stanley McChrystal, over Vice President Joe Biden and US ambassador to Afghanistan, Karl Eikenberry, in that it secured the President's approval for 30,000 additional troops until 2012. This strategy certainly sought to address some of the shortcomings discussed above. It emphasised protection of the main population centres, institution building and the relationship between good governance, reconstruction, security building and Pakistani compliance. It underlined the importance of the accelerated capacity building of the Afghan Security Forces (ASF), and aimed at expanding military operations into the heartland of Taliban territory with an escalation of cross-border operations into Pakistan to target Taliban and al-Qaeda leaders and sanctuaries. At the same time, however, another key element of the revised strategy was a presidential commitment to transfer all security operations to the ASF and withdraw most of the American forces from Afghanistan by the end of 2014 – a goal that most of America's allies with military involvement in Afghanistan welcomed, and over which the Taliban and their supporters rejoiced. Many serious analysts of Afghan politics and society could not believe that this limited time frame would allow enough time for the change in approach to remedy the mistakes of the past.

Meanwhile, US efforts in Afghanistan suffered from a transient and ill-coordinated leadership. The chief architect of President Obama's counter-insurgency approach, General McChrystal, who was appointed to command the NATO forces in Afghanistan in June 2009, was fired from his position only a year later. In a July 2010 article published in *Rolling Stone* magazine, McChrystal and his advisors openly mocked President Obama's civilian team's policy approach to the complex Afghan situation. Two figures bore the brunt of McChrystal's vindictive: Vice President Biden and Ambassador Karl Eikenberry. Before holding the post of American ambassador to Afghanistan from May 2009 to July 2011, Eikenberry was the former Commander of US forces in Afghanistan. McChrystal accused Eikenberry of betrayal for having opposed his 2009 proposal for the deployment of more troops.[13] Although he subsequently apologised to the President for his 'error of judgement', one wonders whether McChrystal himself had developed serious doubts about the chances of US-led NATO success in Afghanistan and saw his *Rolling Stone* outbursts as his own personal exit strategy. Due to McChrystal's substantive role in formulating and revising US policy in Afghanistan, his dismissal could not but cause a significant dent in Obama's strategy on the ground. McChrystal's personal influence was considerable. He had succeeded in building a good rapport and working relationships with his Afghan partners at the governmental, provincial and tribal levels and had managed to gain Karzai's confidence, which had been pierced by Eikenberry's pressure on him to engage in serious political reforms and to adopt a tougher anti-corruption stand.

McChrystal's replacement, former Commander of US forces in Iraq, General David Petraeus, lacked the personal touch and nuanced approach of his predecessor. Moreover, Petraeus's commission was cut short by his appointment as Director of the Central Intelligence Agency (CIA) in September 2011, a position from which he resigned in November 2012 following an episode of sexual misconduct. Petraeus's successor, General James Allen, also served a short time in the role. Amid controversy surrounding his inappropriate email exchanges with a female socialite friend of Petraeus, he was replaced by Marine General Joseph Dunford by mid-November 2012. The revolving door of military leaders at the very top of the US command, and the time necessary for each leader to adjust to conditions on the ground, proved to be an unsettling factor in the operational situation in Afghanistan.

Throughout all of this, the United States continued to reassure the world of its efforts to strengthen local Afghan security forces such as the Afghan National Army (ANA), the Afghan National Police (ANP), the Border Guard and the Afghan Local Police, with a view to increasing security responsibilities. The ANA, which achieved a strength of more than 200,000 troops by the end of 2012, has certainly acquired the capacity to participate in some operations, but it has not been able to engage in any large-scale military engagement without the support of foreign forces. A December 2012 Pentagon report painted a bleak picture, stating that only one of the ANA's 23 brigades was 'able to operate independently without air or other military support from the United States and [a] NATO partner'.[14] The ANA was not only trained and built up in a piecemeal fashion by different foreign forces, but has also suffered from a notable degree of desertion, internal ethnic, cultural and sectarian divisions, suspect loyalty to the central government and a high casualty rate since taking on increased security operations. By the end of 2013, there was little reason to expect this situation to improve dramatically. The ANP, meanwhile, grew into a quite unreliable and corrupt organisation, and the Border Guard remained underdeveloped and poorly equipped for the task of ensuring the security of Afghanistan's borders, especially the long and treacherous Pakistan frontier. In addition, the Afghan Local Police that the United States and its allies, in conjunction with the Karzai government, established to operate locally in different parts of the country, was plagued by a notoriously self-serving culture.[15]

With the total strength of all Afghan security forces reaching 350,000 personnel by the end of 2012, the Karzai government's desire to expand this force developed into a very contentious issue for the United States and its allies.[16] Afghanistan's overwhelming dependence on foreign aid has meant that the responsibility for the annual costs of maintaining such a large force has fallen largely on the United States and its NATO allies, even in the wake of the withdrawal. These actors, unsurprisingly, proposed a reduction in the size of the ANA, the ANP and other forces to a total of 228,000 personnel – a figure that the Afghan government immediately rejected as inadequate, claiming that a force of at least 400,000 would be necessary to maintain national security.[17] Yet even the smaller force was estimated to require an annual expenditure of more than US$4 billion. The question of funding Afghanistan's post-withdrawal security forces has proved a highly contentious issue. The US–Afghanistan Strategic Partnership Agreement, signed by Obama and Karzai on 1 May 2013, failed to resolve these questions in any substantive way. While guaranteeing US support for military, social and economic development in Afghanistan for ten years, the agreement did not commit the United States to any specific level of funding or military assistance.[18] This is despite the concerning fact that Afghanistan's security sector consumed the largest proportion of the national budget as of 2010, accounting for more than 40 per cent of operating expenditures.[19] The government's ability to sustainably fund more recruitment and training in the absence of foreign aid is therefore highly doubtful. The only parts of the security apparatus that have performed with a degree of effectiveness are the numerically limited but well-trained special forces and the National Directorate for Security. But even these forces, like other instruments of state power and the government as a whole, are suspected of being penetrated by armed oppositional elements, and were until very recently entirely bankrolled by the CIA. The Directorate's head and Karzai's close ally, Asadullah Khalid, was critically wounded in an assassination attempt by the Taliban on 6 December 2012, casting some serious doubt on the effectiveness of the organisation.

Compounding the difficulties in ensuring stability in Afghanistan was the belated US recognition of the links between military security and human development. Military efforts, when unaccompanied by good governance and improved living conditions for the population, are unlikely to achieve the desired long-term objectives of a stable political order. US policymakers in particular have demonstrated a poor understanding of Afghanistan's history, and the social, cultural and regional complexities that this legacy has produced. Exalted by its military prowess and world power status, the Bush administration gave too much primacy to coercive operations. This approach undermined the possibility of a viable post-Taliban political order and impeded accelerated reconstruction processes. It also resulted in significant human rights violations, including the killing and dishonouring of thousands of Afghan civilians – a problem that continuously eroded the initial popular support for the international forces and constricted Karzai's relations with Washington.

With a lack of political willpower necessary to sustain the Coalition's efforts, and the growing desire of a number of US allies to end their involvement in Afghanistan as soon as possible, NATO decided at the Lisbon summit of November 2010 to end combat operations within the next four years. The United States began drawing down its forces in 2012 with the departure of Obama's authorised 30,000 surge troops. Meanwhile, as General Allen expressed a preference for keeping the US troop level at 68,000 until 2013,[20] there was a growing conflict between military objectives and political interest in view of mounting domestic pressure in the Obama administration for the withdrawal of more troops sooner rather than later. In October 2012, Republican congressman Walter Jones called for the speedy removal of US troops after 11 years of what he viewed as incurable Afghan incompetency: 'You can train a monkey to ride a bicycle in that length of time,' he remarked.[21] The view that quietly gained saliency in Washington and amongst US allies was that the Afghan War, which had lasted longer than the Second World War, the Vietnam War and the Soviet occupation of Afghanistan, had become unwinnable; therefore, the sooner the allies withdrew, the better.[22]

To this end, from 2011 the foreign forces accelerated their efforts to prepare the Afghan security forces and various local power-holders for life without foreign combat support, with the United States and some of its allies also concluding strategic partnerships with Afghanistan to provide assistance in matters of security, reconstruction and finance beyond 2014. They affirmed their commitment to these objectives in the NATO Chicago Summit on Afghanistan and subsequent conference on Afghanistan in May and July 2012 respectively. Throughout his presidential campaign for a second term, Obama had repeatedly expressed his confidence in and commitment to a complete US withdrawal from Afghanistan on schedule.[23] His re-election only increased the pressure on him to fulfil his promise to the American public. However, by the end of 2013, as Afghanistan's security situation remained highly fragile, the capacities and commitment of the United States and its allies to guarantee Afghanistan's security beyond 2014 remained unclear.

Reconstruction strategy

The United States and its allies fared no better in their attempts to achieve a significant degree of progress in the field of reconstruction. Washington initially conveyed mixed messages about the US role in rebuilding Afghanistan. Whereas on 25 September 2001, President Bush said that he was not 'into nation-building' in Afghanistan, Secretary of State Colin Powell mentioned 'reconstruction', and the Secretary of Defense Donald Rumsfeld insisted that the United States was only considering immediate humanitarian aid.[24] Washington also shunned the idea of a 'Marshall Plan' for Afghanistan because of its belief that a small amount of money could go a long way in that country.[25] After reported prompting by British Prime Minister Tony Blair, Bush appeared to have come around to the idea, by October 2001, that it might be wise to offer more substantive help to Afghanistan. This was reflected in his comments at the time: 'I think we did learn a lesson from the previous engagement in the Afghan area', and 'that we should not just simply leave after a military objective has been achieved'.[26] Even so, the

Bush administration failed to draw up a comprehensive and coherent programme of reconstruction for Afghanistan. The approach that it adopted was piecemeal, poorly coordinated and badly implemented. The Bush administration's strategy in Afghanistan was designed largely to benefit the United States, and American companies, rather than to target Afghan needs in accordance with realities on the ground.

As of 2011, of the more than US$90 billion pledged by international donors to Afghanistan after 2001, over US$30 billion remained to be delivered.[27] According to a major report by the Agency Coordinating Body for Afghan Relief in 2008, 40 per cent of the aid funds distributed between 2002 and 2008 went back to the donor countries in consultant fees and expatriates' pay, with most of the remaining funds being spent on UN and NGO operations and on foreign contractors and subcontractors. This ensured a flow of capital out of the country so large (between US$1 billion and US$2.5 billion) that it made up one-quarter of Afghanistan's gross domestic product (GDP) in 2010.[28]

The same report added that 'while the US military alone spent [US]$100 million a day' in Afghanistan, the average amount of aid spent by all donors combined was just US$7 million a day between 2001 and 2008.[29] Until 2008, far less money was invested, per capita, in the reconstruction of Afghanistan than in each of the three other states experiencing political upheaval during that same period: Bosnia, Kosovo and Timor-Leste. Even access to life-saving necessities was neglected. For humanitarian needs relating to water, sanitation and hygiene, funding was short by US$33 million in 2009; in the same year education received no funding at all.[30]

The international community, through the 2006 Afghanistan Compact and 2008 Afghanistan National Development Strategy, aimed in vain to reconcile its various approaches with those of the Afghan government. Aside from addressing security, the Compact defined cooperation on issues of governance and economic and social development as priorities and established a Joint Coordination and Monitoring Board, co-chaired by the government and the UN, to oversee these efforts.[31] The 2008 Strategy called for the realignment of international interests with domestic imperatives, giving the lead to the Karzai government in formulating and dictating policy.[32] However, the national budgeting structure utilised by the international community continued to seriously undermine the Afghan government and to pose an obstacle to overall reconstruction planning. From 2002 to 2009, three-quarters of foreign aid bypassed the government's own core budget system through an external budget, a fact that at least in part reflected the donors' distrust of the Afghan government.[33] As 90 per cent of the national budget, both governmental and external, was (and still is) provided either directly or indirectly from foreign aid, it was no surprise that the Afghan government's lack of control over external donors, and the frequently clashing interests of the donors themselves, entailed a disconnect between national objectives and budget expenditure.[34] Coupled with these tensions, the consistent inability of the government to properly allocate resources (for example, in the 2009–10 fiscal year, the government only managed to spend 38 per cent of its budgeted expenditure) contributed to the reluctance of donors to shift their aid delivery to the core budget.[35] Consequently, a majority of Afghans have experienced no positive change in living conditions as a result of post-Taliban reconstruction efforts. After more than a decade of foreign involvement, they came to have little reason to remain supportive of either the Karzai administration or its foreign backers, and yet at the same time to view the NATO troop withdrawal with fear and apprehension rather than with hope.[36]

From 2006, recognising substantial underfunding in the development sector, Washington found it necessary to change tack, with Ambassador Eikenberry leading the way in policy revisions. As a result, US non-military assistance to Afghanistan leapt from US$1.1 billion in 2006 to US$4.2 billion in 2010.[37] However, while this assistance achieved some substantial outcomes, the aforementioned issues with aid delivery and project implementation continued to hinder actual reconstruction. Considering the Afghan government's dependence on foreign aid and its inability to extract substantial revenue from domestic taxation, as has been predicted, Afghanistan is set to suffer from a severe economic depression after the departure of foreign troops and many NGOs.

Civil society and democratisation
Meanwhile, the process by which *substantive* democracy was to be developed was left largely undefined in US strategy. As part of what was dubbed a 'light footprint' approach, neither the US government nor international bodies such as NATO and the United Nations chose to draft a specific plan for the development of a functioning civil society or

the improvement of human rights, individual liberty, or freedom from violence for the Afghan people. As such, the role of NGOs, development organisations, aid groups and new government agencies, such as the Afghanistan Independent Human Rights Commission, remained poorly defined, resulting in frequent confusion, overlap and contradiction.

What little direction was propounded by US democracy promoters in Afghanistan often hindered rather than helped the rebuilding of civil society. American NGO workers and aid officials persistently gave preference to secular NGOs and shied away from supporting overtly Muslim organisations.[38] This resulted in a complete 'othering' of Muslim organisations, even those whose focus was on providing basic humanitarian aid. The proportion of divestment of aid, civic education and financial support toward expansive organisations such as the UN Office for the Co-ordination of Humanitarian Affairs, the World Health Organisation and the World Bank increased at the expense of some well-intentioned, local NGOs, which had more expertise in the country. Finally, the blurring of civil and military action in Afghanistan greatly influenced the public perception of civil society. US and NATO forces strategically matched military interventions with humanitarian campaigns to win over the 'hearts and minds' of the population.[39] In characterising NGOs as their 'eyes and ears on the ground', as 'force multipliers', or as a 'build' component within their counter-insurgency strategy, US and NATO forces caused humanitarian workers to be seen as legitimate targets for insurgents.[40]

The promotion of civil society in Afghanistan is further complicated by the operational guidelines of the various international NGOs and agencies. There has been a disconnect between the three key groups in this process: foreign workers, Afghan workers hired by NGOs, and the majority of Afghans who live in abject poverty.[41] By lavishly rewarding their workers out of all proportion with general living standards in the country, international organisations fed a general distrust of NGO and development workers among the general population. It is unsurprising but no less unfortunate that a United Nations Office on Drugs and Crime (UNODC) report found in 2010 that 54 per cent of Afghans believed that international organisations and NGOs are corrupt and are only in the country to get rich.[42]

From 2008, the Secretary-General's Special Representative (SGSR), head of UNAMA, was given the lead role in the civilian reconstruction effort, with a mandate for democratisation of the Afghan polity and the promotion of cooperation between the United Nations, the United States, NATO, the Afghan government and the multitude of other actors in the country. Parallel to this empowerment was a budget increase to US$250 million in 2009 compared with US$86 million in 2008.[43] Although viewed locally as an impartial and inclusive institution with the majority of its staff recruited from the Afghan population, this shift in priority proved to be a case of too little, too late. The international community, having fully invested its political capital in Karzai's leadership, seemed unwilling to speak out against his increasingly authoritarian tendencies. Both the selection of Kai Eide over Paddy Ashdown as SGSR in 2008 and the dismissal of Peter Galbraith, previous deputy SGSR, over his criticism of the 2009 election that brought Karzai to power for another term, are reflective of this. In February 2010, Karzai managed to remove UNAMA's power to appoint three of the five members of the Electoral Complaints Commission (ECC), empowering himself in the process.[44] The appointments of Staffan de Mistura (2010–12), previous SGSR to Iraq, and Jan Kubis (2012–) in heading UNAMA, showed no clear signs of bringing the urgently needed change to the mission, although Kubis expressed his eagerness to ensure a clean presidential election in 2014. Karzai, who constitutionally could not run for a third term, sought to circumvent Kubis's efforts in this respect by setting the election date for April 2014. This decision drew criticism from various political opposition factions, which had recently sought to unite within several coalitions, on the grounds that most of northern Afghanistan, which forms the main power base of the opposing factions, would be snowbound at the time. The opposition groups also voiced their lack of confidence in Karzai's ability to put the necessary electoral and political reforms in place for a fair and free election.

Far from achieving the democratic transition that had initially been envisioned, US involvement in Afghanistan served only to intensify sectarian divisions and exacerbate political factionalism. Furthermore, the ways in which the United States and its allies approached the Afghan transition fostered a culture of dependency and complacency that has not only dominated the government but also gripped large segments of the population. Many Afghans have become accustomed to looking to foreigners, rather than to themselves, in order to achieve improvements within their country. As many of these actors were not driven by altruistic aims, their activities enhanced rather than diminished the culture of corruption and nepotism among the Afghans. As such, external assistance and influence do not appear to have helped the situation in the country to a desirable extent.

Social Issues

A host of social issues plague Afghan society as a whole. Given the high rate of violent incidents affecting civilians, further displacement of civilians on top of the estimated (as of mid-2013) 486,000 internally displaced persons is to be expected.[45] Displaced families face an uphill battle; coping mechanisms and support networks are disrupted and unreliable. In addition to this widespread problem of national insecurity, a majority of Afghans live under threat from security operations, suicide bomb attacks and improvised explosive devices. These constant difficulties are compounded by a chronic shortage of food, shelter, water, sanitation and access to meaningful education.[46] John Ging, Director of Operations for the UN Office for the Coordination of Humanitarian Affairs, illustrated the severity of the current situation when he pointed out that the level of malnutrition in Afghanistan stood at 59 per cent as of June 2012.[47]

The continued plight of women in contemporary Afghanistan also serves to disprove the self-aggrandising rhetoric of Washington and the Karzai government. According to former First Lady Laura Bush, as early as 2001, the US intervention had restored to the women of Afghanistan the 'rights and dignity' taken from them by 'terrorists'.[48] The reality on the ground tells a different story. Most Afghan women have remained repressed by and shackled to traditional practices in the name of either Islam or cultural norms, or both. If there has been some change in their living conditions, it has been confined mostly to a select number of women in the main urban centres, Kabul in particular. Many of the women's NGOs operating in Afghanistan, such as the Afghanistan Women's Education Centre, the Afghanistan Women's Network and the US-based Women for Afghan Women, belong to what Thomas Carothers calls 'advocacy NGOs' as opposed to 'development' or 'reconstruction' NGOs.[49] A 2008 report by Amnesty International, whose conclusions remain relevant today, found that 'Afghan women and girls still face widespread discrimination from all segments of society, domestic violence, abduction and rape by armed individuals, trafficking, forced marriages, including ever younger child marriages, and being traded in settlement of disputes and debts.'[50] A study undertaken by the NGO Global Rights in the same year found that 58.8 per cent of Afghan women were living in forced marriages, with around 40 per cent reporting physical domestic violence at least once in the past year.[51] There were more women and young girls in jails around the country for 'moral crimes' in 2013 than ever before since the end of Taliban rule, with Human Rights Watch reporting a rise of over 50 per cent since mid-2011.[52] A presidential decree banning violence against women, child marriages and forced marriages was issued in 2009, but when put to the *Wolesi Jirga* (the Lower House of the Afghan parliament) in mid-May 2013 for legislative support, the debate was aborted by the conservative legislators to the disgust of all the women members and their supporters who had initiated the move.[53] Karzai's reluctance to undertake positive action in this direction was linked to his growing need to win over conservative factions, including the Taliban, in the lead-up to the US withdrawal.[54] The overall picture for women in Afghanistan, even after over a decade of international intervention, indeed remained exceedingly grim.

Dysfunctional Governance

US and international policy alone cannot answer for the current state of Afghanistan. Karzai's leadership and the political system that he generated have been just as serious obstacles to the achievement of a stable political order. His approach and policies gave rise to politics of patronage, corruption and inefficiency in both the civilian and military spheres at all levels. As a result, Afghanistan has remained beset by poor governance and the multiple problems this has engendered.

Some noticeable progress has doubtless been made in Afghanistan since the US-led intervention of 2001. This includes limited improvements in such areas as political pluralism, freedom of expression, print and electronic media outlets, infrastructural development (such as building roads and the supply of clean water and electricity), communication, education and health, and construction of industrial enterprises. What limited success was achieved by the end of 2013, however, took place more or less on an *ad hoc* basis. Little consideration was given to the implementation of a national plan that could aid the consolidation of a political and economic order that would systematically improve living conditions in Afghanistan. Nor was any substantial effort made to promote cooperation between the central authority and local societies, and indeed among these societies themselves, in order to achieve the kind of confidence necessary for the pursuit of national unity.

Strong executive and executive–legislative divide

The model of political change adopted by the Karzai government, from the outset and under Washington's influence, aimed at generating a strong presidential system of government more akin to the American model than anything else. Both the Karzai government and Washington obstinately ignored the repeated warnings of seasoned scholars of Afghan politics and society, who argued that such a system was unlikely to work in a war-torn country like Afghanistan with a myriad of tribal, ethnic, linguistic and sectarian divisions. Such a system in the Afghan context was seen as dangerous on the grounds that it would typically produce one winner and many disgruntled but powerful losers with a capacity to challenge, undermine or otherwise manipulate the victor, and with the latter becoming vulnerable to unsavoury practices in order to maintain power. A more suitable alternative proposal was to create a somewhat decentralised parliamentary system of government, with the executive power resting with a prime minister and his/her cabinet to be drawn from the parliament that could enable citizens to connect with the central authority at different levels, from village to capital.[55]

Karzai's uncompromising push for a strong presidential system was nevertheless successful. In this bid, Karzai was backed by Zalmay Khalilzad, the Afghan-born, American presidential envoy (2001–02), ambassador to Afghanistan (2002–05) and self-confessed neoconservative, as well as by a number of joint Karzai–Khalilzad hand-picked ministers and members of the Constitutional Commission. At the December 2003–January 2004 'Constitutional' *Loya Jirga* (traditional Afghan grand assembly), pressing issues of government were left unaddressed as discussions focused on the role of Islam within the polity.[56] Advocates for a centralised government brushed aside the possibility of parliamentarianism. Even in the midst of virulent opposition to a strong presidential system by regional 'strongmen', and from across the political spectrum by groups such as *Jamiat-e Islami, Junbash-e Milli Islami, Hezb-e Motahed-e Milli* and the royalist *Harakat-e Wahdat-e Milli*,[57] pro-Karzai factions, with US backing, managed to win the day.[58] The new constitution prescribed a highly centralised presidential system of government, entrusting the executive arm with enough powers to be able to marginalise the legislative and judicial branches whenever it deemed desirable and under the 'right' circumstances.[59]

Under the same constitution, Afghanistan was given a two-chamber parliament. The lower and more powerful chamber, the *Wolesi Jirga*, was elected on a non-party basis in 2005 and 2010. Both parliaments have been far from perfect, reflecting partly the mosaic nature of the Afghan society and partly Karzai's original opposition to party politics. Members of parliament have tended to operate within informal groupings and *ad hoc* alliances, based mostly on tribal, sectarian, factional and ethnic loyalties. To make matters worse, among the members of the 2010 Afghan parliament were many 'strongmen' with varying records of human rights violations who shared a common determination to do whatever was necessary to protect themselves from public scrutiny and prosecution. The Afghan political system also suffers from a flawed electoral law, adopted in May 2004, which prescribes a voting system known as the 'single non-transferable vote'. This system is only used in a few other countries, such as Vanuatu and Jordan, and is notorious for its perversity. Simple on the surface, it can produce bizarre outcomes.[60] This voting system has contributed to the emergence of a legislature that is largely unrepresentative of the votes cast; in 2005, only an estimated two million of the six million votes cast were for winning candidates, resulting in over four million 'wasted' votes.[61]

The executive sought vigorously and persistently to marginalise parliament's role in the processes of governance. Karzai did little to build an effective working relationship between the executive and legislative branches. He sought to incapacitate parliament to make it his tool, rather than seeking to strengthen it as an effective arm of the government and to make it a genuine check on executive power. He frequently exploited the *Wolesi Jirga*'s internal divisions, and induced and bought off its members through nepotistic and patronage practices, in order to prevail over the chamber and override its legislative responsibilities and decisions whenever he found it desirable. The relationship between the two sides, as a result, became unnecessarily adversarial and distrustful.

The 2010 parliamentary election served only to deepen the executive–legislative divide. Accusations of systematic fraud, ballot stuffing and intimidation led the UN-backed Electoral Complaints Commission (ECC) and Afghan-led Independent Election Committee (IEC) to take action which seemingly marginalised the Pashtun vote, with the IEC discarding 1.3 million ballots out of 5.6 million cast,[62] and the ECC disqualifying 21 winning candidates. The results in the mixed Pashtun-majority province of Ghazni proved a case in point, with Hazara candidates sweeping all 11 seats. Soon afterwards, Karzai protested against a perceived lack of Pashtun representation in the lower house. Under pressure from domestic constituents and the international community, he eventually swore in the new parliament in January 2011, yet he continued to contest the latter's legitimacy by establishing a 'Special Court on Election Complaints', a body outside the jurisdiction of the Afghan courts, to question the election process and the IEC's activities.[63] According to a study by the Afghanistan Research and Evaluation Unit, the 2010 parliamentary election and subsequent intra-governmental squabbling damaged even further the legitimacy of the government and electoral institutions in the eyes of the people.[64] Only in October 2011, after months of sustained international pressure, did Karzai annul the 'Special Court' and acknowledge the legitimacy of the IEC.[65]

The growing lack of trust between the executive and legislative branches seriously undermined the processes of building inter-institutional cooperation and institutionalisation against the entrenchment of personal politics in Afghanistan. The centrality of political personalities, as opposed to political institutions, in Afghan political culture remains a deep-seated issue for political stability and continuity. As a result, political institutions have risen and fallen with personalities instead of governing and regulating the behaviour of these individuals. Following the fall of the Taliban, Karzai, backed by greater international support than any of his predecessors, had a unique opportunity to turn a new page in Afghan history in this respect. Instead, he opted to act in ways that perpetuated dysfunctional Afghan political traditions.

Patronage politics
Karzai's political behaviour came progressively to resemble that of a Pashtun *khan* or tribal leader. He increasingly used his governmental

powers and international support to run the Afghan state along the lines of the patronage network he fostered, with political prominence depending largely on Karzai's personal favour or disfavour.[66] He surrounded himself with a number of entrepreneurs and businessmen, many of whom were more interested in protecting their ill-gotten position of power and privilege than in boosting national unity, reconstruction and security. Most of them acted as self-seeking, corrupt functionaries rather than as visionaries, with little inclination for strategic thinking and planning. Karzai remained throughout his period in office as one of the most protected heads of state in the world. As he increasingly bottled himself up in the presidential palace, some of his ministers succeeded in turning their ministries into disconnected and largely ethnic-based fiefdoms. There was little reform to create a unified, viable administration, armed with a well-trained and effective bureaucracy. The 'old guard' persistently deprived the better-educated and home-grown generation of young Afghans of the opportunities to play an effective role in the nation's transition. The fact that Karzai and many of his functionaries received annual and intermittent funding from the CIA, MI6 and the Iranian government also blotted Karzai's domestic reputation as the Afghan leader on 'the payroll' of foreign intelligence services. Karzai publically sought to weather the scandal by openly welcoming such contributions, claiming that they were in the interests of the country. But the Afghan people have historically viewed such a leader as a disgrace and stigmatic. Some Afghan analysts have compared Karzai with one of his nineteenth-century predecessors, Shah Shuja Durrani, who assumed the rulership of Afghanistan twice – from 1803 to 1809, and from 1839 until his assassination by one of his courtiers in 1842 – and who was renowned for being on the British payroll and for having been a servant of a foreign power.[67]

Despite his initial promise to downplay the role of ethnicity in order to create national unity, Karzai became increasingly prone to privileging his own ethnic Pashtuns and, more specifically, his Durrani tribe. By leaning towards the Pashtuns, he precipitated Afghanistan towards a politics of ethnic imbalance. This caused growing concern among the non-Pashtun segments of the population, whose opposition to Taliban theocracy had been partly stirred by the discriminatory policies of this predominantly extremist Pashtun Islamic group.[68] Concerns about corruption and malpractice was scarcely assuaged by the rise of a 'Karzai cartel', dominated by close relatives of the president. Until his assassination by his head of security in July 2011, the president's half-brother, Ahmad Wali Karzai, had a reputation as the 'Kingpin of Kandahar', and was accused of being a notorious extortionist, drug-trafficker and CIA agent.[69] Karzai's four remaining full and half-brothers, in particular Quayum, Mahmood and Shah Wali (who replaced Ahmad Wali in Kandahar), have been involved in highly lucrative economic, commercial and industrial dealings (with considerable investments abroad, in Dubai in particular) and political machinations. The sprouting of their sudden wealth, which amounts to millions of dollars, is very suspicious, as the brothers are reputed to be deeply involved in a number of illicit activities. Whoever carried the surname Karzai reaped maximum benefit from his or her association with the president, who did not hesitate to protect them whenever necessary. As the Karzai era drew to a close and the 2014 presidential election and NATO troop withdrawal loomed, the president's eldest brother, Quayum, formerly a restaurateur in the United States, and two close loyalists became presidential candidates to succeed him in the April 2014 election. Meanwhile, signs of internal business and financial squabbling within the Karzai faction became evident, with his brothers, especially Shah Wali and Mahmood, engaging in acrimonious activities against one another in order to safeguard their interests.[70]

Despite his growing unpopularity, or perhaps because of it, Karzai seemed to have mastered the art of political duplicity, patronage and co-optation. He used his office and foreign resources to protect his family and to recruit 'strongmen' to enhance his election chances irrespective of their often unsavoury records. It was through these mechanisms that Karzai managed to win the presidential election of August 2009, which was widely rigged in his favour.[71] Under pressure from the international community, Karzai finally agreed to a second round against his main political rival, former foreign minister Dr Abdullah Abdullah, but ultimately refused to meet Abdullah's calls for a fair and free run-off. He rejected Abdullah's demand to fire the head of the IEC, who was accused of being a Karzai crony and involved in the rigging. Abdullah withdrew from the run-off in protest, and Karzai was triumphantly declared the victor. Yet Karzai's victory was based on winning a little more than half of the four million votes cast out of 12 million voters who had registered. This result could hardly be seen as providing legitimacy, particularly after the UN-backed election watchdog commission, the

ECC, found that one million of the four million votes cast were null and void.[72] Karzai therefore had no claim to a respectable base of popular legitimacy for his second term, putting many of his international backers, most importantly the Obama administration, in a very embarrassing and precarious position. Initially, Washington appeared to have many reservations in dealing with Karzai in the wake of his election scandal, but ultimately found it expedient to support him. The two sides' relations nosedived in late 2013, when Karzai decided not to sign the US–Afghan Bilateral Security Agreement (BSA) to regularise the status of the limited number of troops that the US could leave in Afghanistan after 2014 for another decade for training and counter-terrorism purposes. Although his hand-picked *Loya Jirga* ratified the BSA as an expression of the will of the Afghan people in November, Karzai publicly preconditioned the signing of the agreement on the US assuring Afghanistan's security, respecting Afghan lives and securing a political settlement with the Taliban. Otherwise, he said his successor could deal with it. However, beneath all this, he wanted to be remembered in history as a nationalist rather than an American subordinate, to protect his future and that of his family, and to let his successor take the blame for whatever may go wrong as a result of the agreement. Consequently, relations between Karzai and the Obama administration plummeted to an all-time low, prompting the latter to consider a 'zero-option' withdrawal scheme that would see the removal of all US troops by the end of 2014, with possibly serious security, economic and reconstruction repercussions and uncertainty for Afghanistan.[73]

Karzai's presidency resulted in highly damaging political intrigues, rivalries and malpractices that permeated his administration at all levels. Serious rifts occurred even within his inner circle. In 2010, he forced two of his top security men – the Minister of Interior Hanif Atmar, and the head of the Afghan intelligence Amrullah Saleh, both of whom were perceived by Washington as highly capable – to resign. Policy disagreements with Karzai, particularly over approaches to the Taliban, were the main reason for their forced resignations.[74] Karzai had pushed desperately for a political deal with the Taliban; Atmar and Saleh, in contrast, opposed such a deal at any cost. Since then, both figures have joined the political opposition. Karzai indeed presided over not only a highly corrupt and dysfunctional government, with limited control beyond Kabul, but also a divided and conflict-riddled governing elite. The control by 'strongmen' over vast swathes of Afghan territory severely limited Karzai's writ and made him highly dependent on the goodwill of these figures and on meeting their demands. In addition, Karzai's administration was vulnerable to penetration by oppositional factions and various foreign intelligence services at both civilian and military-security levels, with his cabinet discussions and decisions allegedly leaked within hours. This, in turn, fed back into Karzai's paranoia and sense of vulnerability. His growing conviction about the existence of plots against him further exacerbated his authoritarian tendencies.[75]

Inefficiencies at all levels of Karzai's government contributed significantly to its poor reputation among the international community and the Afghans themselves. The inability of the government to effectively allocate resources had as much to do with failings at a governmental level as it had with instability in the provinces. In particular, the lack of overall direction and communication between the various tiers of government and external agencies severely restricted effective resource allocation. The disconnect between the executive and legislative branches often paralysed action, as the parliament twice rejected large numbers of Karzai's nominees for the cabinet in 2010 and 2011, with several ministries continuing to function under acting heads as late as 2013. It is therefore no surprise that when NATO assessed local governance in roughly 120 districts across the country in 2010, it was rated 'unproductive' in one-third of the districts, 'dysfunctional' in one-quarter, and in 17 districts was simply described as 'non-existent'.[76] An 'unproductive', 'dysfunctional' or, even worse, 'non-existent', government presence is unlikely to inspire local confidence in the Afghan state.

Ideologically, the Karzai government lacked a clear direction. What precisely it stood for remains ambiguous: did it represent a pro-Western, pro-capitalist democracy with an Islamic face, capable of meeting the preferences of the United States and its allies, but unsupported by a great majority of the Afghan people who are unable to identify with it? Or was it a blend of Western and Afghan values and practices, topped up by assorted Islamic traditions of authoritarianism, viewed with confusion and ambivalence by a majority of the Afghan population? The answers to these questions are yet to be clearly resolved, and are unlikely to be for quite some time yet.

Corruption

Problems at the elite level have been echoed within the population at large. Years of turbulence, bloodshed, uncertainty and unpredictability, which have seen at least four different ideological groups seizing power in Afghanistan since the pro-Soviet communist coup of April 1978, have led many ordinary citizens to place a high premium on the art of self-preservation. In doing so, they have engaged in a variety of activities which have involved deceitful and corrupt practices.[77] Sadly, the result of this is that Afghan society as a whole has become, in many ways, as dysfunctional and corrupt as the state. Whilst in many aspects the state–society dichotomy has become entrenched, at least in this respect the two have come to have much in common.

Rampant corruption has seeped into the everyday lives of the Afghan people. The 2010 UNODC report cited earlier claimed that 59 per cent of Afghan citizens see corruption as the most prominent problem for the country. More indicative of recent trends is the fact that 80 per cent of rural dwellers believed it had significantly increased from 2005 to 2010.[78] In the same report, Afghans claimed that 40 per cent of the time they had contact with senior politicians they were solicited for a bribe. During 2009, one Afghan out of every two had to pay kickbacks to a public official. In that year, Afghans as a whole paid out US$2.5 billion in bribes, accounting for an astronomical one-quarter of Afghanistan's GDP.[79]

Corruption has reportedly been lower in the larger metropolitan cities,[80] in the presence of Afghan and international watchdogs such as the High Office of Oversight and judiciary anti-corruption units.[81] But the same cannot be said about the provinces, as these watchdogs lack sufficient reach in Afghanistan's periphery. Even then, only 9 per cent of city dwellers have ever bothered reporting an act of bribery to the authorities, a clear reflection of the state's inability to redress legal grievances and of the resignation of many Afghans to the existence of corruption in daily life.[82] While the Karzai government attempted to counteract this issue through pay and grading reforms and an increase in ANA and ANP salaries, two facts indicate that money alone will not be sufficient to root out this malaise, which has become so embedded in Afghan society. First, government operating budget expenditures already doubled between 2006 and 2010.[83] Second, the large sums demanded in bribes by highly placed enforcement officials suggest that greed, rather than necessity, is often the major motivation.[84] The difficulty of rooting out corruption in a country where domestic politics and international interests have been so closely intertwined yet often conflicting is significant. The case of Mohammad Zia Salehi may be taken as exemplary. As the chief of administration for the Afghan National Security Council and a close Karzai confidant, Salehi came under investigation for corruption after wiretapping caught him soliciting a bribe.[85] Although Salehi was quickly released from prison (through Karzai's personal intervention) and charges were soon dropped, the event caused considerable embarrassment to the United States and particularly the CIA, on whose payroll Salehi seems to have remained at least until 2011.[86] A further example is that of the Kabul Bank, whose US$900 million deposits have been embezzled by culprits ranging from Hamid Karzai and his Vice President Mohammad Fahim to Mahmoud Karzai. Afghanistan's poor governance is clearly and intrinsically linked with the flawed US and NATO approach to rebuilding the country. Transparency International's annual list for 2013 named Afghanistan along with North Korea and Somalia as the world's most corrupt countries.[87]

The Economy

Natural resources

In the midst of these political debacles, Afghanistan faced the urgent need of addressing shortcomings within its domestic economy. Investment in both natural resources, and those of the Afghan people, are of the utmost importance for Afghanistan if it wishes to have a fighting chance of becoming an independent and viable state in the long run. The Pentagon's 2010 announcement that Afghanistan could be sitting on untapped mineral resources worth US$1 trillion did not come as a surprise to most Afghan observers, who had some knowledge since the late 1960s of the country's extensive iron, copper, gold and oil deposits.[88] Whether this wealth amounts to US$3 trillion or more, as suggested by the Afghan Minister of Mines Wahidullah Shahrani,[89] or closer to US$500 million, as suggested by experienced geologists who strongly question the announced discoveries of lithium and niobium deposits,[90] it is clear that mineral exploration in Afghanistan will prove a worthy investment.

While mining was only a US$52 million a year industry as of 2010, the China Metallurgical Group's (CMG) Anyak copper mine, when and if it comes to full fruition, is expected to bring in US$1 billion of annual revenue for Kabul, and CMG has agreed to invest US$3 billion in the project.[91] However, even though some geologists believe that the Aynak copper field may be the world's largest undeveloped copper mine, the same obstacles that prevented it from being developed in the last 30 years could prevent CMG from meeting its production goals there as well.[92] Infrastructure difficulties are quite clear: US$500 million needs to be invested in an electrical power plant and a large amount in constructing a railroad. There have also been complications in the removal of archaeological and cultural artefacts, and issues over the disposal of toxic waste. The immense investment needed, complicated by insurgent attacks, has made the overall mineral auction process difficult. For instance, tendering for the Haji Gak iron ore field (the largest untapped mine in Asia) in the central Afghan province of Bamiyan, with an estimated two billion tons of iron ore, failed in its first attempt in 2009. The contract was ultimately won by an Indian company in partnership with an Afghan firm, largely owned by Karzai's brothers.[93]

The current government's focus on mineral extraction as a lynchpin of Afghanistan's economic growth may also likely stifle local entrepreneurship and foster public dependence on the state.[94] In this sense, the Pentagon's description of Afghanistan as possibly the 'Saudi Arabia of lithium' may prove to be an inaccurate prediction. If mineral wealth becomes the driver of the Afghan economy, poor governance, corruption and local conflicts over resources are likely to become even more entrenched in the country. On the other hand, without a source of income, the Afghan economy is likely to remain hostage to foreign handouts, and the narcotics and drugs industry. With the withdrawal of foreign forces, Afghanistan is expected to experience a severe economic downturn.

A narco-state

With opium cultivation in 2013 increasing for the third year running and set to become the nation's major economic activity in 2014, Afghanistan has for all practical purposes become, once again, a narco-state.[95] The poppy trade, which was estimated to constitute 30 to 50 per cent of the Afghan economy in 2009, comprised around 15 per cent of the nation's

GDP as of April 2013.[96] Given the wide range of motivations that drive Afghanistan's opium economy, which accounts for more than 90 per cent of the global supply of heroin,[97] this trend is unlikely to be reversed even if the Taliban are eliminated.[98] The 2013 Opium Risk Assessment Report, issued by UNODC, predicted a further increase in opium production over the ensuing 12 months, particularly in the south, where the surge occurred and where the Taliban are present.[99] The number of Afghan addicts has now reached an alarming proportion, with serious long-term social consequences for the country.[100] Proceeds from opium, heroin production and drug trafficking have become a main source not only for funding the operations of the Taliban and other private militias, but also for enriching government officials, many of whom have been heavily involved in the industry. Afghanistan's current status as a 'narco-state' also has important regional and global ramifications. At the March 2009 Shanghai Cooperation Organisation Conference on Afghanistan, the Russian foreign minister, Sergey Lavrov, stated that drug trafficking had become the most serious threat for Russia and Central Asian countries. At that time, some 12 tons of pure heroin, enough for about three billion single doses, were arriving in Russia each year from Afghanistan.[101]

While 500,000 families were estimated to be involved in opium poppy cultivation in 2008,[102] many analysts and even UNODC have arrived at the conclusion that poppy cultivation is becoming disassociated from poverty and increasingly linked to the insurgency and corruption.[103] In other words, the destruction of the opium industry has become less and less likely to endanger the well-being of poor families. Instead, it is the 'well-being' of entrenched elites, drug barons and insurgent groups that is at risk, especially in the areas of the Pashtun south. It is widely reported that some of Karzai's relatives and cronies, including the late Ahmad Wali Karzai, have been among the main culprits. Poor governance, corruption and narcotics are completely intertwined as the revenue from poppy cultivation finds its way into the pockets of hundreds of police chiefs, judges and senior Afghan officials.[104]

A variety of issues drive farmers toward the planting of poppies. The lack of credit facilities and accessibility to drug barons who provide loans provides one economic incentive, but the virtues of the poppy plant yield others. Poppy is less prone to spoilage than other crops and therefore easier to transport on debilitated roads; it is also a hardy crop, making it a preferable choice in dry regions where irrigation is poor.[105] Finally, and most importantly, the cultivation of opium yields exponentially greater returns per acre than cereal crops, such as rice or wheat.

Three overarching and largely unsuccessful strategies have been variously employed by NATO and the Afghan government to combat poppy production since 2001: compensated eradication, interdiction and 'resolute' eradication. Compensated eradication, which involved a cash payment by NATO and Afghan officials for crops, proved to be a massive failure. If farmers receive cash for poppies, they keep the money and grow poppies again the following year in order to earn more cash. Such a 'perverse incentive' has never worked anywhere in the world.[106] Interdiction, a strategy framed in 2004 around targeting large drug traffickers and 'strongmen', created a vacuum in the market and allowed the Taliban to re-enter the business. By the time 'resolute' eradication had become a strategy, disagreements between the United Kingdom (the lead nation on counter-narcotics), the United States and the Afghan government led to a disjointed and often uncoordinated counter-narcotics effort which prevailed until near the end of the occupation.[107] In addition, each policy failure led to a stronger response from the international community, which in turn alienated the local population and increased support for the Taliban and other insurgent groups. The management of Afghanistan's narcotics sector is set to be a great and ongoing problem for the country.

Counter-Systemic Actors and Tensions

Poor governance, elite fragmentation and corruption, societal divisions and problems and a flawed international approach to Afghanistan's transition have interacted inauspiciously over time to generate space and conditions for a number of counter-systemic actors. Chief among them are the Taliban, with three noted spoilers on their tail: the *Hezbi Islami* (Islamic Party) of the former maverick *Mujahideen* leader, Hekmatyar; the Jalaluddin *Haqqani* network; and al-Qaeda. Contrary to popular belief, the Taliban – one of whose closely associated lethal groups is the *Haqqani* network – are not necessarily a united movement, as they are divided between various groups. Nor are they the best-trained, best-equipped and best-led force. The Taliban cluster is instead largely made up of self-styled but poorly trained, fed and clothed *jihadis*, with only the Pakistani ISI behind them. Unlike the *Mujahideen,* who enjoyed the support of the United States and its allies in the 1980s, the Taliban are not backed by any world power. They have become formidable again largely because the failures of the Karzai administration and of its foreign allies have generated a massive political and security vacuum. The Taliban and their Pakistani backers have drawn skilfully on these failures at both strategic and operational levels to mount and sustain a serious challenge from outside the system. The Taliban's projection of themselves as the forceful defender of faith, country and honour, as well as harbingers of social justice and improved security and living conditions, has gained substantial historical and cultural resonance among many ethnic Pashtuns, and among some other disfranchised elements of other Afghan communities. A May 2010 US Department of Defense report surveyed 92 districts across the country to gauge their feelings toward the government. Out of the 92, the respondents in 44 expressed a neutral opinion and 48 were sympathetic to the Taliban.[108] Meanwhile, the Taliban and other counter-systemic actors became increasingly confident in their approach in the years following the invasion, signified by an alarming trend in 2011 that witnessed a 105 per cent increase in the targeted killings of government officials, aid workers and civilians perceived to be supportive of the Karzai government or ISAF.[109] The greater the disarray in the Karzai government and US-led strategy, the more the Taliban and their supporters felt encouraged to maintain their resistance.

Against this backdrop, the Karzai and Obama administrations found it imperative in 2010 to launch an earnest policy of reconciliation and settlement with the Taliban. Washington and its allies provided the Karzai government with an initial pledge of US$160 million to enable it to buy off as many Taliban as possible.[110] Karzai outsourced the task of negotiating with the Taliban to a 'High Peace Council', which was headed by former President Burhanuddin until his assassination by insurgents in September 2011. Burhanuddin was replaced by his relatively young and inexperienced but determined son, Salahuddin.[111] Attempts at some kind of negotiated settlement proceeded in spite of the intermittent labelling of the Taliban by the United States and its allies as an al-Qaeda-linked terrorist group, and the rejection of Karzai as a Western 'puppet' by the Taliban and their affiliates.

The Karzai and US policy of reconciliation and the efforts of the High Peace Council initially seemed somewhat promising. In January

2012, senior Taliban officials arrived in Qatar to open a political office in the country. This was seen as a potential breakthrough in negotiations between the Karzai administration, the Taliban and the United States.[112] However, these efforts soon proved untenable in the aftermath of two critical events in Afghanistan. In February 2012, the media reported that copies of the Qur'an were burnt at a US military base. While this did not directly affect negotiations with the Taliban, with a spokesperson for the group specifying that 'this issue will not affect [the] process in Qatar',[113] the killing of 17 civilians by a US soldier in Kandahar in the following month cemented the end of a short-lived experiment.[114]

In many ways, however, this negotiation process seemed doomed to failure. First, the possibility of reconciliation with the Taliban set off jitters among Afghanistan's non-Pashtun population and women's rights groups. Second, the Taliban leadership continued to insist that it would talk with the government only when all foreign forces had left Afghanistan. Alternatively, the Taliban signalled the possibility of negotiating solely with the United States without the input of the Afghan government – a proposition that predictably angered the Afghan president. Third, Karzai's approach was undermined by a fundamental contradiction in US and NATO policy that encouraged reconciliation with the Taliban while at the same time focused on fighting and killing as many of them as possible. Fourth, Karzai used the High Peace Council as a means to reward his supporters, and silence and marginalise his opponents.

Even when the Taliban finally agreed (although it is not clear which group of the movement did so) to send two representatives from their Qatar office to attend a two-day meeting with their counterparts from various non-governmental Afghan political factions at the invitation of a French think tank, the Foundation for Strategic Research, in late December 2012 in Paris, the meeting amounted to nothing more than what the Taliban spokesperson called an 'exchange of views'. The Taliban delegation not only reiterated their past demands, but also asked for a new Afghan constitution which would be in accordance with their own interpretation of Islam as well as with their preferences for their labelling of the country as the 'Islamic Emirates of Afghanistan'. Despite the gloss put on the meeting by the United States and Pakistan as an 'ice breaker', with the US and allied troops' withdrawal nearing, the Taliban and their supporters were clearly in no rush for a political settlement.[115]

The Taliban's official opening of a political office in April 2013 in Qatar, for the purpose of facilitating direct negotiations with Washington and possibly the Afghan government, proved similarly disappointing. The Taliban's projection of their office as a diplomatic mission of the Islamic Emirates of Afghanistan, as well as Washington's initial benign attitude to this, prompted Karzai to denounce the whole development and refuse to back any American dialogue with the Taliban without his government's full participation. After months of unsuccessful negotiations and stand-offs that led more than once to the closing of the Taliban's Doha office, the group's elusive leader, Mohammad Omar, announced on 6 August 2013 that the Taliban would not take part in presidential elections and would continue to wage war until all foreign troops withdrew.[116]

The Afghans, who have traditionally been in the grip of an authoritarian political culture, have remained caught between two forces in the aftermath of the US-led invasion. The first is the US- and NATO-backed corrupt and weak governing elite that has sought to lead them down a path of semi-secular political change, an ideology which fails to resonate with a majority of Afghans. On the other side are the Taliban and their associates, who want all Afghans to embrace a radical version of political Islam as the only viable ideology of salvation. The Taliban and their Pakistani backers have all along had strong reason to believe that despite their public rhetoric, the United States and its allies will not be able to empower Afghanistan to ensure its own security. They seem to be assured of this despite a pledge by the United States and its allies at the Chicago summit and international donors conference in Tokyo to provide Afghanistan with some US$8.1 billion in security and construction assistance until at least 2016, and willingness by them to leave a residual force behind until 2024, provided that the Karzai government meets certain benchmarks in terms of instituting serious political, social, economic and anti-corruption reforms, and sign a bilateral security agreement with the United States. However, in July 2013, a meeting of major donor nations concluded that the Karzai government had not met its end of the bargain, as it had so far fulfilled only three of the seventeen benchmarks. It severely criticised Karzai for appointing unqualified and partisan people on Afghanistan's Independent Human Rights Commission.[117] Lingering doubts about the capacity of the Karzai government to meet the benchmarks, and the willingness of the United States and its allies to meet their commitments, served only to reinforce the resolve of the Taliban and their affiliates to hold out against a political settlement.

International Relations and Foreign Interests

While Afghanistan's stability and security is far from assured, the US-led intervention has nonetheless once again reinforced the country's geostrategic importance and lately highlighted its potential as a natural resource-rich but narcotic-saturated state. Despite being one of the world's poorest and most conflict-ridden countries, these imperatives, along with the potential threat of Islamic extremism emanating from within the Afghan borders, have served to create interlinked interests between regional neighbours and major powers in relation to the country.

China's growing interest in Afghanistan is largely grounded in ideological and economic considerations. It perceives Afghanistan to be a possible source of pan-Islamic militant groups that could influence its Muslim Uighur population and affect the security environment of the predominantly Sunni Muslim Xinjiang Province, which borders Afghanistan.[118] In addition to its involvement in the Aynak copper project, China is estimated to have invested around 900 million yuan in Afghanistan,[119] to have abolished tariffs on many of Afghanistan's exports and to have participated in a number of business enterprises in the country. Its investment has focused on the irrigation, infrastructure, telecommunications and power sectors. In December 2012, China also signed a multi-billion-dollar agreement with Kabul to explore and exploit oil in the Amu bastion in north Afghanistan over the next two decades. Beijing finds it desirable to see a stable Afghanistan, and signed a China–Afghan declaration of 'bilateral strategic partnership' in June 2012.

Russia has both political and economic reasons for retaining an interest in Afghanistan. It seems eager to regain some of its past influence in the country, in line with its broader desire to re-establish a strong foothold in the former Soviet Central Asian republics, or what it calls 'Near Abroad' – a development which Washington and, for that matter, Beijing, would find adverse to their interests.[120] The Russian government is in the process of planning a Collective Security Treaty Organisation or 'CSTO-Afghanistan' oil pipeline which would run throughout Afghanistan,[121] and has a vested interest in the destruction of the poppy fields which fund both the Taliban and, more importantly for Russia, radical Islamic groups with links to Chechen and Dagestani Islamic networks.

Iran and India are united in their interest in containing and limiting Pakistani influence in Afghanistan. For Iran, Pakistani Sunni influence appears as a direct threat to its Shi'a revolutionary ideology. Iran has worked on fostering economic, trade, cultural and political ties with the western provinces of Afghanistan, with which it shares deep historical and cultural ties. For India, curtailing Pakistan's support of the Taliban and other Islamic extremist groups is a pressing security prerogative, as demonstrated by the 2008 Mumbai bombings and continued violence within Indian-controlled Kashmir. India also aims to build a bridge to Central Asia through Afghanistan and has invested around US$150 million in completing the Zaranj–Delaram road project, which effectively links India and Iran to Central Asia through southern Afghanistan.[122] It has also established electricity lines from Uzbekistan to eastern Afghanistan, including Kabul, financed the new Afghan parliament building and constructed many roads.[123] Coming on top of this is India's lion's share in the Haji Gak iron ore project. With India expected to invest some US$10 billion in Afghanistan over the next 30 years, this could result in stronger relations between the two countries.[124] To enhance security ties, India and Afghanistan also signed a strategic partnership agreement in September 2011, enabling New Delhi to provide military and police training and potentially wider security assistance to Afghanistan if necessary.

India's growing involvement has invoked the ire of both the Afghan Taliban and their effective backers in the Pakistani ISI. A leaked US military report suggests that the ISI paid the Taliban-linked *Haqqani* network US$15,000–US$30,000 to eliminate Indian nationals working on the road project and to target both engineers and road workers.[125] Even though both the March 2009 UN-backed Hague Conference and January 2010 London Conference suggested that regional countries should play a greater role in stabilising and developing Afghanistan,[126] a stable Afghanistan dominated by a secular regime is not currently considered by Pakistan to be in its strategic interests. Utilising the Taliban as a strategic tool in its rivalry with India, Pakistan has continually resisted India's growing influence in Afghanistan and worked towards a political settlement of the Afghan conflict that could empower its proxy Taliban-led forces in one way or another. As a result, the Karzai administration's efforts to position Afghanistan as a hub of trade and connectivity between its neighbours and within the greater region have not resulted in concrete positive outcomes.[127]

Russia has historically had similar interests to Iran and India in Afghanistan. All three lent support to the United Front from time to time against the Taliban during the latter's rule of the country, and all have developed a common interest in an Afghan government that is not dominated by the Taliban or a Taliban-partnered group.[128] In fact, it was only with very great reluctance that Moscow agreed to Taliban participation in the December 2012 Paris meeting. Nevertheless, the underlying support, whether overt or behind the scenes, of these three countries, plus China (which has also traditionally maintained close strategic ties with Pakistan), for the US and international agenda in Afghanistan is contingent on the implementation of policies which they believe will decrease the Islamic Sunni extremist threat and on the potential to reap economic dividends. Pakistan, on the other hand, has long shared historical linkages with Afghanistan. Its policy toward the latter, both complex and often misunderstood, is discussed in depth in Chapter 3. What is clear, however, is that the role played by regional actors in Afghanistan will become more important when the United States and its allies withdraw most of their troops from the country.

The Way Forward

There is an urgent need for serious inter-elite dialogue and a national consensus within Afghanistan itself. Following the US-led invasion, both the Karzai government and the political opposition remained highly fragmented, with no overriding purpose for national unity or agreement regarding the direction that Afghanistan should take. The Karzai leadership became increasingly self-centred and self-seeking, and the same applied to all other political factions, although in varying degrees. The problems of Afghanistan cannot be addressed on an enduring basis as long as the Afghan governing and political opposition clusters remain divided on how to generate an effective and legitimate leadership and move the country forward. Unfortunately, most actors within the government as well as within other political factions have seemed to be predominantly concerned with enhancing and protecting their individual interests. Precious little attention has been paid to what would be required to build solid institutional bases for an enduring inclusive political order and appropriate processes of change and development. Yet this is what is needed in order to endow Afghanistan with a capacity whereby a majority of its citizens could experience positive changes in their living conditions and could defend their country against internal disorder and foreign encroachment.

Afghanistan is badly in need of effective and legitimate leadership, and this can only occur as a result of efforts by the Afghans themselves. The emergence of such a leadership is central to tackling other dimensions of the Afghan crisis. It is only from such a position that an appropriate process of political settlement with the Taliban and their associates could be pursued and that Pakistan's support for them, and consequent leverage in the post-withdrawal Afghan political and strategic landscape, could be curtailed. By the same token, regional rivalries in and over Afghanistan could be constrained.

The long-term success of such developments rests on the successful implementation of a number of factors. Afghanistan needs a diversified, party-based parliamentary or proportionally representative system of governance for two important reasons. First, it would provide for a range of actors to be locked into a framework of national obligations and responsibilities, directing them to participate constructively in national affairs. It would also allow micro-societies a necessary degree of self-regulation in the exercise of their local affairs, while enabling them to relate to the overall political system through their local representative bodies and national parliament. Second, it would remove the burden of responsibility from a single individual (as is currently the case in the strong presidential system), who could easily become the focus of public discontent if things were to go wrong. In the meantime, it would prevent the winner from either using the powers of his office to build a system of patronage, or acting as a delegative leader between elections. The 2004 Afghan constitution provides for a separation of powers, rule of law, checks and balances, effective mechanisms of public scrutiny, and rights and duties of citizens, the implementation of all of which are necessary for the transition of a state from total disruption to stability and viability. However, they have all meant little in the face of empowering the president to do what he deems desirable to manipulate and maintain power in the context of a highly divided society. To change the Afghan system would require a substantial modification of the Afghan constitution of 2004. This, in turn, would require a new constitutional *Loya Jirga* to be convened, similar to the one that ratified the present constitution.

The emphasis on democracy, which initially dominated the US approach to reconstruction in Afghanistan, has thus far proved unhelpful. A more constructive focus might be on creating a workable government, with a culturally relevant national manifesto of state building that could help generate good governance as a prelude to democracy. Elections are too often equated with democracy. In a country like Afghanistan, which lacks democratic traditions and has historically been subjected to traditionalist, authoritarian rule, elections must for the moment be seen as simply one of many tools for creating legitimate government, with a gradual approach to fostering manageable political pluralism, civil society activities and national reconciliation. This approach could include temporarily delegating considerable informal decision-making power to local communities, until such time as the central institutions in Kabul have reformed into legitimate and functional bodies. Effective local governance does not necessarily need a strong central government.[129] The role of UNAMA might be adapted to this approach. Only then could the country secure the foundations for the growth of substantive democracy in the long run.

It is also necessary to return to, and formally reaffirm, Afghanistan's traditional neutrality in world politics in order to reassure the country's neighbours, especially Pakistan and Iran, that Afghanistan will not pose any threat to them or act in the interest of any outside power against them. As part of this, Afghanistan would be required to modify the strategic partnership agreements that it has signed with various countries, especially with the United States, into 'strategic friendship agreements' whereby they would not be viewed as actionable defence pacts vis-à-vis the interests of the neighbouring states. The sooner Kabul is able to disentangle Afghanistan from the Indo-Pakistani and US-Iranian rivalries, which have somewhat moderated since the mid-2013 change of government in Iran (see Chapter 4), the better for Afghan and regional stability. These imperatives, in conjunction with the Afghan leaders getting their act together to produce an effective leadership for Afghanistan as their first priority, could instrumentally help a process of regional consensus to consolidate on Afghanistan, provided that the process is led by the UN Secretary-General and backed by the five permanent members of the UN Security Council.

Further, the conflict within Afghanistan since 2001 has been essentially an intra-Pashtun one, with the majority of the non-Pashtun population having remained largely aloof. It is important to engage in such processes of state building that could focus on two objectives. One would be to reduce the vulnerability of the Pashtun population, who have borne the brunt of the fighting since the US-led intervention, to ideological extremism as expounded by the Taliban and their supporters. Another would be to prevent the non-Pashtun Afghans from sliding deeper into a situation that could compel them to take up arms once again in order to defend themselves against a Pashtun-dominated government in Kabul. In this context, whatever political accommodation is reached with the Taliban and their affiliates would need to have the support of a wide cross-section of Afghanistan's mosaic society.

It might also be best to focus on a diverse set of narcotics problems rather than a 'narcotics problem' as such. Considering the variety of 'micro' issues which drive the production of the poppy, and as the Afghan government and outside actors have not come up with a common approach to tackle the problem,[130] it might be more productive to address core local issues rather than attempting to tackle the monster of Afghanistan's narcotics problem as a whole. The correlation between instability, lack of governance, and strong drug trafficking networks on the one hand, and widespread poppy cultivation on the other must be taken into account in any attempt to combat narcotics production. Finally, regional differences must be considered. Five Afghan provinces, all in the south, accounted for 95 per cent of the country's poppy cultivation in 2009.[131] A two-pronged strategy, therefore, might prove useful – one in the north and one in the south.

A diversified economy and decisive anti-corruption campaign are also crucial for the country to reach its economic potential. Improvements in agriculture, an industry currently worth US$3.3 billion, would be prudent, as this sector employs more than 40 per cent of Afghans.[132] The 22.5 per cent GDP growth during the 2009–10 fiscal year was largely attributed to a strong rebound in the agricultural sector, which was aided by ample and well-distributed rainfall. However, improvements in agriculture will not help every community. The poverty rate in Afghanistan is, on average, higher in the mountainous regions of the country in the west, which is home to one-fifth of its population.[133] Industrial growth continues to be pulled down by modest manufacturing and construction sector growth rates. The Karzai leadership promised much but did little to reduce corruption. This problem must nevertheless be tackled from the top, with the Afghan leaders paving the way for others.

Without meeting challenges in these areas, Afghanistan's future appears to be as bleak as the country's past, especially since the pro-Soviet communist coup of April 1978. This may be the case whatever role the Taliban and Pakistan, or the United States and its allies, might play in the country. The future of Afghanistan now rests very much with the Afghan leaders and their factions. The sooner Afghanistan has a widely mandated and visionary leadership as the core element in its transformation, the better its chances of digging itself out of its crisis. All local power-holders and factional leaders bear a special responsibility in this regard. They have the option of leaving behind either a dark and destructive legacy or a forward-looking and constructive situation on which an enduring, stable, progressive and sovereign Afghan state could be built. As the situation stands, the future of Afghanistan hangs very much in the balance.

PAKISTAN

Fragile and Violent

Introduction

Both the 1979 Soviet invasion of Afghanistan and the subsequent 2001 US-led intervention in the country seriously impacted on neighbouring Pakistan which, although a nuclear-armed state, is at the same time domestically fragile and volatile. Developments in the two countries have been so intertwined that some analysts and policymakers have opted to lump them together under the joint designation, 'Af-Pak'. The 11 September 2001 al-Qaeda attacks on the United States, and the ensuing American 'war on terror', came at a noteworthy time for the then President of Pakistan, General Pervez Musharraf, who had seized power in a military coup in 1999. Diplomatically ostracised by the international community in the wake of his coup, Musharraf was understandably quick to comply with US demands for assistance in Afghanistan in exchange for the United States legitimising his rule and providing material support to his regime. Pursuing a Janus-like agenda, he attempted to position himself as the backer and beneficiary of the 'war of terror' while manoeuvring to manipulate this war against US objectives in pursuit of his own interests and those of Pakistan, as defined by himself and a close coterie of senior generals. As it turned out, his overriding domestic goal was the creation of a stronger and more unified Pakistan under his own centralised military rule. Regionally, Musharraf sought merely to maintain the status quo and therefore made no meaningful structural adjustments in Pakistan's foreign policy priorities and objectives.

In the face of an ultimatum from the George W. Bush administration either to join the United States or be counted among its terrorist enemies and, according to Musharraf himself, be bombed into the 'stone age', Musharraf pragmatically threw in his lot with Washington.[1] In declaring Pakistan a US partner in Bush's self-proclaimed 'war on terror', beginning with 'Operation Enduring Freedom' in Afghanistan, in October 2001, Musharraf forged a new and robust alliance with the United States. Some visible elements of Pakistan's foreign policy posture were altered almost overnight, with considerable impact on the country's domestic political dynamics. Yet it would be a mistake to view these developments as producing any kind of meaningful consensus within Pakistani politics. Since the renewal of the US–Pakistan alliance, establishing a situation more or less identical to that which was the case during the Soviet occupation of Afghanistan in the 1980s, the interests of various social, political and religious groups interacted to produce divergent and competing trends in the realms of governance and economic management at the expense of coherent and effective policies. The existence of an often corrupt, ineffective and dysfunctional elite, coupled with the rise of ideological extremism within Pakistan, contributed to a spike in domestic terrorism and violence in the years after 11 September 2001. The shift to a civilian government and the rise of Asif Zardari to the presidency following the 2008 election did little or nothing to alter this state of affairs. If anything, it made the situation even worse. President Zardari had a long and well-documented history of corruption, and the military and the Inter-Services Intelligence (ISI) continued to exercise substantial power from behind the scenes. Far from ebbing slowly away, violence and extremism has continued to reap a devastating toll on Pakistanis. Overall fatalities from domestic 'terrorist violence' increased from 1,471 in 2006 to a peak of 11,704 in 2009.[2] Although these figures subsequently stabilised, they remained extremely sobering. Over 1,000 civilians were killed by suicide bombings in 2010 alone,[3] and the number of civilian deaths rose from 1,796 in 2010 to 2,738 in 2011, and 3,007 in 2012.[4]

The killing by the US of the nominal and spiritual head of al-Qaeda, Osama bin Laden, on 2 May 2011, brought to a head a number of divergent and often contradictory Pakistani objectives. Having succeeded in locating bin Laden in Abbottabad, a city well known for its high-standard military establishments, the United States opted to conduct a covert and illicit operation to kill him without the knowledge or involvement of the Pakistani military and the ISI. The consequences of this action, which amounted to nothing less than a transgression of Pakistani national sovereignty, combined with increased US drone and other cross-border attacks, were immense. The Pakistani government resolved to publically castigate the United States for its actions, and the Army's Chief of Staff, General Ashfaq Parvez Kayani, made it clear that any further violations of Pakistan's sovereignty would present a substantial threat to future cooperation between the Pakistani intelligence and military and the United States.[5] From the other side, American policymakers began to question the nature of the US–Pakistan relationship, especially with regard to the vast sums of American money that had been provided on the pretext of a somewhat conspicuously inconspicuous fight against 'terrorism' and 'extremism'. In the face of persistent domestic extremism and faltering international relations, the situation in Pakistan deteriorated.

What brought Pakistan to this point? Why has Pakistan not been able to reconcile its interests in its declared alliance with the United States? What factors can explain why the situation has been getting worse for the Pakistani people, and what might the future hold for them? In two respects, the problem in modern Pakistan has closely resembled that faced by its Afghan neighbour. Since its creation in 1947, Pakistan has been beleaguered by a number of issues similar to those of Afghanistan, and those of the region more broadly. They range from the historical legacy of its mosaic society to dysfunctional elites, poor governance, corruption, ideological extremism, flawed foreign policy priorities and objectives, and contradictory attempts by the United States to influence the country according to its geopolitical preferences.

Social Divisions

Pakistan, like Afghanistan, is a true patchwork of cultures, ethnicities and linguistic groups. According to most official estimates, the total population of Pakistan was over 185 million as of 2012.[6] Of this figure, Pakistan's largest ethnic groups – the Punjabis, Sindhis, Pathans (or Pashtuns, as they are called on the Afghan side of the border), and Baluchis – were estimated respectively at 91 million, 55 million, 27 million and 13 million.[7] Linguistic identities follow from these ethnic differences: Punjabis claim Punjabi as their first language, Pathans claim

Pashto, and so on. However, the national language, Urdu, is spoken and understood by a majority of the population, and the same applies, though a less extent, to the official language of state, English. The latter is often the key to upward social mobility and more frequently associated with the 'upper classes'; Urdu, with close historical and contemporary ties to the spread of Islam, is more widely spoken, and is more or less the 'language of the street'.[8]

As in so many post-colonial states, the borders of modern-day Pakistan, drawn up decades ago by the machinations of British colonialists, fail to correspond in any meaningful way to existing linguistic, cultural or ethnic units. Indeed, the limits of the state of Pakistan cut across many such groups, with the result that a number of Pakistanis living on the fringes of the state continue to identify with populations beyond the country's borders. On both sides of the Indian–Pakistani border exist Punjabi and Sindhi ethnic groups; the Baluchis inhabit a territory that runs into Pakistan, Afghanistan and Iran; and the Pathans, some of whom have over time become largely assimilated into Punjabi society, populate Pakistan's Khyber-Pakhtunkhwa province (previously known as the North-West Frontier Province – NWFP), the Federally Administered Tribal Areas (FATA) along the border with Afghanistan, and much of northern Baluchistan, which also borders Afghanistan.[9] At different moments, and for various reasons, particular ethnic groups within Pakistan have risen up against each other, or against the state. In addition, as is the case in most Muslim majority states, the Sunni–Shi'a cleavage often rears its head in Pakistan. Similar to Afghanistan, around 80 per cent of Pakistan's Muslims are followers of Sunni Islam, while most of the remainder belong to the Shi'a sect. As a whole, Muslims constitute 96.4 per cent of Pakistan's total population.[10] There are also small numbers of Ahmedis (a self-identifying Islamic sect considered heretical by mainstream Muslims), Christians and Hindus, who collectively form less than 4 per cent of the populace.

In addition to intra-provincial tensions, mostly aimed at the majority Punjabis, bitter ethnic rivalries exist within provinces. The Muhajirs – Urdu-speaking families who migrated to Pakistan following independence and who have become increasingly frustrated as a consequence of their marginal position in Pakistani society – are in a struggle with the native Sindhi population in the south. The Baluchi and Pathan tribesmen have become embroiled in competition for the natural resources of Baluchistan.[11] Another serious difficulty for the state has been the sub-nationalist movement of the Baluchi people. Baluchistan, one of Pakistan's richest provinces in terms of natural resources, is nevertheless home to the nation's poorest people. In 2008, although Baluchistan provided Pakistan with 45 per cent of its energy needs, 63 per cent of its population were living below the poverty line, with 85 per cent lacking access even to safe drinking water – a situation which has not changed substantially to date.[12] Unsurprisingly, the Baluchis have become increasingly resentful of the one-sided relationship between the province and the state. Feelings of exploitation and injustice have been exacerbated by the state's siding with the Pathans in intra-provincial disputes, feeding into a growing sub-nationalist movement among the Baluchi people that manifested itself in a full-blown insurgency launched in 2005. At the same time, the growing discontent and allegiance to an extreme form of Islam among the Pathans, nurtured mostly by the Pakistani state in the context of the long-running conflict with India, the ongoing conflict in Afghanistan, and wider regional geopolitical ambitions, have morphed into a Pathan-dominated Taliban insurgency in Khyber-Pakhtunkhwa and FATA. This insurgency, on the rise since Musharraf's coup of 1999, had, as of 2012, tied down over 120,000 military and paramilitary forces in the region.[13] By 2013, the insurgency had showed little sign of abating; if anything, it had reached a level that threatened the integrity of the Pakistani state.

Historical Legacy

Colonialism, post-colonialism and quasi-democracy

The state of Pakistan was born out of the All-India Muslim League's focus on Muslim and minority rights in Hindu-dominated India. The leader of the Muslim League and one of the central figures of the Indian independence movement, Muhammad Ali Jinnah, had consistently advocated a 'two-nation theory' that envisioned the creation of a separate Muslim homeland in the wake of Indian independence from Great Britain. It was to Jinnah's demands that the British colonialists acceded in 1947, instigating a hasty and ill-prepared partition of the dominion. The Indian Independence Act created Pakistan by partitioning the former provinces of Bengal and Punjab along confessional lines between Hindu-majority India and Muslim-majority Pakistan. Carved out of the two Muslim majority wings of British India, the new state of Pakistan comprised West Pakistan (modern-day Pakistan) and East Pakistan (modern-day Bangladesh), which bookended India at its western and eastern borders. The partition led to communal riots and often violent mass migrations as panic-stricken Muslims and Hindus poured across the borders of the newly formed countries of India and Pakistan.[14] Hundreds of thousands of deaths resulted from religiously motivated violence and the newly formed government found itself struggling with a refugee crisis of gargantuan proportions.[15]

Although in no way commensurate to the staggering and tragic human cost that it had to bear as a consequence of the partition, the Pakistani government did receive a share of British India's state assets. However, unlike India, which could count on building on the British structure of governance that it was handed as the successor to the British colonial state, Pakistan inherited neither a credible federal structure nor the political machinery necessary to integrate the new nation-state. Pakistan, in other words, emerged from the partition lacking the basic infrastructural elements needed for the running of a government. These chronic problems of poor governance, weak infrastructure and inadequate finances were compounded by the obvious difficulty of governing a country that was separated by 1,600 kilometres of Indian territory.[16]

Soon after partition, the political status of the princely state of Jammu and Kashmir sparked the cycle of Pakistani–Indian animosity that has endured for more than half a century. As part of the partition process, it was agreed that princely states would be allowed to join India or Pakistan, or opt for independence. The Hindu ruler of Jammu and Kashmir, Hari Singh, aimed to remain independent, although his subjects were 77 per cent Muslim. Following incursions from Pakistani tribesmen, which may or may not have been supported by the Pakistani government, Singh agreed to join India in return for protection. This provoked great consternation in Pakistan and led to the outbreak of the 1947 Indo-Pakistan War, whereby Pakistan occupied one-third of Kashmir and India the remaining two-thirds.[17] Since the first Indo-Pakistan War, and therefore effectively since its inception, Pakistan has continued to view India as its paramount strategic threat. From the early days, Pakistani leaders found it expedient to look to the Muslim world, specifically the oil-rich Arab states, led by Saudi Arabia, and the United States, to shield itself against what it perceived as threats from India and Afghanistan, with which Pakistan has also had a long-standing border dispute. The vagaries of the Cold War played their role in the process, as Kabul and New Delhi developed close ties with the Soviet Union. These factors led to Pakistan's growing ties with Saudi Arabia and its membership of both the US-backed Baghdad Pact and its successor, the Central Treaty Organisation (CENTO), from the mid-1950s to the early 1970s, as well as the similarly US-sponsored South East Asian Treaty Organization, which operated over roughly the same time frame as CENTO.

In 1970, tensions between West and East Pakistan came to a boil. East Pakistan, primarily composed of ethnic Bengalis, had been subjected to political, social and military domination and discrimination by West Pakistan. Running on a platform of securing a political voice for the East, the Awami League, based in East Pakistan, secured a majority of seats in the national elections that took place that year, the first in Pakistan's history. Despite this, the party was unable to form a government. Both Pakistan's military ruler and president, General Yahya Khan, and prime minister, Zulfikar Ali Bhutto, proved unwilling to cede power to Sheikh Mujibur Rahman, leader of the Awami League. This failure, coupled with the military's decision to stifle dissent in the East, created a firestorm of events that led eventually to Indian intervention, the 1971 Indo-Pakistan War, the complete and utter defeat and surrender of Pakistani armed forces in the East, and the creation of Bangladesh.[18] Pakistan, which had lost half its territory and over half of its population as a consequence of the war and East Pakistan's subsequent secession, would henceforth lag even further behind in its military competition with India.

Continued tensions with India provided the necessary pretext for the military, right from Pakistan's early years, to divert an ever-increasing proportion of state finances to itself and to involve itself substantially in political affairs. The Pakistani military has intermittently seized the reins of government from the civilian leadership, frequently on the pretext of the latter's alleged corruption and inefficiency. Field Marshal Ayub Khan (1958–69) and General Yahya Khan (1969–71) were amongst the earliest examples of this trend in Pakistan's brief post-colonial history. General Zia ul-Haq followed suit in 1977 by toppling the

founder and leader of the ruling Pakistan People's Party (PPP), Prime
Minister Zulfikar Ali Bhutto, and establishing martial law. Following a
controversial and protracted trial, Bhutto was convicted of murdering
the father of a dissident PPP politician. Having it within his power to
commute Bhutto's sentence, Zia nevertheless had him hanged on 4 April
1979, allegedly stating 'it's either his neck or mine'.[19] In the context of
a growing influence of public religiosity in Pakistan, Zia ul-Haq found
secular military rule ill-suited to his attempts to consolidate his grip on
power and to promote Pakistan's national identity. He therefore opted to
move Pakistan increasingly towards an Islamised polity during his rule
(1977–88).

Ideological Islam

The debate on the relationship between Islam and democracy flourishes
in Pakistan, as in any Muslim-majority state. Until 1977, most of the
ruling elite were inclined towards a liberal perspective, which viewed
Islamic teachings as a source of guidance for law-making rather than
as providing for a specific structure of governance. Orthodox and
conservative members of the clergy, who favoured the 'establishment of
a puritanical Islamic state with an emphasis on the regulative, punitive
and extractive role of Islamic injunctions', were effectively sidelined.[20]
This changed dramatically with the advent of General Zia ul-Haq.

Zia's rule represents a prominent example in recent history of the
implementation of political Islamism from above.[21] The General pursued
a systematic programme of Islamisation in Pakistan, encompassing all
aspects of life from national laws to public policy and popular culture.[22]
As a result of these measures, whose implementation was facilitated
by Pakistan's status as a key proxy in the United States- and Saudi-
financed jihad against the Soviet invasion of Afghanistan, Pakistan was
transformed into a wellspring of Islamic extremism, whose ideologies
and movements were nurtured by its interventionist and extremely
influential military intelligence agency, the ISI, in the service of foreign
policy.[23] Islamist groups have been viewed by the Pakistani military as a
tool to boost the country's national cohesion and regional position as part
of an overall approach that aimed at creating and exploiting a favourable
external environment whenever possible,[24] especially in the context of
the Pakistani–Indian strategic rivalry. General Zia's death, along with
the US ambassador to Pakistan, Arnold Raphel, in a mysterious air

crash on 17 August 1988, opened the way for another period of civilian rule in the country. By this time, however, the ISI and the military had developed into a government within the government, with close links to a number of powerful Islamist groups. They were still dominant in many aspects of Pakistani domestic and foreign policy at the time of Zia's unexpected death, and their capacity to puppeteer civilian governments and shape the nation's Afghan and Kashmir policies was not negated as a result of his passing away. [25]

Islamabad scored an important success in relation to Afghanistan, where it backed the *Mujahideen* against the Soviet invasion, but more importantly, the medievalist Islamic Taliban from late 1994 onwards in their bid to take over the country in Pakistan's regional interests. Pakistan's 'creeping invasion' of Afghanistan resulted in a bloody conflict between the Taliban and the anti-Taliban forces. The latter were headed by Ahmad Shah Massoud, a former *Mujahideen* commander widely celebrated for his role in successfully resisting the Soviet occupation of Afghanistan in the 1980s.[26] Until the arrival of the Taliban, Massoud had been crucial to, and at the centre of, government operations in Kabul. Islamabad's efforts in Afghanistan enabled the Taliban to dislodge Massoud's forces from Kabul and transform the country into a hub for international terrorism, based on an alliance between the Taliban and al-Qaeda under the ISI's patronage.

ISI interventionism in Indian-held Jammu and Kashmir, which had been based on supporting a separatist movement through an array of radical Islamic groups, was also considered an early success. Through their sponsorship of militant groups, most notably the *Lashkar-e-Taiba* (LeT) and *Harakat al-Ansar* (subsequently renamed *Harakat al-Mujahideen*), Pakistan was able to put pressure on India at little to no cost to itself. Yet Pakistani involvement in Jammu and Kashmir was also a substantial factor in the outbreak of the Indo-Pakistan Kargil 'mini-war' of early 1999 which, according to some analysts, brought the two sides to the edge of nuclear conflict. Although the antagonists pulled back from the brink under intense pressure from a number of major powers, especially the United States, relations between them have not progressed beyond what might be described as an uneasy calm. Domestically, it became clear that ISI strategies were formulated not only to further Pakistan's geopolitical interests but also to shore up the military's domestic credentials with Islamic forces to guarantee the latter's loyalty to the military and ISI against the state's civilian actors. The extent to which the ISI has relied on the cooperation of Islamic extremist groups in its operations is highlighted by the events of the 1990s. During this time, the agency deployed extremist forces to limit or undermine the position of two elected prime ministers: Benazir Bhutto, who served two non-consecutive terms (December 1988–October 1990, October 1993–November 1996) as the PPP's leader; and Nawaz Sharif, who also served twice in a similar fashion (November 1990–July 1993, February 1997–October 1999) as the leader of the Pakistan Muslim League-Nawaz (PML-N).[27] Bhutto and Sharif were played off against one another, manipulated and dismissed twice at the behest of the ISI and the military. Meanwhile, sectarian and terrorist violence raged across Pakistan and Kashmir, and there were even two attempts on Sharif's life by extremist groups with links to the military.[28] Before long, however, another military coup would take place in Pakistan: that of General Musharraf in 1999.

By the 1990s, there was a growing concern that ISI activities were getting out of hand. The agency's support of Islamic extremism had also given rise to a plethora of other radical home-grown groups – *Jaish-i-Mohammed* and *Sipah-i-Sahaba*, among others – that had become entrenched within the mosaic of Pakistani society. Its major proxy in Kashmir, the LeT, was beginning to grow beyond the ISI's control.[29] The LeT, and many other such groups, had become aware of the self-interest and duplicity of the ISI, prompting them to become autonomous actors in their own right. The growing divisions between a number of religious groups and the Pakistani military did not, however, contribute to a decline in either sectarian violence or in Islamic extremism. The systematic 'Islamisation' of society achieved under Zia, along with the ongoing pre-eminence of the military in domestic affairs and Pakistan's misplaced foreign policy priorities, would continue to affect and strangle Pakistani governance long afterwards.

Flawed Governance

Power of the military and dysfunctional elite

Following the death of Zia ul-Haq, Pakistan failed to establish anything more than a quasi-democracy under the premierships of Bhutto and

Sharif, and the presidencies of Musharraf and Zardari. Troubled relations with India, the threat of sectarian unrest, the expanding Pakistani Taliban insurgency and the Afghan conflict entailed a prioritisation of internal and external security in questions of policy, which was typically characterised by the 'centralisation of power, impatience towards dissent and strengthening of the military ... [contributing] to the atrophy of civilian institutions and democracy'.[30] The military and more specifically the ISI continued to act as the main determinant in Pakistani politics even after Musharraf's fall from grace in 2008.[31]

Musharraf's downfall came fast, following the assassination of the popular head of the PPP, Benazir Bhutto, in December 2007. The 2008 parliamentary election of Yousaf Raza Gilani as Prime Minister and subsequent election of Zardari as President, both members of the PPP, seemed to promise a unique opportunity for democratic forces to reverse the militarisation of Pakistan and to conduct reform in the nation's political arena. In November 2008, the new government closed the military's most obstinately meddlesome arm – the ISI's political wing. In April 2010, Zardari signed off on sweeping constitutional reforms (the Eighteenth Amendment) which curtailed presidential powers and empowered the office of the prime minister, discarded a wide range of autocratic powers and allowed for an improved system of checks and balances between the government's executive and legislative bodies.[32] These ambitious programmes to restrict military influence in Pakistani politics were also encouraged by a general perception of Musharraf's successor as army chief, General Kayani, as a 'soldier's soldier', who was unlikely to interfere in political affairs.

The picture, however, was not as rosy behind the scenes. The balance of power, in many ways, reflected the same old quasi-democratic system that had become entrenched in Pakistan, and the situation held little hope for real improvement. It may indeed have been the case that the military opted for a period of retrenchment rather than confrontation with pro-democratic forces in the immediate wake of Musharraf's fall. The central role of the judiciary in the demise of Musharraf was aimed at promoting the accountability of governments and leaders. In this context, the military might have done well to recognise the relative weakness of its position in the face of an apparently resurgent civil power. If this was indeed the trend, it seems that it soon began to move in reverse. Commentators began to view General Kayani as the most powerful man in Pakistan,[33] a claim given further weight following the three-year extension of his post in June 2010. A former Director-General of the ISI, Kayani already had a strong base of support prior to his appointment as Army Chief of Staff. His successor at the ISI, Lieutenant General Ahmad Shuja Pasha, was especially loyal and indebted to him. The man who succeeded Pasha in March 2012, Lieutenant General Zaheerul Islam, also had close ties with Kayani, who retired on 29 November 2013. As Shuja Nawaz of the US-based Atlantic Council argued, the advent of a civil government in Pakistan 'wouldn't makes [sic] a great deal of difference ... [as] instructions will continue to come from the army chief'.[34]

In addition, Kayani had built up a strong rapport with the US military and NATO, and, with the 'success' of the Swat and South Waziristan military campaigns against the Pakistani Taliban (discussed later in this chapter), also gained substantial popular backing. Ironically, by weakening the presidency, the Eighteenth Amendment also removed a potential check on the military's power. Unlike President Zardari, Prime Minister Gilani, who was dismissed from office in June 2012 by Pakistan's Supreme Court, was also said to be on good terms with Kayani. National and internal security issues, the remit of which can be quite expansive, remained clearly under the purview of the General.[35] It was therefore not surprising that many remained concerned that Kayani's increasing prominence was undermining civilian authority,[36] despite the General's public pronouncements of his commitment to strengthening democracy in Pakistan.

The judiciary and the civil service, two cornerstones of the state, have also emerged in recent years as leverage against the central government. Musharraf's declared state of emergency in 2007 and subsequent Provisional Constitutional Order polarised the judiciary into competing blocks, with 12 of 17 Supreme Court judges unwilling to take a new oath under the Order. The subsequent lawyers' movement and restoration of the judiciary to its standing in 2009, along with the passing of the Eighteenth Amendment, empowered the judiciary to act as an effective check on both the government and the military. In December 2009, the restored Supreme Court declared unconstitutional the 2007 National Reconciliation Ordinance, which had granted amnesty to politicians, political workers and bureaucrats for crimes committed between 1986 and 1999. This paved the way for a substantive challenge not only to

Zardari's tenure as president,[37] but also to other prominent political leaders such as former Prime Minister Sharif. The Supreme Court under Justice Iftikhar Chaudhry, a bitter opponent of Musharraf, continuously championed the cause of the rule of law in Pakistan. In 2011–12, it even challenged the military when it heard a number of cases related to the security forces and intelligence agencies, especially the ISI, over the disappearance of a number of political activists in Khyber-Pakhtunkhwa and Baluchistan. One of the most prominent cases with which the Supreme Court dealt was that of a former army chief, General Mirza Aslam Beg, and an ex-chief of Military Intelligence and the ISI, Lieutenant General Asad Durrani. The Court recommended that action be taken against Durrani and Beg for their role in sponsoring the right-wing *Islami Jamhoori Ittehad* (Islamic Democratic Alliance) and bribing politicians in the 1990 general elections. The landmark ruling constituted a clear warning to the military.

The judiciary's assertive role was accompanied by the development of a more robust media, which widened the space for freedom of expression and criticism in Pakistan. The court rulings and greater transparency in the Pakistani media prompted Kayani to issue a series of statements to reassure the civilian government that the military did not intend to bid for power. At the same time, he issued veiled criticisms of the judiciary and the media by inferring that their actions had weakened rather than strengthened the rule of law and the Constitution.[38] In 2012, the Supreme Court attracted international attention for its actions against Prime Minister Gilani. Gilani repeatedly blocked the Court's attempts to investigate corruption charges against President Zardari, persistently refusing to write a letter to the Swiss authorities that would enable the investigations to proceed. Zardari was accused of stashing away US$60 million from a cargo contract into a Swiss bank account. This represented just one of many corruption allegations against him, going back to when his wife Benazir Bhutto was Prime Minister. Following Gilani's conviction in April 2012 for failing to implement the Supreme Court's directives regarding reopening corruption cases against Zardari, the Supreme Court passed a ruling on 19 June 2012 that stripped Gilani of the premiership and barred him from holding further office.[39] The increasing assertiveness of Pakistan's judiciary has, therefore, proved to be an important check on excesses committed by both politicians and military leaders.

At the same time, the Civil Service of Pakistan (CSP) has continued to play an important role in Pakistan's politics, albeit not as pervasively as the military. While the CSP may have felt threatened by the 'unprecedented' appointments, during the Musharraf era, of serving and retired military officials into its ranks,[40] it has historically seen the military as its natural ally against the government. Prior to the 1970s, effective rule over Pakistan lay with the military–CSP alliance. However, the loss of credibility suffered by the Pakistani military as a consequence of the 1971 war, coupled with widespread public disenchantment with the corruption-ridden and inefficient civil service, presented Prime Minister Zulfikar Ali Bhutto with the opportunity to clip the wings of the CSP.[41] In 1973, he introduced a series of sweeping reforms intended to subordinate the CSP to the government's policies. The inevitably hostile reaction of the CSP was heightened by Bhutto's politicised appointments, which seemed to many to make patronage a more important criterion for promotion than expertise or seniority.[42] Bhutto ultimately succeeded in his objective of weakening the civil service, but it came at the cost of a neutral and competent bureaucracy.[43] The process of reversing Bhutto's reforms began in 1977 with General Zia's military takeover, since which time the CSP has re-emerged as a formidable counterweight to the Pakistani government. The Zardari–Gilani government tried to weaken the CSP, but the Supreme Court intervened to ensure the right of the civil service to resist the dictates of politicians in a ruling of 12 November 2012.[44]

Pakistani politics is a complex and multifaceted, yet systematic game, in which competing actors continue to secure and change alliances based on a historical pattern that has become deeply embedded in the nation's dysfunctional political culture. Intermittent military rule has always begun with accusations of the corruption, ineptitude and predatory instincts of the civilian politicians in power and ended with denouncements of militarisation and personalisation of political authority. Civilian rule, on the other hand, has been marked by politicisation of the civil service and judiciary, nepotism, corruption and, at times, accusations of extrajudicial killings of political opponents. Two parties, the PPP and PML, have dominated the political scene since 1971, with the Sindh-based PPP reflecting a more secular centre-left ideology, and the Punjab-based PML reflecting a centre-right, more Islamist and urban constituency. More recently, the emergence of cricketer-turned-politician Imran Khan's *Pakistan Tehreek-e-Insaf* (Pakistan Movement for Justice) party, which seeks the same centre-right, urban vote-bank as Nawaz Sharif's PML-N, has created a third force in Pakistani politics, as will be discussed in more detail later.

The Local Government Ordinance (LGO) initiated by the Musharraf government in August 2001 provides a snapshot of the complexity and challenges surrounding the democracy project in Pakistan. The LGO devolved considerable authority from provincial to district governments, and at the district level from civil servants to elected *nazims* (mayors). This both undermined the provincial government structure and dealt a serious blow to the elitist District Management Group, the civil service authority that had previously exclusive oversight of local governance through their district commissioners.[45] As such, while aiming to extend democracy to the local level and to create a proactive citizenry, the LGO also served to weaken Musharraf's political opponents at the provincial level and allowed him to stamp his authority on the civil service. It is therefore not surprising, but nevertheless unfortunate, that the LGO has been allowed to lapse since the toppling of Musharraf in 2008, stripping many local governments of their legal cover.[46] The case of the LGO, whereby a military government ostensibly promoted democracy by delegating power to local organisations, shows that Pakistan's democracy project is clearly not black and white.

Despite being deeply ensconced in a very difficult and complicated domestic and foreign policy position, Pakistan was able to hold fair and free general elections on 13 May 2013. The elections signified a crucial step towards the possibility of nurturing a genuinely democratic political order. They marked the first instance in the nation's history of a democratic transition from one civilian government that had completed its full five-year term to another. Although the pre-election period was marked by considerable violence, primarily stemming from the targeting by the Pakistani Taliban of a number of secular parties such as the PPP, the Muttahida Quami Movement and the Awami National Party, Pakistanis turned out in impressive numbers to vote. According to official estimates, the voter turnout was as high as an unprecedented 60 per cent.[47]

Nawaz Sharif's PML-N won the largest number of seats in the National Assembly and comfortably formed a government with a simple majority in the federal parliament. The PML-N also won an overwhelming majority of provincial seats in Punjab, the country's most populous and politically most important province. Yet Sharif's victory, however significant, was far from marking the end of Pakistan's political woes. Rather, the newly elected president faced many of the same problems as his predecessors: that of delivering a stable and effective government capable of solving Pakistan's formidable economic, social and security-related problems, as well as ending endemic corruption and wresting control over key areas of foreign policy from the military.

Patronage politics and corruption

Pakistan's dysfunctional elite, where members of the military, political parties, civil service and judiciary are perpetually locked in competition to secure resources and power, is a product not just of the political system but also of the entrenched political culture in which it operates. By encouraging patronage and corruption, this culture, as in Afghanistan, Iraq and to a large extent Iran, has greatly undermined the capacity of Pakistan's political elite to form a working consensus on governance.

Politics of patronage and entrenched corruption have a long history in Pakistan, dating back to the colonial era. The British first institutionalised patron–client political relationships between the bureaucracy and local elites.[48] Abstract notions of loyalty – to the state, a political party or a legal system – have not embedded themselves in Pakistani culture, with many today arguing that much of Pakistan's value system is still based primarily on kinship, family, *zat* (lineage group), *quam* (occupational group) and tribe.[49] As the primary focus of loyalty, the interests of family networks often take precedence over professional or other rational codes of conduct or laws. In reflecting on the role of patronage politics in Pakistan, former Pakistani Foreign Minister Abdul Sattar once said, 'for friends everything, for enemies nothing and for the rest strict application of rules'.[50]

While rapid urbanisation, revolutionary advances in communications and the change towards a market economy have weakened the role of patronage and, arguably, somewhat undermined the power of aristocrats and 'feudal' families in Pakistani politics, it will arguably take generations to nurture popular belief in the fairness and usefulness of the political system.[51] Devoid of independent and visionary leaders, the Pakistani people have constantly faced a choice between a selection of familiar and largely discredited political figures, on the one hand, and dynastic leaders, on the other. Zardari, who is also the co-chair of the PPP, was known as 'Mr 10 per cent' during Benazir Bhutto's two terms as prime minister, due to his having generated over US$1.5 billion in illicit profits through kickbacks in virtually every sphere of government activity, ranging from the sale of fighter planes to rake-offs from state welfare schemes.[52] Bilawal Bhutto Zardari, still in his twenties, is the eldest son of Benazir Bhutto and Asif Zardari, and that appears to have been his only qualification for appointment as chairman of the PPP in 2007. At the opposing end of the spectrum, Nawaz Sharif, chair of the PML-N and current president, saw his governments sacked and toppled in 1993 and 1999 on accusations of corruption, nepotism and extrajudicial killings.

These issues have become endemic not only within the political arena, but also through the ranks of the civil service. By the late 1990s, the Customs Service had become so corrupt that a Swiss agency was brought in to assess customs at departure points.[53] The Water and Power Development Authority was so politicised that the army was called in to run it. As of 2011, bribes were still commonplace at the Public Works Department. The Federal (previously Central) Board of Revenue has been described as 'rotten to the core'. The Board of Revenue's chairman, Riaz Naqvi, apparently reported to Musharraf in 2004 that he wanted to sack 90 per cent of the Board of Revenue's staff for corruption.[54] This pestiferous problem within government departments has often been attributed to the fact that civil servants in the officer grades are paid considerably less than similar roles in the private sector. The compression of salary scales over time is a serious problem that affects not only recruitment and retention at the higher levels, but also increases the personal incentives of civil servants to take bribes and kickbacks.[55]

These quandaries, so disruptive to the processes of state, are compounded by ineffective departmental structures and policies. For instance, newly recruited civil servants in Pakistan are usually placed in the core secretariat divisions, with the result that young section officers and deputy secretaries often find themselves formulating policies. Senior and more experienced specialists, usually placed in attached departments, have the responsibility of implementing policy.[56] This cultural and generational disconnect between those formulating policy and those implementing it has often led to bitter confrontation within various departments. In another example, the civil service's attempt to ensure diversity within its ranks has meant that the best and the brightest do not necessarily get the right jobs; in 2009, only 10 per cent of new recruits at the national level were selected purely on the basis of merit, compared to 90 per cent on the basis of ethnic quota policies.[57]

Inept governance has led to a major failure in servicing the needs of the Pakistani people. For every step forward, Pakistan takes two steps back. As such, even though the implementation of the aforementioned LGO saw improvements in transportation infrastructure, sewage and sanitation management, clean water supply and health services, there has also been a loss of household satisfaction regarding agricultural services, electricity provision and gas supply.[58] State failure has created a power vacuum for counter-systemic actors, such as Islamic extremists, to step in to provide for the people what the government cannot. The Zardari government's slow response to the 2010 summer floods, the worst in 80 years, created the space for radical Islamic charities to spring into action. These charities reacted immediately to the disaster by sending 4,000 volunteers to Nowshera in Khyber-Pakhtunkhwa to rebuild homes.[59] These actions, and similar forms of humanitarian assistance, have understandably increased public support for hardline Islamic groups.

The Economy

The increasingly corrupt and poorly functioning government finds little relief in surveying the dismal outlook of Pakistan's economy. Before the 'war on terror', the country's economy as a whole was already suffering. In 1997, Pakistan's GDP growth rate was a mere 1.8 per cent and had only risen to 2.5 per cent in 2001.[60] Between 1990 and 2001, the incidence of poverty increased from 26 per cent to 32 per cent.[61] Although Musharraf's decision after 11 September 2001 to align with the United States appeared at first to come with vast economic benefits, it ultimately proved to be only a temporary cure. Like Afghanistan, Pakistan's economy has become increasingly dependent on foreign (particularly US) aid, a tendency that has fed into problems of political corruption while doing little to effect substantial improvements in infrastructure within the country. In the three years following 9/11, the United States provided Pakistan with something close to US$4.2

billion in the form of military aid and reimbursements. In comparison with US aid between 1998 and 2001 (US$9.1 million), this signified a 50,000 per cent increase.[62] Total US military, economic and development assistance to Pakistan between 2002 and 2011 amounted to more than US$20 billion.[63] Most of the money came from what the US Department of Defense calls the Coalition Support Fund, a fund facilitated by the Pentagon as 'reimbursement' for Pakistani military support and therefore not closely tracked by Congress.[64] As a result, Pakistan's real GDP jumped 5.1 per cent per annum between 2002 and 2004, with all economic sectors – from agriculture to industry – registering healthy growth, giving rise to a degree of economic and social activity that Pakistan had not experienced for some years.[65]

Whilst US backing led to an impressive economic performance in the 2001–07 period, instability within the country and in the political arena, compounded by the rising cost of tackling the insurgency on the Afghan–Pakistani border areas, led to a loss of economic confidence in the country, capital flight and a greater awareness of the structural problems affecting Pakistan. From 1998, imports began to rise at a much faster rate than exports, producing a drastic rise in the trade imbalance, most recently from $15.6 billion in 2010–11 to $21.3 billion in 2011–12.[66] Even with foreign aid, the current account deficit per year continued to increase, reaching almost 2 per cent of GDP in 2012.[67] Pakistan was only able to save its foreign currency reserves with the intervention of an International Monetary Fund loan, which pushed its debt from US$46.4 billion in 2008 to US$55.1 billion in 2010.[68] As a result, the country's economic growth from 2001 to 2007 did not alleviate the burden of government expenditure on interest payments, which has remained constant at around 30 per cent.[69] Considering that Pakistan spends around one quarter of government revenue on defence – a figure unlikely to decrease as long as the military remains powerful – the amount of revenue available for spending on other critical social and humanitarian areas remains desperately low.[70] In 2012, education spending by the government amounted to a mere 1.8 per cent of GDP, an all-time low, and spending on health was even worse at only 0.75 per cent.[71]

For the average citizen, inflation, followed by unemployment, have become particularly painful problems.[72] In 2008, the latter increased to 12 per cent from 8 per cent the previous year and stayed steady at that rate through 2012.[73] In addition, with rapid population growth, natural resources have been increasingly placed under stress. Pollution is also becoming a major environmental concern, with conservative estimates suggesting that environmental degradation cost the country at least 6 per cent of its GDP in 2007 and that these costs fall disproportionately upon the poor.[74] As such, and in light of the 2005 earthquake and 2012 floods, Pakistan's environmental policies have been increasingly questioned. And while these national disasters created a push for a two-year freeze on Pakistan's national debt, with charities from around the world calling for a more concerted effort in aiding flood victims, international donor fatigue has settled on Pakistan just as it has with Afghanistan.[75]

International Relations and Foreign Policy

Much of this fatigue can be attributed to the fact that the 2008 change to a civilian government failed to produce structural domestic reforms and any serious revisions in Pakistan's conduct in international affairs. The power and influence of the military and entrenched civil service, compounded by the fact that Pakistan's foreign policy dilemmas are indeed pressing and vital to the security of the state, has ensured a remarkable continuity in foreign policy posture over time. The policies of the Pakistani government, whether civilian or military, have often been dictated by the legacy of Islamic extremism, and following the 11 September 2001 events, by the continuation of the 'war on terror' as well as conflict with India and troubles in Afghanistan. As such, and despite the advent of civilian government, Pakistan's foreign policy has remained largely within the framework established by the ISI and General Musharraf, both before and after the turn of the century, although by the end of 2012 there were some signs that the military would focus more on enhancing domestic security than on engaging in regional adventures.[76]

Musharraf's legacy

The parameters of Pakistani foreign policy under the post-2008 civilian governments were largely set by the military leader, General Musharraf (1999–2008). To directly deter its more powerful nuclear neighbour, India, Pakistan felt constrained to adopt a credible first-use nuclear posture. This 'asymmetric escalation' policy was adopted after the 1998 Indian nuclear tests, which pushed Pakistan to view India as an existential threat.[77] While this posture effectively deterred India from retaliating militarily following later attacks on India's parliament in 2001 and in Mumbai on 26 November 2008 – both of which were staged by Islamic extremists trained and equipped in Pakistan – it also did little to ease tensions between Islamabad and New Delhi or to promote and facilitate a well-founded rapprochement. Whilst making a series of proposals for a resolution of the Kashmir problem, all of which were rejected by India, Musharraf did not substantially deviate from Pakistan's historical support for the Kashmiri people's right to self-determination. As an extension of this, he also did not back away from the ISI's continued backing of groups that had engaged in cross-border violence. In addition, he reinforced Pakistan's alliance with an ascendant China. US–India relations and the booming Indian economy have combined to make China more interested in pinning down India than in embracing her as a partner in the region.[78] As a result, Musharraf was able to rely on tacit Chinese support for ISI strategy toward India, a strategy that has bound half a million Indian troops in Kashmir along the border with Pakistan.

With regard to containing the predominantly Shi'a Iran, Musharraf counted on the support of a number of Arab countries, especially Saudi Arabia and the United Arab Emirates (UAE), as well as the United States. He was able to do this for a number of reasons. Saudi Arabia has long championed the cause of Sunni Islam, enjoyed a close friendship with the United States and been engaged in a serious sectarian and political rivalry with Iran's Shi'a Islamic regime. The UAE, a close partner of Saudi Arabia in the Gulf Cooperation Council (GCC), which was formed in 1981 as a response to Ayatollah Khomeini's calls for the export of Islamic revolution to the Persian Gulf, has also been involved in a territorial dispute with Iran over three strategic islands in the Gulf – Abu Musa, and the Greater and Lesser Tunbs. Its Sharjah and Ras Al Khaimah emirates have respectively claimed sovereignty over the islands, which were taken over by Iran under the Shah, based on a secret deal between Tehran and London as part of the British withdrawal from east of Suez, in 1971.[79] Iran's refusal to return them has been a persistent source of tension in Iran–UAE and, for that matter, Iran–GCC relations, and is a problem that remains unresolved. Abu Dhabi has constantly sought ways and means to pressure Tehran over the issue, and this motivation partly explains its support for the Taliban during their rule

of Afghanistan. Meanwhile, the United States was keen to maintain its
policy of containment toward the Iranian regime, which it has pursued
since the rise of Khomeini's Islamic government and the infamous
hostage crisis (discussed in detail in Chapter 4).[80] The United States'
hostility toward Iran emboldened Musharraf to continue his policy of
support for the Taliban, confident that Washington's need for regional
allies against Iran would eclipse its growing agenda for undermining
the Taliban.

Musharraf therefore stood firm on Pakistan's support of the Taliban
(and by implication of the Taliban–al-Qaeda alliance) right up until
the attacks on the United States in 2001. He described his support for
the Taliban as a 'national security imperative' for Pakistan.[81] Having
promised Washington in 1999 to pressure the Taliban to change
direction and hand over bin Laden, Musharraf quickly reverted to
a policy of unwavering support. Eventually this became as much a
matter of constraint as a question of choice. Increasingly dependent
on the military and pro-Taliban Islamic groups for political survival,
Musharraf was in no position, even if he had wished to do so, to rein in
the ISI, which strongly supported the Taliban. As would ironically later
be the case with Afghan President Karzai, Musharraf found himself in a
position where he was forced to compromise with a number of non-state
actors, many of them unsavoury, in order to retain his political power.
He pleaded repeatedly to the international community to recognise the
Taliban as the legitimate government of Afghanistan, as Pakistan and
two of its close Arab friends – Saudi Arabia and the UAE – had done. He
shared the military and ISI view of Afghanistan as a source of 'strategic
depth' in the event of a confrontation with India, and as an important
corridor for Pakistan's access to the former Soviet Central Asian Muslim
republics. A strong alliance with Afghanistan was seen both as a way
to promote a wider regional economic and strategic role for Pakistan,
and as a means of denying India and Iran an opportunity to enhance
their influence in the region. Musharraf's government played a dubious
balancing act by, on the one hand, criticising international efforts to
isolate the Taliban and calling on the latter to moderate some of their
actions, while, on the other hand, nevertheless rejecting any criticism
of Pakistan's role in Afghanistan and continuing to deny the facts of its
military involvement in the country.

The US 'war on terror'

While presenting himself as an 'enlightened' Muslim, Musharraf was in fact eager to promote secular politics within Pakistan. As he points out in his autobiography, he had always been deeply impressed by the secularist founder of modern Turkey, Mustafa Kemal Ataturk, and entertained the desire to style himself after Ataturk as a military-cum-civilian reformer.[82] Ideologically, therefore, he stood at odds with his military predecessor, Zia ul-Haq, and unlike him, could not have felt privately comfortable with Pakistan's support of radical Islamism (and the Taliban) as a major strand in Pakistani politics. Yet the circumstances that had propelled him to power had at the same time severely impaired his legitimacy and ability to manoeuvre easily against the situation. During the first two years of his rule, he was personally languishing as a pariah in world politics, and Pakistan was struggling under the growing weight of political, economic and social quandaries. Musharraf was badly in need of an external circuit-breaker.

That circuit-breaker came in the form of the 11 September 2001 events and the Bush administration's declaration of the 'war on terror'. While Musharraf's decision to publically side with the United States was framed within the constraints of Bush's ultimatum, he knew from the start that this new alliance was based on the politics of mutual vulnerability and leverage which, if shrewdly managed, could be highly advantageous to his regime and to Pakistan.[83] He perceived in his partnership with Washington an opportunity to consolidate power and lead Pakistan out of the dire predicaments in which it was placed. From the American point of view, the Bush administration needed Pakistan as a key state not only in order to overthrow the Taliban and achieve their goals in Afghanistan, but also to successfully execute its 'war on terror' strategy with wider aims than what it wanted to achieve in Afghanistan.[84] The benefits that Musharraf was able to extract from the new alliance proved to be greater than anybody could have originally anticipated. By presenting himself as a champion against extremism and terrorism, Musharraf was able to rapidly build an externally driven basis of legitimacy for his military rule and to gain a degree of international acceptability that otherwise would not have been within his reach.

Continuity in Pakistan's foreign policy posture

Throughout his rule, Musharraf skilfully (although in the eyes of many analysts also manipulatively) focused on achieving a number of subtly self-serving foreign policy priorities and objectives. These objectives would continue to underlie the foreign policy dynamics of Pakistan for many years after Musharraf's downfall.

Pakistan's relations with India have continued to be double-edged, in a manner that complements to a large extent Pakistan's position on Afghanistan and the 'war on terror'. Urged by Washington to improve relations with India, Pakistan has ceded ground, but only the minimum amount required to please the United States. Pakistan would later find it necessary to deflect the need for a resolution by making its usual claim that any additional US pressure on Pakistan would endanger Pakistan's stability and would therefore compromise America's success in the 'war on terror'.

As a result of the 'war on terror', Pakistan was therefore able to position itself, despite its misdeeds, as a central player on the regional and international scene. For this, the Musharraf regime (and for that matter the Zardari government) pursued a double-act approach. The emphasis was on a normative commitment to expunging Pakistan of Islamic extremism by reforming religious teaching and schools, bringing educational establishments under government control, and de-linking Pakistan from Islamic extremist groups in the region and beyond. At the same time, like Musharraf, Zardari sought to promote an image of Pakistan as a pro-Arab and pro-Sunni bulwark against the predominantly Shi'a and anti-US Iran and other hostile forces, and therefore as central to defending US interests in the region. While announcing some measures to deal with Islamic extremism at home, the Zardari leadership constantly emphasised to Washington its need to maintain its Sunni Muslim status as a means of retaining its close ties with the United States' oil-rich allies in the Persian Gulf and mainly Sunni-profiled friends in Central Asia. It intimated that any action that could compromise these relationships would undermine Pakistan's ability to assist the United States in containing possible Iranian predatory actions in Afghanistan and the Central Asian republics. This was despite the fact that the Zardari regime publically pursued friendly relations with Tehran.

Pakistan took advantage of the post-Taliban situation to focus on carving a critical niche in relation to the drive by the Karzai government and its international supporters to strengthen reconstruction and security in Afghanistan on the basis of promoting economic cooperation and integration between Central Asia and South Asia. Similar to the Musharraf regime, the Zardari leadership went to great pains to make sure that this drive did not result in either an emergence of a strong Afghanistan, or the expansion of Indian influence in the country, where this could possibly impinge on Pakistan's role as a central regional player. In this respect, Pakistan was especially mindful of Kabul's close ties with New Delhi as a counter to Pakistan, and of Afghanistan joining the South Asian Association for Regional Cooperation. Pakistan has approached reconstruction in Afghanistan with two key objectives in mind. The first has been to ensure that the reconstruction linkages created between Afghanistan and its regional neighbours will not limit Pakistan's manoeuvrability as a pivotal actor in the process. The second is to guarantee that Pakistan remains in an influential position vis-à-vis the creation of these linkages and to obstruct them if this is deemed necessary. Therefore, although the Zardari regime (similar to that of Musharraf) was seen as a strong supporter of regional economic cooperation,[85] it was also known to shape this cooperation in a way that proved to be quite frustrating for Kabul and New Delhi.

Whilst publicly backing the Karzai government, Islamabad under the Zardari government continued Musharraf's policy of privately maintaining pressure on Karzai to give Afghanistan's ethnic Pashtuns the lion's share in the post-Taliban power structure. Similarly, Islamabad pressured Karzai to rid his government of the influence of those non-Pashtuns who had formed the bulk of the anti-Taliban resistance within the United Front (the Northern Alliance) and which had played a critical role in the US-led ground war and in Karzai's interim and transitional governments (2001–04).[86] After winning the first presidential election in late 2004, Karzai caved in to Pakistani pressure by replacing some of the key figures of the Front with his Pashtun allies in the cabinet. This was not enough to satisfy the Pakistani leadership, which continued to agitate for expanded Pashtun influence in the Afghan government. In September 2006, Musharraf even went as far as to make the grossly inaccurate claim that the Pashtuns constituted almost 60 per cent of the Afghan population, whereas the Tajiks formed a mere 5 to 7 per cent minority.[87] In fact, the Pashtuns have never been estimated to be more than 42 per cent of the Afghan population, and the ethnic Tajiks come a fairly close second with 25–30 per cent, as was documented in the previous chapter.

These foreign policy priorities and objectives remained largely unchanged under the Zardari government, and in fact gained strength, as the inability of the United States and international forces to contain the Taliban-led insurgency in Afghanistan became more obvious. As the Taliban and their affiliates continued to be resilient and assertive, Karzai and, for that matter, the United States and its allies, ceased to see much prospect of defeating them.[88] Islamabad had anticipated all along that foreign forces would eventually leave Afghanistan, and that the prospects for Afghanistan's transformation into a stable state were unlikely to improve substantially. It therefore found it imperative to place itself in a position whereby it could safeguard its interests against any adverse developments in Afghanistan and the region in the foreseeable future. Despite its public utterances to the contrary, Pakistan has therefore remained committed to maintaining strong leverage in the form of the Taliban and associated groups in order to influence Afghanistan's post-2014 fate according to its preferences. It is this consideration that has also guided Islamabad's approach to any political settlement of the Afghanistan conflict.

The Taliban and Pashtuns

Under the Zardari government, Pakistan provided both sanctuary and material assistance to elements of the Taliban and one of its lethal associates, the *Haqqani* network (which is closely linked to the ISI and which was declared a terrorist organisation by the United States in 2012), contrary to repeated demands by the United States and its allies to cease entirely all such support. General Kayani and the ISI emphasised the importance of brokering a deal between the Karzai government and the Taliban and *Haqqani* network.[89] However, Pakistani policy towards the Taliban and its associates has been anything but straightforward; it has been calculating, deceptive, manipulative, and often characterised by conflicting aims and objectives. With the strength of the Taliban-led insurgency resting on the willingness of local people, primarily Pashtuns, to support it, there has been a gradual and dangerous twinning of the Taliban Islamic extremist and Pashtun nationalist narrative. The end result has been the emergence of a religious and ethnic conflict in the border regions which has bedevilled not only Afghanistan, but also Pakistan itself.

The Taliban

All the anti-Taliban measures that Musharraf had announced – ranging from deploying troops along the border with Afghanistan, and fighting both the foreign and tribal backers of the Taliban on the Pakistani side of the border, to fencing parts of the Afghan–Pakistani border and closely cooperating with the US-led coalition and NATO forces to enhance border security – amounted to little more than an attempt to impress Washington with his commitment to fighting the 'war on terror'. In reality, Musharraf discreetly allowed the Afghan Taliban to continue to receive shelter and logistical assistance from Pakistan, especially through the ISI and the Pakistani Islamic radicals in FATA, Khyber-Pakhtunkhwa and also to some extent in Baluchistan.

By 2004, however, the United States had caught onto Musharraf's double game. Around the same time, the Pakistani leader himself was also becoming concerned with the growth of the Pakistani Taliban. Whilst pressured by the United States to instigate a sustained crackdown on Islamic extremism on Pakistani territory, Musharraf was obliged to change tack to some extent in order to maintain his image as a valuable US ally and a strident opponent of extremism. Yet, despite deploying some 80,000 troops to the Afghan border, Musharraf wavered again in the face of mounting military casualties. By adopting a policy of negotiation and truce, he ensured that the Taliban and their supporters on both sides of the border were able to operate freely and expand their armed struggle.[90]

As the Pakistani Pashtun militants coalesced into an organisation of their own – the *Tehrik-i-Taliban Pakistan* (TTP) or the Pakistani Taliban, in FATA – its mounting insurgency challenge to Islamabad led in 2009 to the intensification of Pakistani military efforts in the border regions of both Afghanistan and Pakistan under Musharraf's successor as army chief, Kayani, and the new US President, Barack Obama. The Swat campaign, launched by General Kayani in May 2009, was supposed to be the start of a long military assault to eliminate the Taliban, opening a new chapter in Pakistan's short but turbulent history. It resulted in the killing and injuring of many civilians, the destruction of Swat's main city, Mingora, and the displacement of some two million people, causing a massive humanitarian crisis. Perhaps more importantly, in the long term, by essentially pitting the country's Punjabi-dominated army against the predominantly Pathan (Pashtun) people of the region, the Swat campaign introduced a new ethnic dimension to the border conflict. For the Pathan civilians of the Swat region, the campaign was a bitter reminder of Punjabi political and military supremacy in Pakistan. Consequently, the campaign, which was extended to the wider Taliban front in South Waziristan, enabled the Taliban and their cohorts to whip up the ethnic issue as a means of galvanising Pashtun unity and support. Admittedly, the Pashtuns also make up a good proportion of the Pakistani army, but this has not prevented the Taliban from exploiting the ethnic factor to the maximum.

Pakistan's anti-TTP campaign was accompanied by even more determined efforts by the United States and its allies to fight the Taliban in both Afghanistan and Pakistan. The purpose in the short run was to stabilise the situation for the Afghan presidential election on 20 August 2009. However, the long-term goal focused on reducing the Taliban insurgency to a manageable level, so that the danger of extremism in both Afghanistan and Pakistan could be minimised, which would enable foreign forces to scale down in Afghanistan sooner rather than later. However, the United States and its allies failed to achieve their objectives of sweeping the Taliban from their heartland in southern and eastern Afghanistan and blocking escape routes into Pakistan. The Taliban and their supporters, whose ranks swelled with those who fled the parallel Pakistani military campaign, have indeed proved to be very adaptable and resilient.[91] In addition, a great number of Afghanistan's Pashtun population, like their Pakistani counterparts, have inevitably been subjected to greater dislocation and suffering.

While the 2009 Pakistani Swat and South Waziristan campaigns gave rise to the belief that the Zardari regime and the ISI would indeed crack down on the Taliban, the conduct of the campaigns and subsequent ISI actions toward the Taliban once again suggested a more nuanced and complex policy. ISI strategy distinguishes between the Afghan Taliban – those targeting the Karzai regime or the International Security Assistance Force in Afghanistan – and the Taliban engaged in actions against the Pakistani state.[92] It has therefore buttressed militant groups deeply engaged in the Afghan insurgency, but has opposed the TTP, which explicitly targets the Pakistani state.[93] Thus, for instance, the Pakistani army rejected the idea of a campaign in North Waziristan, a strategy adamantly pushed by the United States, in favour of a negotiated peace with various Taliban elements there. As an example of the ISI's double-handed policy, while working with the United States to capture a top Afghan Taliban leader, Mullah Abdul Ghani Baradar, the ISI quietly freed two other senior Afghan Taliban figures,[94] one of whom was reportedly a top military commander, Abdul Qayum Zadir. It is often said that the ISI utilises such 'catch and release' tactics to keep various Taliban elements in line with ISI priorities.[95]

The persistently divisive strategy of the ISI in relation to Taliban elements, coupled with increasing interaction between various Taliban factions, the entrenchment of the Taliban within tribal structures, and the growing salience of Islamic radicalism as an alternative uniting ideology in FATA and Khyber-Pakhtunkhwa, has left the door wide open for various Taliban elements to promote their own vision of Pathan nationalism among the disaffected communities of Pakistan's border regions.

Pashtun (Pathan) nationalism
The intense efforts by the Afghan and Pakistani governments, backed by the United States and many of its allies, to expunge elements of the Taliban movement, have carried the risk of Pashtun political and social alienation. This has only provided greater impetus to the Pashtun militancy spanning the Afghan–Pakistani border, with serious political, security and territorial consequences for both countries.

Although divided along family, clan and tribal lines, the Pashtun people that straddle Afghanistan and Pakistan have historically shown a flair for self-rule or independence. Originating from what is today southern Afghanistan, the Pashtuns form an 'ethnie', or what Anthony Smith defines as 'a named population sharing a collective proper name, a presumed common ancestry, shared historical memories, one or more differencing elements of common culture, an association with a specific "homeland" and a sense of solidarity for significant sectors of the population'.[96] As such, they constitute an ethnic-based nation in the classic sense of the term.

One of the Pashtuns' patrimonial codes of conduct is *pakhtunwali*, which centres upon such notions as honour or *nang*, involving the protection of sexual propriety, which is of utmost importance to a Pashtun; the principle of revenge, or *badal*, which is intimately associated with the notion of honour and upholds the dictum of 'an eye for an eye and a tooth for a tooth'; and hospitality, or *melma*, which underlines the importance of maintaining loyalty to friends and allies, and providing protection to whoever seeks it, including an enemy, for so long as a person is in the realm of a Pashtun's home.[97] Another shared characteristic since the end of the seventh century has been the Pashtuns' adherence to Islam, predominantly to the Sunni sect, although they have traditionally tended to embrace a relatively moderate form of Islam, as expounded by the Hanafi school of thought.[98]

The Pashtuns' 'home territory' has historically stretched northwards from the Indus River, which runs from Kashmir through Pakistan and to the Arabian Sea, to the Hindu Kush ranges that dissect Afghanistan into north and south. The Afghan capital of Kabul, which has been very much a multi-ethnic city for a long time, falls to the south of this dividing range; it is therefore also located in the traditional homeland of the Pashtuns. The Pashtun nation is today divided by the 2,640-km-long border between Pakistan and Afghanistan, known as the Durand Line, a frontier that came into existence only in 1893 as a result of an agreement between the British Empire and the then monarch of Afghanistan, Abdul Rahman Khan. It is noteworthy that the Durand Agreement has never been ratified by either Pakistan or Afghanistan, and that the Afghan Taliban defiantly refused to acknowledge its validity throughout their stint in power, despite pressure from their sponsors in Islamabad to do so. The contested border, a legacy of British colonialism, has periodically inflamed relations between the Afghan and Pakistani states, as well as between the Pakistan government and its ethnic Pashtuns.

In 2012, an estimated 13 million Pashtuns formed about 42 per cent of the total population of Afghanistan,[99] and some 30 million made up around 16 per cent of the total citizenry of Pakistan.[100] Many Pashtuns, however, continue to strongly adhere to a notion of Pashtun identity, as was reflected in 2010 with the successful demands of the 75 per cent Pashtun ethnic majority in the former NWFP to rename the province Khyber-Pakhtunkhwa ('Pakhtunkhwa' meaning 'Pashtun Quarter').[101]

Yet the Pashtuns have never had an independent state of their own. They have constantly suffered from foreign subjugation, which has instilled in them an acute perception of deprivation and victimisation. All this has come to lay the necessary historical foundations for a distinct Pashtun identity and codes of behaviour, and, therefore, for the growth of what can be termed Pashtun nationalism in pursuit of self-rule and independence.

The Pashtuns have rarely acted as a coherent collective. They have often been fragmented into various social segments, at times in serious feuds and conflicts that have often been drawn along personality, family, clan and tribal lines. Attempts by some of their leaders to unite them in pursuit of independence have, in general, proved futile. Nevertheless, during exceptional periods of history, particularly when they have either been engaged in successful military offensives and territorial conquests, or seriously threatened by an outside force, the Pashtuns have shown themselves capable of ethno-tribal solidarity.

The Soviet retreat from Afghanistan in 1989 and the collapse of the communist regime in Kabul three years later did not result in the political empowerment of Pashtuns in the country, as Pakistan had hoped would be achieved through their backing of the Pashtun warlord Gulbuddin Hekmatyar. The ISI then raised the Taliban as a radical Sunni Pashtun force, intended, at the very least, to link the Afghan territory organically from the Pakistan border to the Hindu Kush into Pakistan for wider national and regional purposes.

Although the Afghan Taliban projected themselves as a radical Sunni Islamic movement, the militia's Pashtuniate (Pashtun-centred) identity was undeniable. While they did not officially recognise the Durand Line, their rule was always confined within the national boundaries of Afghanistan.[102] Yet the Taliban's rise to power also produced an Islamic pincer among the Pashtuns on the Pakistan side of the border, providing Islamabad with a potent means to shift the basis of Pashtun nationalism from ethnic and cultural solidarity to Islamism. This, however, only played into the hands of the Afghan Taliban. The success of the Islamist parties under the electoral alliance of *Mutahhidah Majlis Amal* in 2002, in the then NWFP and in Baluchistan, reflected for the first time a large political divide between Pashtuns and the rest of Pakistan, which failed to substantially support the alliance.[103] While the main Pashtun ethnonationalist parties in Pakistan – the Awami National Party and the *Pukthunkhwa Milli Awami* Party – have not supported the insurgency, whether in Afghanistan or Pakistan, the TTP and other elements of the Pakistan-based Taliban have stood directly in contrast, attempting to Islamify Pashtun nationalism in order to utilise the narrative under their banner.[104]

Both the Pakistani and Afghan Taliban undoubtedly espouse an extremist ideological disposition, and have not hesitated to employ draconian methods of cajoling and intimidating the Pashtun population into silence and submission. Such methods have extended even to the killing of tribal elders on trumped-up charges of being Pakistani and American spies, in order to strengthen the Taliban's position as an alternative source of leadership.[105] Nevertheless, the Taliban have had considerable popular support among their fellow Pashtuns in Afghanistan and Pakistan, which has been critical in enabling them to remain a potent force whose activities have proved extremely expensive to NATO and Islamabad operations. The Taliban may have been driven out of parts of Helmand and Swat, but this has not appeared to have reduced their capacity to continue the fight on a long-term basis. According to *pakhtunwali*, it has long been accepted that those who oppose a government can seek asylum on the other side of the border if their efforts fail.[106] This means that the Afghan–Pakistani border, which is long, rugged, full of treacherous terrain and not clearly defined in some sections, is conducive to constant criss-crossing by members of the Taliban.

The difficulty of securing such a border, either by Afghan or Pakistani forces, is compounded by the fact that both sides of the border are awash with light and heavy weapons, and are the domain of goods smugglers and drug traffickers, some of whom have their own private militias. Tension along the border has even resulted in a number of exchanges of fire between the Afghan and Pakistani border guards, with Kabul accusing Pakistan of making a forward thrust into Afghan territory in 2003–05, 2007, and 2011–12. The most serious early clash was reported in July 2003, and provoked anti-Pakistan demonstrations in Kabul and recriminatory exchanges between Kabul and Islamabad.[107] More cross-border clashes occurred in mid-2012 to mid-2013, when Pakistani forces intruded into Afghan territory, inviting Afghan retaliation and prompting both sides to lodge official protests against one another.[108] In the case of Afghanistan, the lower house of parliament censured Karzai's veteran Defence Minister, Abdul Rahim Wardak, and Minister of the Interior, Bismillah Khan Mohammadi, for their lack of decisive action to stop Pakistani intrusions. Karzai, who wanted a cabinet reshuffle anyway, approved parliament's vote to dismiss both ministers, although he reinstated Mohammadi in place of Wardak.[109]

These clashes have reinforced a long-standing view among many Afghans that Pakistan continues to harbour predatory ambitions toward Afghanistan. Karzai trod a fine line with Islamabad in this respect. On the one hand, he repeatedly criticised Pakistan for its support of the Taliban and their affiliates and for its role as a key source of extremism and terrorism. On the other hand, mindful of the need to secure Islamabad's cooperation in order to stem the tide of the insurgency, he sought brotherly friendship and good neighbourly relations with Pakistan. One senior Pakistani official recently described Karzai's approach as erratic and confusing. Whatever the case, effective military cooperation between Kabul and Islamabad against the Taliban and their supporters is unlikely to materialise in the foreseeable future.

As a result of these factors, the Taliban are now potentially positioned to present themselves as the repository of the nationalist aspirations and interests of the Pashtun population as a victimised people. Many Pashtuns across the Afghan–Pakistani border see themselves as squeezed between adversarial forces encroaching upon their religion, land, resources, honour, cultural and social norms and values and, therefore, upon their whole way of life. Whereas before 2001 many Pakistani Pashtun tribal factions, such as the *Mehsud*, *Wazir* and *Karlandri*, were unresponsive to the Taliban's programme, Islamabad's willingness to send troops into the area and its alliance with the United States, which aimed to kill off al-Qaeda and the Taliban leaders in the area, has provoked outrage.[110] In the absence of a return to peace and stability in their lives and lands, the Pashtuns' sense of common desperation and victimisation has the potential to provide a powerful and dangerous incentive for them to brush aside their historical divisions and rally behind the Taliban leadership in pursuit of their historical goal of a united and independent 'Pashtunistan'.

The relationship between operations against the Afghan and Pakistani Taliban and the risk of fierce nationalist backlash among the Pashtuns is something that seems to have been missing from the strategic calculations of the Afghan and Pakistani governments, as well as their international backers, even though a history of the Pashtun regions suggest that an increase in foreign footprints is more likely to rally the tribes *against* rather than *for* the Pakistani or Afghan state.[111] In addition, the Pakistani Taliban, irrespective of continued military pressure, can be expected to flourish as long as the tribes are somewhat united. This sobering fact is evidenced in the failure of the death of TTP leader Baitullah Mehsud in August 2009, and his successor, Hakimullah Mehsud, in 2013, to dent TTP efforts.[112]

Counter-Systemic Actors and Tensions

Prospects for a variety of other counter-systemic actors, ranging from anti-Punjabi nationalists to non-Taliban Sunni extremists, have increased in the post-11 September 2001 context due to the security vacuum caused by the growing appeal of radical Islam and the fragility of the Pakistani state.[113] Links between the Taliban and Sunni extremists in Punjab, the most populous and prosperous province in Pakistan, were originally fostered with the tacit support of the ISI, which viewed the Taliban's radical Sunni Islamism as a possible outlet that would help curb Pashtun nationalism in the former NWFP.[114] Today, groups such as the LeT or the *Jaish-i-Mohammed* run mosques and seminaries in the heartland of Pakistan – centred in the Punjab – blurring the distinction between various Sunni extremist groups and the Taliban.[115] It is said that 'Punjabi Taliban' were behind the 28 May 2010 assault on the Ahmadi sect that claimed the lives of over 90 people during Friday prayers.[116] The 3 September 2010 Quetta blast, which killed 43 Shi'a Muslims, was the second attack on the Shi'a community in a week.[117] While sectarian attacks declined somewhat in 2011, they certainly picked up in 2012 and 2013, with one taking place, on average, every two to three weeks, at the cost of hundreds of lives.

Coupled with growing 'extremism' in Punjab have been persistent tensions between the Punjabi majority and the Sindhi and Baluchi minorities. Of all the minority groups, the Sindhis are the most 'accepting' of the current order. The Sindhi nationalist movement is relatively weak, due largely to the supremacy of the *waderos*, the traditional landowning chieftain class. These *waderos* are linked to the state through ties of patronage, giving them a vested interest in the current system.[118] In contrast, there has been a simmering Baluchi insurgency in western Pakistan. The Baluchis subscribe to a tribal code similar to that of *pakhunwali*, which makes tribalism and clan ties a very important factor in their dissatisfaction with the state.[119] However, being a relatively smaller ethnic group, and because of their position on the periphery of the state, the Baluchis have been left behind in Pakistan's modernisation drive. As outlined above, they have also been angered by what they perceive as government and military exploitation of their natural resources and usurpation of vast sections of their land, which have yielded little return for their communities, and by Islamabad's apparent support for the 'Pashtunisation' of Baluchistan.

Islamic militancy and sectarian tensions have produced rising instability in Pakistan, causing great concern for international intelligence and security agencies, and producing a strong deterrent to potential investment in the country. There is a real risk that extremists will gain access to Pakistan's nuclear arsenal either through penetration of the armed forces or during transportation of nuclear components. The Pakistan military's persistent concern with its lack of strategic depth has ensured an absence of robust negative controls on the nuclear arsenal, which seems disconcertingly designed to allow quick release of nuclear weapons in the case of an Indian attack or National Command Authority decapitation.[120] Since the December 2008 attacks on Afghanistan-bound freight through the Khyber Pass, where 12 per cent of total freight 'disappeared', the United States and NATO have been pressured into establishing new transit corridors, such as the Northern Distribution Network through Central Asia, in order to bypass the dangerous Pakistan Ground Lines of Communication supply route into Afghanistan whenever necessary.[121]

Not only the Pakistani government, but also the United States, must be mindful that the more they apply brute force to quell the Taliban and their supporters, the more they carry the risk of inflicting collateral suffering on Pakistan's Pashtun population as a whole. It is important that every care be taken not to alienate them further and push them deeper towards the very force that Pakistan and the United States have sought to destroy.

The Way Forward

The counter-terrorism card has too often been played to promote Pakistan as a pivotal force in shaping the regional geopolitical landscape in interaction with changing world politics. The fear of what an extremist Pakistan can produce has been used to perpetuate the rule of a dysfunctional elite and to maintain international support for it.

There is an urgent need for structural changes in Islamabad's policy approach. After Baluchistan, Khyber-Pakhtunkhwa is the least represented province in Pakistan's power structure. Nor have either of these two undergone as much social and economic development as Pakistan's other two provinces, Punjab and Sindh, the former in particular. Whilst the Punjabis (and to a limited extent the Sindhis) have come to exert dominant control of the levers of political, military and economic power, the same cannot be said about the Pashtuns and the Baluchis. In the past, a number of Pashtun personalities have reached the pinnacles of power, most famously Field Marshal Ayub Khan, who ruled Pakistan from 1958 to 1969, and several others who have reached senior federal political and military posts. But this on its own cannot compensate for the deeper political grievances and lack of sufficient educational, social and economic development among Pakistan's Pashtun population. For example, the per capita income of Khyber-Pakhtunkhwa was 30 per cent lower than the national average in 2007,[122] and the 2008 literacy rate in FATA stood at an appalling 17 per cent, compared with 56 per cent in the rest of the country.[123] The same inequalities hold true for Baluchistan. The two provinces are nevertheless among Pakistan's richest in terms of natural resources. Whilst Khyber-Pakhtunkhwa's natural wealth has recently been enhanced by the discovery of new oil and gas reserves, Baluchistan boasts enormous coal deposits among other minerals. Yet these resources have been exploited primarily for the benefit of the Punjabi, thereby aggravating the grievances of the provinces' predominantly native populations against the central government. The Pashtuns of Khyber-Pakhtunkhwa and the Baluchis have repeatedly demanded higher royalty rates, and a greater investment in the social and economic development of their provinces and federal power structure,[124] but to little avail. It is not only the Pakistani Pashtun Taliban that have remained resilient in pursuit of violent operations, but also the Baluchis, whose resurgent resistance movement has become increasingly militaristic in response to government crackdowns. The more the Pakistani government attempts to use violence to suppress Pashtun and Baluchi dissent in the provinces, the stronger the grievances and demands of these peoples have become.

The distancing of the military and the ISI from Pakistani politics is important if the country is to have any hopes of attaining a functional democratic government. The power of the ISI to manipulate ethnic relations and tensions and to use radical Islamism as an instrument of policy direction and implementation has been deleterious to harmony within the country and the region. Yet in order to achieve this, a necessarily cautious path of reform must be pursued. Although there is general popular support in Pakistan for civilian control over the military, there is considerable variation in views over the form that this control should take. Furthermore, there is some ambiguity regarding the Pakistanis' view of legitimate military power, with 69 per cent of the population reporting in 2009 that they believed the military had a right to take over control of the state 'in an emergency', whatever that might mean.[125] A further problem is that many external powers have become more trusting of the military as an institution than its civilian counterparts. China, a crucial ally of Pakistan, has historically seen the Pakistani military as a principal guarantor of its interests.[126] Other international players, the United States in particular, also retain an interest in ensuring that the Pakistani military remain predominant in politics. Reforms that could be initiated, however, might begin with curbing the influence of vast industrial empires controlled by the military – the *Fauji*, *Bahria* and *Shaheen* Foundations – that hold various companies in different sectors of the economy.[127]

A fundamental reassessment of Pakistan's geopolitical strategy is also needed. The ISI has pointedly chosen to ignore the fact that conflicts following the seizure of power by a cluster of pro-Soviet communists in Kabul in April 1978 profoundly changed the Afghan political and social landscape, empowering the non-Pashtun segments of the population to resist any return to past Pashtun supremacy. The majority of Afghanistan's neighbours are also wary of Pashtun predominance, with Iran and India worried that Pakistan's push for increased Pashtun representation would be at the expense of other minorities in the country, and China and the Central Asian republics wary of its potential to exacerbate Islamic extremism within their own borders.[128]

An added impetus for this reassessment came with the marked deterioration of relations between Washington and Islamabad, stemming from the controversial killing of bin Laden within Pakistani sovereign territory, and the ISI's backing of the *Haqqani* network and other Taliban elements. In July 2011, the Obama administration suspended hundreds of millions of dollars of aid to the Pakistani military, despite having pledged a further US$7.5 billion of aid to Pakistan through 2014, in the midst of an increasingly aggressive Taliban-led insurgency.[129] The November 2011 NATO air strikes on two Pakistani military posts on the Afghan–Pakistani border only served to add fuel to the fire.[130] In retaliation for this incident, Pakistan closed NATO supply routes into Afghanistan, further undermining its relationship with the West. Although a thaw came to prevail in US–Pakistan relations from mid-2012, when the United States finally formally apologised for the killing of the Pakistani soldiers, these events have caused both sides to be distrustful of each other, and their relations are prone to serious fluctuations and disruptions. Whilst being careful not to make ground-based military incursions from Afghanistan into Pakistani territory, the United States has carried out frequent drone attacks on Pakistan's border areas, targeting al-Qaeda, the Taliban and other elements identified as hostile. The drone operations have proved controversial and have carried with them the cost of very high civilian casualties.[131] Although quietly consenting to the operations under Musharraf and Zardari, Islamabad has publicly protested and condemned them, in line with the generally outraged opinion of the Pakistani public.[132] The increasingly popular leader of the *Pakistan Tahreek-e Insaf* Party, Imran Khan, has reaped dividends from this situation. Khan's vehement opposition to the drone attacks, coupled with his overtly anti-American posture, has struck a common chord with many Pakistanis,[133] as was borne out by the results of the May 2013 national elections, in which the PTI won a majority of seats in Khyber-Pakhtunkhwa. The electoral victory of Nawaz Sharif's PML-N in the same year was an encouraging development in Pakistan. Yet the victory by no means ensured the advent of stable and effective government capable of pursuing major structural reforms, which requires a very solid parliamentary majority.

Sharif, who served two previous non-consecutive terms as prime minister in the 1990s, cannot have been unaware of the challenges before him following his third electoral victory. In 1992, during his first term as prime minister, Sharif's attempts to negotiate a power-sharing peace settlement between seven Afghan *Mujahideen* leaders collapsed due to sabotage by some Afghan *Mujahideen* leaders and the ISI.[134] A rather different set of challenges confronted the Pakistani industrialist upon his 2013 re-election: that of enlisting support from factions within his own country, such as Imran Khan's PTI and the PPP, as part of building a national consensus, one that has historically eluded Pakistan's political elite. Sharif and Zardari were bitter rivals during the life of the last PPP-led parliament, while Imran Khan represents the aspirations of the young generation of Pakistanis. This put Imran Khan at odds with Sharif, who in many ways is tied to the 'old guard' Punjabi majority. Sharif is likely to lead an uneasy government, deprived of the kind of across the board support to enable him to effectively address the deep-seated challenges that confront Pakistan. Ideologically, however, he may stand a better chance of success than the secularist PPP-led government did in seeking a settlement with the Pakistani Taliban to rein in violence. Imran Khan's electoral win in Khyber-Pakhtunkhwa, where the Pakistan Taliban has its roots and the Afghan Taliban and their affiliates have safe havens, can help Sharif in this respect, provided that the two forge close cooperative ties.

Meanwhile, a major question mark remains over the potential for a Sharif-led government to tame the military and ISI, and wrest from them control of Pakistan's Afghanistan and Kashmir policies. Given Pakistan's myriad domestic problems and foreign policy complications, the task of limiting the political space for the military and the ISI is not going to be easy. Sharif's decision in June 2013 to prosecute Musharraf for treason could not ease the process either, as the military would not be pleased to see one of its former heads being humiliated and punished.

A further critical issue for Sharif has been relations with the United States. In the aftermath of the election, Sharif was quick to call for better relations with India, Afghanistan and the United States. However, major breakthroughs cannot be expected in the short run, given the complexity of the issues involved in these relations.

In order for Pakistan to overcome its domestic and foreign policy problems and dilemmas, the country's civilian government, military and the ISI must re-evaluate their policy of using Islamic extremism for internal and external purposes. Serious reforms are required to address such critical issues as that of a dysfunctional elite, a flawed quasi-democratic system, widespread corruption and massive social and economic disparities, which in 2011 placed Pakistan at 145 out of 187 countries on the United Nations Development Programme (UNDP) Human Development Index.[135]

All of these problems have deep roots in Pakistan's short but troubled history, and cannot be eliminated overnight. The relatively seamless experience of the previous election, as well as the tentative signs of growth in Pakistani civil society, provide some cause for optimism with regard to the nation's political future. Yet Pakistan's elites, which, as in Afghanistan, have proven to be notoriously self-serving and bitterly fragmented, have done far too little in the past to inspire confidence in their ability to institute the necessary reforms in pursuit of goals of national unity, good governance, social and economic prosperity and viable foreign policy.

While Islamabad cannot be expected to accomplish many reforms rapidly, given the political incongruities and vested interests that underpin the country's system, current governing elites bear the immediate responsibility for setting the process in motion. The Sharif government needs to enact an honest and forthright evaluation of the current political order, build effective government structures and discard a 'rogue state' approach to foreign policy. If it does so, it should be able to avoid a possibly debilitating Pashtun – or, for that matter, Baluchi – nationalist and religious extremist backlash, and to improve the national conditions to the extent necessary to stabilise Pakistan as an enduring functioning state. Pakistan is badly in need of strengthening its viability and improving on its long-standing image as a dangerous source of tension and instability, both in the region and for the world. It is a nuclear armed but impaired state, and this goes to the heart of the problem.

IRAN

Between 'Sovereignty of God' and 'Sovereignty of the People'

Introduction

The oil-rich and predominantly Shi'a Islamic Republic of Iran is indeed unique. Melding electoral processes and religious traditions, and combining Islamic and nationalist ideas, the country's Islamic regime has attempted to marry what are often seen as conflicting and contradictory trends in order to establish a two-tiered Islamic system of governance that enjoins the 'sovereignty of God' with the 'sovereignty of the people'. However, the country's Islamic regime has been scorned and sidelined by the United States and its allies, Israel in particular, which have accused it of aiding international terrorism, harbouring intentions to develop nuclear weapons and exerting a destabilising influence in the region. Iran has been castigated by its enemies for the perceived ambitious approach to its neighbours, as well as for repeated attempts to export its version of political Islam to the Muslim Middle East and Central Asia. The United States and its allies have viewed Iran's actions as validating the need for an approach characterised by unrelenting suspicion and constant vigilance. In turn, Tehran has lambasted Washington for hegemonic behaviour for its own geopolitical interests, including US support for what Tehran has branded as the aggressive Zionist Israeli state. It is only with the election of moderate-reformist cleric, Hassan Rouhani, since mid-2013 that some promising signs of a thaw in US–Iran relations have emerged, although many obstacles remain in place.

Situated at the crossroads of East and West, Iran (known in the outside world exclusively as Persia, although inside the country as

Iran, prior to 1932) has historically occupied a significant geostrategic position. Bordering Afghanistan to the east, Iraq to the west, Turkmenistan, Azerbaijan, the Caspian Sea and Armenia to the north, and the Persian Gulf to the south, Iran has traditionally proved critical to the construction of a sustainable regional order in world politics. Distinguished by its remarkable heritage and cultural richness, its lands have seen the rise and fall of many powerful empires in history. Yet Iran, like so many other states in the region, has also been subjected to intense major power rivalry and external interference. The latter tendency has been particularly pronounced in Iran's modern history, and has exerted a decisive influence over the evolution of the Iranian state from the late nineteenth century to the present day. During the late nineteenth and early twentieth centuries, Iran was carved into zones of interest and spheres of influence by Imperial Russia and Great Britain. Proud of their heritage and determined to preserve their historical independence and identity, Persians began to oppose with growing tenacity the cultural and economic domination of Western powers in their homeland in the early twentieth century. Nationalist ideas, imported from the West and combined with home-grown secularist and Shi'a Islamic ideologies, gave structure and intellectual coherence to many Persians who sought to reclaim 'their' land for themselves and to repel encroaching foreign influences. It is only in this context that Iran can be fully understood: external intervention in the twentieth century has been largely responsible for making confrontation and conflict the norm rather than the exception. The CIA-orchestrated overthrow of the popularly elected and reformist Prime Minister Mohammad Mossedeq in 1953, the Iran–Iraq War (1980–88) and the continued estrangement of Iran from the international community since the Iranian Revolution of 1978–79 drove the consolidation of the Iranian state under an exceptional blend of Shi'a Islamism and nationalism. The process of consolidation and blend has been largely shaped by the perceived threat of the 'other' (i.e., non-Iranian), which today forms the basis of the Islamic Republic's often defensive, but perceived as 'aggressive', behaviour toward outside actors.

The controversy over the 2009 presidential elections and the fracturing of the government elite brought many political issues out into the open. The struggle between *jihadi* (exertive traditionalist Islamist) and *ijtihadi* (reformist Islamist)[1] forces at all levels of the system was made far more public than ever before, pitching both clusters against one another, and causing a critical split within the ruling clerical elite to the point of posing a serious threat to the Islamic regime. However, the election of the moderate, centrist candidate Hassan Rouhani to the presidency in June 2013 seemed to mark a new phase in Iranian politics. Here, the religiously conservative middle classes and young reformists came together in an apparent rejection of hardline *jihadi* politics to confer a landslide victory on the reformist cleric. Rouhani quickly made clear his commitment to engaging in domestic reforms and foreign policy openness in order to improve the living conditions of all Iranians, resolve the nuclear impasse and end Western sanctions against Iran. Yet Rouhani's commitments must be considered in light of the Iranian regime's very complex system of Islamic governance and its long-standing, although largely unsuccessful, attempt to seek international approval for itself and its nuclear policies. This chapter, therefore, focuses on a country where the interplay between various forces has created a unique political and social system that is unlikely to be replicated elsewhere and which may well hold the key to stability in the entire region.

Social Divisions

Centralised and legitimised Persian rule in the context of a mosaic society has defined the framework in which Iran has operated throughout history. Although Iran is less socially fragmented than Afghanistan, Pakistan or Iraq, minorities have nevertheless created difficulties for state consolidation. Of some 79 million people of Iran, the majority Persian ethnic cluster makes up 65 per cent. The Azeris and Kurds, concentrated in the north, make up 16 and 10 per cent respectively. Of the remaining minorities, only the Arabs (3 per cent), who reside predominantly in the south-western, oil-rich province of Khuzestan, and the Baluchi tribes (2 per cent), who dominate the south-east, are of significance.

Historically home to a multitude of religions, the period since the 1978–79 Revolution that resulted in the overthrow of the pro-Western monarchy of Mohammed Reza Shah Pahlavi, and its replacement by Ayatollah Rohullah Khomeini's Islamic regime, witnessed the political ascendency of Shi'a Islam in the Iranian polity. Today, 90 per cent of Iranians are Shi'a and around 8 per cent are Sunni. The most prominent non-Muslim religious minority, the Baha'is, were estimated to number between 150,000 and 300,000 in 2000, and are subject to ongoing marginalisation and alleged persecution.[2] Iran's Christian and Jewish communities continue to dissipate as followers migrate to more preferred countries.

With a relatively consolidated Shi'a community and a concentration of Persian stock in the centre of the country, Iran has therefore managed to build itself into a centralised state even in the absence of ethnic congruity, and despite regional and historical differences among the Persians themselves. Nearly all Iranians are fluent in Persian, with linguistic conformity fostering a shared sense of culture and identity that in some ways transcends ethnic divisions. Unlike neighbouring states, where identity has coalesced around tribal, sectarian or religious symbols, the notion of 'Iran' appears to have firmly entrenched itself in the consciousness of most of the country's citizens.

Historical Legacy

Although this centralised mosaic nature has persisted under the Islamic Republic, the regime's ideological orientation and political perspective represent a radical departure from and reaction to the reign of Mohammad Reza Shah Pahlavi (1941–79). Ayatollah Khomeini, the founder of the Islamic Republic, formulated his religious worldview in the framework of dialectic opposition to what he condemned as the repressive, secularist 'Western' outlook of the Shah. Since the Revolution, the Iranian Shi'a clerical establishment has strived to implement Khomeini's vision, with arguably little to no concrete success in relation to what Khomeini may have desired. The attempt by President Mohammad Khatami (1997–2005) to build an inclusive and reformist society under the auspices of Khomeini's legacy only served to highlight the divide existing within the ruling clerical–political elite. A return to inward-looking and conservative domestic politics and defiant foreign policy under Khatami's successor, President Mahmoud Ahmadinejad (2005–13), further fragmented the elite and caused Iran unprecedented international isolation.

The Shah's rule: authoritarianism and Western interference

The beginning of the end for the Pahlavi dynasty in Iran dates from the bitter power struggle between the Shah and the veteran Iranian nationalist reformist politician, Mohammad Mossadeq, in the early 1950s.[3] Mossadeq had pushed for a revolutionary process of change that would transform Iran into a constitutional monarchy, nationalise Iran's oil resources (a British monopoly since the early 1900s) and implement long overdue social and economic reforms. With these goals in mind, he also sought to undermine the traditional Anglo-Russian rivalry to which Iran had been subjected since the late nineteenth century, although as in Afghanistan the intensity of this dynamic was markedly lessened in the 1920s and 1930s following Russia's transformation into a communist state in the wake of the 1917 Bolshevik seizure of power. The Shah was opposed to Mossadeq's approach, especially where it came close to infringing on the traditional powers of the monarch, who drew much of his strength and legitimacy from the historical institution of the Shah, which had existed in Persia for some 2,500 years. After Mossadeq's accession to the premiership, based on his rainbow group, *Jabhe-i Melli* (the National Front), emerging as the largest political force in the *Majlis* (National Assembly), on 30 April 1951, and his nationalisation of the British controlled Anglo-Iranian Oil Company (AIOC) shortly thereafter, the Shah found himself increasingly sidelined in policymaking, and was ultimately forced to go into exile to Switzerland in August 1953.

Despite his initial reluctance, the Shah quickly gave his support to a coup d'état in his own country, engineered and executed by the American CIA and supported by the British Secret Intelligence Service, MI6. The British were fundamentally opposed to Mossadeq's nationalisation of the AIOC, and the United States perceived a unique opportunity to act in support of their own global geopolitical interests, with a focus on containing their archenemy at the time, the Soviet Union. Within a week of his exile, the Shah had been brought back to Iran by the CIA. He was reinstalled on his throne – not to reign, but to rule Iran at the behest of the United States,[4] at the cost of Mossadeq being put under house arrest where he died in 1967, and Iran drifting rapidly into the US orbit.

The CIA's intervention was widely resented within Iran and in the region. The Shah imposed a military dictatorship and did not hesitate to maintain it through the extensive use of a secret police called the Organization of Intelligence and National Security (*Sazeman-e*

Ettela'at va Amniyat-e Keshvar, commonly known as SAVAK), set up
for him by the CIA and the Federal Bureau of Investigation (FBI) in
cooperation with Israel's Mossad. The United States provided massive
financial, economic and military assistance, and signed various bilateral
agreements with Iran to shore up the Shah's regime. It also acted
centrally in setting up an international consortium, operational from
late 1954, that would ensure the maintenance of British and US interests
in Iranian oil. This new body, Iranian Oil Participants Ltd, gave equal
prominence to British Petroleum and five American oil companies in
running the Iranian oil industry while remaining under the nominal
tutelage of the National Iranian Oil Company, established by Mossadeq
in 1951. Iran was also brought into the US-backed regional alliance
of the Baghdad Pact in 1955 and its successor, the Central Treaty
Organisation, two years later – all part of a US-driven strategy to put an
international ring of containment around the Soviet Union. Headed by
an unpopular monarch who relied heavily on US support for political
survival, Iran lost its traditional neutrality in world politics. In the eyes
of US strategists, Iran had become a front-line bulwark against Soviet
communism. The US–Iran relationship was rapidly transformed into
that of 'patron–client', underpinned by enduring structures of Iran's
dependence on and vulnerability to Washington. Even in the 1970s,
when billions of dollars of oil revenue might have made it possible for
the Shah to extricate himself from his dependent position, he proved
incapable of doing so.

Following his empowerment by the CIA, the Shah pursued two
contradictory goals that would lead ultimately to his overthrow in the
Iranian Revolution. The first was to make himself pivotal to the operation
of Iranian governance through a process of political centralisation – a
tactic that had been critical for the survival of the Persian monarchy for
centuries. The second was to engage in a pro-capitalist secular mode
of national socio-economic development and foreign policy that would
complement his special relationship with the United States. However,
by the late 1950s, both Washington and the Shah had come to the
conclusion that it would be necessary for the Iranian monarchy to widen
its support base if its long-term survival and uncritical US backing were
to be ensured. The Shah thus put a formal end to martial law in 1959.
Subsequently, under pressure from the John F. Kennedy administration,
he intensified efforts to secure a wider base of popular legitimacy by

inaugurating what he called the 'White Revolution' or the 'Revolution of the Shah and People'.[5] Ali Amini, who had been imposed on the Shah as the US choice of prime minister, was in fact responsible for initiating the White Revolution by implementing a programme of land reform. Yet Amini was quickly forced out of office by the jealous Shah, who was unable to stand the idea that Amini might eclipse him as Washington's number one man.

Whatever steps the Shah might take to entrench himself at the centre of Iranian politics, he could never expunge the indignity of being put on the throne by the CIA, bridge the contradiction in his goals, or transform his relationship with the United States into one of interdependence in order to elevate his rule in the eyes of most Iranians and the countries of the region. He continued to rule by suppression, co-optation, patronage and divide-and-rule politics. He projected an image of SAVAK as all-powerful and ever-present, to the extent that many Iranians became convinced that most of their compatriots were either members or informants of the organisation. This perception reached the point where 'people could not trust people'.[6] The explosion of Iran's oil revenues, from US$2 billion in 1970 to close to US$20 billion in 1974, provided a critical opportunity for the Shah to free himself from US influence and bolster his popularity. The so-called 'OPEC (Organization of the Petroleum Exporting Countries) revolution' of the early 1970s had enabled the organisation's members, including Iran, to wrest control and pricing of their oil from the Western international oil companies, which had hitherto had a monopoly over most of the Middle Eastern oil industries. The resulting flood of revenue enabled the Shah to embark on an accelerated programme of economic and military modernisation in order to transform Iran into the world's fifth largest economic and military power by the mid-1980s. Yet the Shah squandered the opportunity to engage in appropriate and productive political, social and economic reforms, preferring instead to embark on a poorly conceived and badly implemented process of modernisation. His programme resulted in tremendous social dislocation (including massive urbanisation), uncertainty and increasing disillusionment, and soon proved unviable. The reforms of the 1970s had more to do with the Shah's desire for self-indulgence and aggrandisement than with the needs of the Iranian people.[7]

Roots of the Revolution: opposition to the Shah

By the late 1960s, four major sources of opposition to the Shah's rule had emerged in Iran. The first were the ideological and political opponents of the Shah's rule, including various Marxist and nationalist groups. The second were the pro-democracy reformists, who were generally drawn from the upper stratum of Iranian society. The third were the merchants/petit bourgeoisie (*bazaaris*). The fourth was the Shi'a religious establishment. By the late 1970s, public grievances had also gathered pace among different levels of society that had been adversely affected by the Shah's ill-conceived programme of reform. A deepening rift between two ways of life, one traditional, and one modern and Western, was becoming increasingly obvious in Iran's swelling cities. Disorientated by processes of social change and angered by growing economic inequalities, Iranians of diverse backgrounds felt increasingly alienated from their history and their identity. In this context, the Shah's open embrace of Western culture and uncritical acceptance of Western-style reforms made him the target of even wider resentment.

Of all those disaffected by the Shah's regime, the only group that managed to remain relatively cohesive by the late 1970s were the religious authorities. The Iranian Constitution of 1906 had officially entrusted the Shi'a establishment with the task of ensuring the conformity of the government to the precepts of Shi'a Islam. The *ulama* had felt increasingly impeded in this task by the Shah's promotion of secular politics, which was indeed partly designed to reduce the ability of any religious centre of power to challenge his position. His constant attempts to erode the power base of the Shi'a establishment caused widespread disquiet among the clerics. Many of their leading figures, especially in the city of Qom – a traditional Shi'a seat of learning and political power that had counter-balanced the temporal authority since the early sixteenth century – strongly disapproved of the Shah's regime and its pro-Western secular modernisation drive.

Prominent among the clerics who voiced their opposition to the Shah, but by no means the most senior or well-known Iranian religious figure, was Ayatollah Khomeini. More junior than such clerics as Grand Ayatollah Mohammad Kazem Shariatmadari, Grand Ayatollah Mar'ashi Najafi, Grand Ayatollah Lotfollah Safi Golpaygani or Ayatollah Hossein Ali Montazari in the Shi'a religious hierarchy, Khomeini's portrayal of Iran's political situation in radical religious terms nevertheless found a wide audience in the tumultuous climate of the 1960s and 1970s. Emerging as a leading Islamist and political critic of the Shah's rule from 1961, Khomeini dichotomised the world into *mostakbarin* (the oppressors) and *mosta'zafin* (the downtrodden), and called for empowerment of the latter. From his exile in Turkey, Iraq and Paris (1964–79), Khomeini electrified young clerics by ordaining them to abandon their traditional contentment with overseeing the work of the government in favour of seizing the reins of power themselves. In contrast to the elaborate ideologies of many of the Shah's political opponents, Khomeini's Islamic message was simple and resonated deeply with a majority of Iranians who had been imbued with Shi'a Islamic religious culture over the centuries.[8]

Khomeini's vision and revolution

Pushed by the Jimmy Carter administration's emphasis on human rights in US foreign policy, the Shah had found it imperative to engage in a degree of limited liberalisation intended to mollify the opposition. Instead, the situation snowballed from a wave of protests in October 1977 into a nationwide uprising, and ultimately a popular revolution, within months. While the participants came to include a wide range of social strata, the Shah's suppression of all forms of organised political opposition meant that Khomeini's religious message and mosque network – which remained beyond the reach of SAVAK – proved increasingly influential during this tumultuous period. By the second half of 1978, Khomeini and his supporters, who had secretly formed the anti-Shah Society of Resistant Clerics (*Jame'eh-ye Ruhaniyat-e Mobarez*) in 1977, were able to seize the leadership of the opposition movement. By this point, neither a military crackdown nor the granting of concessions to the opposition could produce a satisfactory outcome for the Shah. The popular uprising, which constituted a genuine mass revolution, had been set in motion largely by the political and professional opponents of the Shah in pursuit of democratic reforms. Yet by November 1978, the movement's leadership had been overtaken by the clerics and headed by Khomeini, who would settle for nothing less than the abdication of the Shah. The Shah was finally forced to hand over power to a prominent figure of the suppressed secular centre-left National Front, Shapour Bakhtiar, and left Tehran on 17 January 1979 for a 'temporary stay' abroad. Khomeini, returning from exile in Paris, received a tumultuous welcome from millions of Iranians two weeks later in Tehran. The Shah's temporary departure became a permanent exile. After controversially being admitted to the United States for medical treatment, he died of cancer in Cairo 18 months later, in circumstances where even the United States was no longer prepared to be closely identified with him.

Khomeini had always entertained a vision of Iran as a Shi'a Islamic state. He could now implement this vision by first transforming the Iranian Revolution into an Islamic phenomenon and then, following a referendum on 31 March 1979, by declaring Iran an Islamic Republic, with an Islamic government, also known as *velayat-e faqih* (Guardianship of the Jurisprudent).[9] He scrapped the Shah's pro-Western secular approach and replaced it with a religious paradigm. Guided by an interpretation of Shi'a Islam, he sought to transform the country into a polity underpinned by both divine law and popular, or earthly, legitimacy. Iran would thus have an Islamic order based on Khomeini's understanding of Twelver Shi'a Islam; yet this would be an order that was to be both participatory and pluralistic within the limits of an Islamic framework. Khomeini envisioned the divine and earthly tiers of the system to be in balance, and at the same time to be organically linked to and dependent on each other. His idea was to enforce a political order in which the divine position of the Supreme Leader (*vali-e faqih*) would provide for overarching continuity and stability, and the government beneath it would embody the will of the people within an Islamic frame, enabling the public to connect and identify with the system.

Although Khomeini's doctrine of *velayat-e faqih* was enshrined as the ultimate source of authority in Iran's Islamic politics, a presidential system of government was also adopted. This system was composed of executive, legislative and judicial branches, and conferred concurrent responsibility on both the Supreme Leader and the people. This two-tiered system of governance was ordained by the country's Islamic Constitution, enacted in October 1979 and amended ten years later. On the one hand, the constitution upheld the 'sovereignty of God' embodied in the position of the *vali-e faqih*. On the other hand, it enshrined the 'sovereignty of the people' to ensure that the Islamic political system also rests on a pillar of popular legitimacy. In social life, the constitution emphasised the need for cultural conformity, and stipulated a compulsory dress code for women and moral codes for everyone.

The sovereignty of the people was to be expressed through a government composed of an elected president and National Assembly (*Majlis*), and an appointed judiciary, providing for public participation and political contestation. The presidential system and National Assembly were complemented by three other powerful bodies. One was the unelected 12-member Council of Guardians, composed of six clerics nominated by the Supreme Leader, and six jurists nominated by the head of the judiciary (himself nominated by the Supreme Leader). Acting as the gatekeeper for the Supreme Leader, it was entrusted with the powers to vet presidential and parliamentary candidates, hold referendums, veto legislation passed in the *Majlis*, and declare the results of elections. The second body was the elected 86-member Assembly of Experts, whose task was to appoint the Supreme Leader, to monitor his performance to make sure that he is on the path of Shi'a Islam, and if required to terminate his appointment. The third body was the Expediency Council, with the ultimate power to adjudicate disputes over legislation between the parliament and the Council of Guardians. Beyond this, various legal, political and security structures and law enforcement agencies, as well as institutional checks and balances, were created. Khomeini therefore put in place a highly complex power structure and system of governance. Nevertheless, the constraints and power-sharing arrangements within the Iranian government were not intended to eclipse the power of the Supreme Leader himself, who was invested with ultimate constitutional authority over the executive branch as well as the general policies of the nation.

While Khomeini was one of many ayatollahs, his leadership and following made him appear a natural choice for the all-powerful position of Supreme Leader, and to function as a *marja'ee taqlid*, or source of emulation – a very high status to achieve in Shi'a Islam. From this position, he could exercise greater authority than any Iranian monarch could ever muster. Both his religious and political status were sanctified to the extent that anyone who questioned the validity of either risked incurring the wrath of his supporters. Other Shi'a leaders, such as Grand Ayatollah Shariatmadari, at odds with Khomeini's vision of an Islamic Iran, sought to promote a gentler and more humane application of Islam than the version promulgated by Khomeini. In spite of the seniority of many such clerics over Khomeini, they were effectively sidelined in the aftermath of the Revolution.

Khomeini initially adopted a *jihadi* (combative) approach to the Revolution, aimed at the forceful Islamisation of politics and society according to his version of Shi'a Islam. This phase dominated the first few years of the Revolution at the cost of thousands of lives, with some estimates of the death toll ranging from 10,000 to 20,000.[10] He pursued this *jihadi* dimension against the backdrop of Iran's centuries-old authoritarian political culture, and within his Islamic worldview of *mostakbarin* (the oppressors) versus *mosta'zafin* (the downtrodden). He labelled all those closely associated with the Shah's dictatorship – whether inside or outside Iran – as 'oppressors' and therefore liable to be punished for their crimes against the Iranian people in particular, and Muslims in general. Those who were known or suspected to have been among the Shah's main functionaries, ideologues and supporters were ruthlessly weeded out. Khomeini considered it to be morally and ethically justifiable to wrest power from oppressors not only by means of persuasion, but also, if necessary, through the use of coercion in defence of Islam.

Once the royalists were effectively defeated, Khomeini turned his attention to the creation of a purified and unified Islamic movement. This involved the dismantling of secular and semi-secular groups that had played a notable part in opposition to the Shah's regime , and with some of them now violently resisting Khomeini's Islamic impositions. The most important of these were the various secularist (and mostly communist) radical groups within Iran, ranging from the *Mujahideen-e Khalq* (the Warriors for the People), a militant group that preached a mixture of Marxism and Islamism, to the militant Maoist *Feda'iyan-e Khalq* (the Sacrificers for the People), to the pro-Soviet communist party *Tudeh* (Masses), as well as Mossadeq's former party, the centre-left nationalist *Jebhe-ye Melli* (National Front). It also involved the targeting and purging of many non-partisan opponents of the Shah who failed to embrace the political ideology of the new Islamic Republic. Khomeini's attempts at purification were then extended to the marginalisation or, in some cases, expunging of those elements within the ranks of Khomeini's followers who were regarded as undesirable or had the potential to challenge Khomeini's particular vision. These elements came to include a diverse range of people. Some had cast doubt on the efficacy of Khomeini's approach; others found themselves unable to agree entirely with his version of political Islam. A number of ayatollahs, including Shariatmadari, were either imprisoned or placed under house arrest.

Even Ayatollah Hossein Ali Montazari, who had initially been anointed by Khomeini as his successor, was eventually marginalised. Khomeini finally revoked Montazari's succession entitlement in 1989.[11] A number of other clerics and their followers were to suffer similar fates.

In the foreign sphere, Khomeini declared the new Republic's policy to be neither pro-West nor pro-East, but pro-Islamic, and therefore totally independent. It was clear, however, that historical legacy and ideological constraints guaranteed that the Islamic Republic would hold an anti-American and also partly anti-Soviet outlook. Khomeini had little time for Soviet Russia, which he condemned as 'the other Great Satan'[12] due to its atheist Marxist ideology. The original 'Great Satan' was, of course, the United States, not only for what Khomeini viewed as its moral decadence, materialism and imperialist ambitions, but also its complicity in the Shah's 'reign of terror'. Khomeini aimed to deprive this 'evil power' of a major strategic foothold in the region,[13] and displayed an antipathy toward those conservative regimes in the region that were either allied with the United States (such as those of Saudi Arabia, Jordan and many other Arab states) or were secular and oppressive (such as Iraq and Egypt), although Syria was not included in this category for broader regional and strategic considerations. Israel, too, was anathema to Khomeini, who saw it as a usurper of Palestinian and Islamic lands.

Apart from urging changes in the regional configuration of forces in the Arab world, against the conservative regimes, Khomeini called for the export of the Iranian Revolution to other Muslim states in order to increase support for Islamic transformation in the region. The chief objective was to radicalise and empower the Shi'a segments both in the countries where they formed a majority but remained oppressed, such as neighbouring Iraq and Bahrain, and in the states where they constituted deprived minorities, such as Lebanon and many other regional Muslim countries. Beyond this, it was also expected that the Iranian revolutionary zeal would have an impact on many Sunni groups which were dissatisfied with their secular governments and with US dominance in the region. While few Sunnis chose to emulate Khomeini's Shi'a leadership and the Iranian Revolution, Tehran scored well among the deprived Lebanese Shi'a, who became increasingly receptive to Khomeini's regime as a source of sectarian inspiration and support. The result was the formation of the militant Islamic movement of *Hezbollah* (Party of God), which would eventually emerge as a very powerful player in Lebanese politics and a notable anti-US and anti-Israeli force.[14] This, together with the Islamic Republic of Iran forging a strategic partnership with Syria – a Sunni majority state but governed by a minority Shi'a-linked Alawite sect – altered the balance of power in the Middle East.

It is not surprising that the new Iran came very quickly to be perceived as a serious threat to the interests of the United States and those of its regional Arab and non-Arab allies. The United States accordingly took to labelling Khomeini's regime as 'fundamentalist'. This disparaging characterisation became especially prominent in the wake of the Iranian hostage crisis – an episode that lasted over a year and caused tremendous embarrassment to the United States. The crisis was instigated when a group of pro-Khomeini militants, with at least the tacit endorsement of the Ayatollah himself,[15] took hostage 52 staff of the American embassy in Tehran on 4 November 1979. The release of the hostages was not secured until the inauguration of President Ronald Reagan on 20 January 1981. While the main purpose of the hostage crisis was to humiliate the United States and to keep the public mobilised behind Khomeini's leadership, it fed Washington's anxiety about and bitterness over the 'loss' of Iran as a significant geostrategic asset in the Middle East, and instigated an enduring American–Iranian strategic rivalry in the region.

Washington's reaction to the seizure of the American hostages was swift. It severed relations with Iran, imposed economic and military sanctions, and increasingly portrayed radical political Islamism as a threat to America and the world order. Soon after, the Iraqi dictator Saddam Hussein seized the opportunity to strike against Iran, a nation in the midst of post-revolutionary turmoil and a diplomatic crisis, in the hopes of destroying Khomeini's rule and establishing Iraq's supremacy in the Gulf – all in the name of defending the Arab nation.[16] Saddam's invasion of Iran on 22 September 1980, which proved an abysmal failure in terms of Iraq's original ambitions, pushed both nations into the longest, bloodiest and most costly war in the modern history of the Middle East. At the same time, American and Arab courtship of and support for Saddam throughout the 1980–88 Iran–Iraq War cemented American–Iranian, Arab–Iranian and Sunni–Shi'a antagonisms.[17]

This initial radical *jihadi* form through which Khomeini consolidated the state, in the midst of war with Iraq, has contributed to a tendency to demonise the Iranian leader while overlooking the elements of his vision which were more reformist, reconciliatory and constructive. After the first few years of the Revolution, Khomeini supplemented his *jihadi* phase with an *ijtihadi* phase in order to build a powerful and modern Shi'a Islamic state,[18] endowed with a pluralist Islamic system of governance capable of standing up to any outside threat. The portrait of Khomeini as both a radical and a reformer fits ill, however, with the simpler caricature of the fundamentalist to which the West had become accustomed.

Rafsanjani's pragmatism

By the time of his death on 3 June 1989, Khomeini had not only entrenched his *jihadi* programme, but also made progress in his *ijtihadi* phase in the Revolution. Ali Khamenei and Ali Akbar Hashemi Rafsanjani, two of his closest loyalists, were now more than ever thrust into the limelight. Khamenei, who was then serving as president, was elevated to the position of *vali-e faqih*, and Rafsanjani ran virtually unopposed for president. However, Khamenei, even more than Khomeini before him, became the source and focus of much controversy within the Iranian clerical establishment. Many Grand Ayatollahs questioned his religious credentials and expressed scepticism as to whether he was qualified for the position. Prior to the death of Khomeini, Khamenei had only held a middling rank in the Shi'a clerical hierarchy as *Hojjtaloleslam* (Authority on Islam), and the quick promotion of his theological rank to Ayatollah by the Assembly of Experts in 1989 did little to appease many clerics.[19] In view of Khamenei's low clerical standing, the charismatic and capable President Rafsanjani, who played a key role in the elevation of Khamanei, became the prominent figure in politics.

Initially, the governing elite had operated within the auspices of the Islamic Republican Party (IRP) and refrained from public display of their differences. However, when factionalist disorder became rife in the IRP in the mid-1980s, Khomeini began to change his views on the role of political organisations within the Islamic state. He reverted to the traditional Islamic dictum that the existence of any kind of political party in an Islamic entity was inappropriate. By 1987, he formally abolished the IRP and decreed Iran to be a non-partisan Islamic Republic, but without calling for an end to political factionalism. It therefore came as no surprise that, soon after his death, under Rafsanjani's presidency, the

Iranian political elite gradually drifted apart, ultimately coalescing into three identifiable ideological clusters.

The first of these, alternately described as the *jihadis*/traditionalists, the conservatives, or the revolutionaries, initially held sway in Iran's political machinations due to their already entrenched position. The *jihadis* had already coalesced around such figures as the new *vali-e faqih*, Khamenei, and Mohammad Reza Mahdavi Kani, by the time of Khomeini's death. They controlled most of the instruments of state power in the Islamic order and had played an active role in the war with Iraq, opposition to the United States and Israel, and promoting the export of the Revolution throughout the region. The *jihadis* argued for the strengthening of the Islamic order and the consolidation of the Revolution's gains through the preservation of traditional lifestyles, the promotion of national self-sufficiency, the maintenance of ideological and cultural purity, and uncompromising hostility toward the United States and some of its regional allies, viewed as both a major threat to Iran and a potential source of Iranian solidarity that could provide backing for the cluster's cause.

The second cluster – the *ijtihadi* (reformist/internationalist) faction, began to evolve in 1987 around such prominent clerics as Mehdi Karroubi and Mohammad Khatami. The latter was a distinguished clerical supporter of Khomeini and had served briefly as Minister of Culture in the early 1980s. United in their support for a pluralistic, democratic Islamic political system, the *ijtihadis* favoured the promotion of Islamic civil society, the relaxation of political and social controls, economic openness, a cultural renaissance and wider interactions with the outside world, including the United States. They were inspired by such Iranian thinkers as Ali Shariati (1933–77), Abdul Karim Soroush (1945–) and Ayatollah Mojtahed Shabestari (1936–), who blended Islamism with Enlightenment ideas in their vision of a modern Islamic society compatible with democratic principles.[20] In March 1988, a number of these reformists formed the Assembly of Assertive Clerics (*Majma'e Rowhaniyun-e Mobarez*), or AAC. They preached pragmatism and reformism in line with the aforementioned vision, which was championed by Khatami. More realists than idealists, the leaders of the reformist cluster emphasised the importance of maintaining a balance of power in domestic politics, hence their limited opposition to policies pushed by Rafsanjani.[21]

Amalgaran, the third cluster on the Iranian political scene, crystallised around the centralist or pragmatist leadership and policies of Rafsanjani. This entity generally occupied the middle ground between the *jihadis* and *ijtihadis* and organised itself into two parties – the Executives of Construction Party (*Hezbe Kargozaran Sazandegi*), which supported the reformists' approach to culture, and the Justice and Development Party (*Hezbe E'tedal va Tose'eh*), which leaned toward the conservatives on cultural issues. The camp as a whole was motivated by the intellectual work of a number of academic economists, and subscribed to a belief in economic modernisation from above, favouring technical and economic relations with the West but with no serious interest in the democratisation of politics. It flip-flopped on many issues, whenever opportune and desirable.[22]

During Rafsanjani's presidency (1989–97), Iranian politics shifted from an initial approach of accommodation and compromise to one of competition and deadlock. Prior to Khomeini's death, these three clusters had both competed and cooperated with one another, and had made alliances on the basis of often overlapping agendas. The conservatives upheld the ideological purity of Khomeini's legacy, but at the same time proved to be both pragmatic and reformist when needed; the reformists sought to popularise and pluralise that legacy and make it palatable to the international community, but without losing sight of their organic linkages with the conservatives; and the pragmatists navigated opportunistically between the two. Fluidity of movement between the clusters during this period acquired an almost routine character, with some individuals changing allegiance quite frequently and their leaders remaining in consultation with one another when confronted with the need to adopt a coordinated position in the face of any serious threat.

The end of the Iran–Iraq War and the death of Khomeini, however, put an end to all semblance of political unity. In his push toward increased economic freedoms and a pragmatic foreign policy, Rafsanjani found himself treading an increasingly fine line between the *jihadi* and *ijtihadi* factions. By the end of his second term, pushed into an ever-tighter political corner, Rafsanjani made efforts to ingratiate himself with the emerging *ijtihadi* faction.[23] While this proved too late to reverse his personal political fortune, it created an opening for the forces of reform and for the ascension of Khatami.

Khatami's Islamic democracy

Swept into power in an astonishing landslide victory in 1997, Khatami assumed office in the firm conviction that the time had come to transform Iran from a political culture of *jihad* to *ijtihad*. To realise this objective, he called for domestic political reforms that would promote 'Islamic civil society' as a precondition for, and in tandem with, 'Islamic democracy', and for a revision of Iran's foreign policy, based on the principles of 'dialogue' between civilisations and cross-cultural understandings within the international system of nation-states.[24] His was a new vision of Shi'a Islam – one that would be adaptive to changing times and conditions. It was a vision, claimed Khatami, that Khomeini would have shared if he had been alive.[25]

Khatami treated Iran's Islamic Constitution as sacrosanct and operated within the framework it had established. At the same time, he consistently stressed not only the enshrinement of his own understanding of civil society and democracy in Islam, but also the commitment of the Iranian Islamic Constitution to the promotion of concepts for the common good. These distinctively Islamic concepts, asserted Khatami, while claiming a different heritage from their Western counterparts, were not necessarily in 'conflict and contradiction in all their manifestations and consequences' with those embraced in Western traditions of rationalism and liberalism.[26] Khatami's broad-reaching political philosophy was structured around a number of key pillars that gave shape to an *ijtihadi* political culture during his presidency. These included a belief in the right of all citizens to determine their own destiny and to hold the government accountable; the conviction that Islamic civil society was one where not only Muslims, but all individuals, were entitled to rights within the framework of law and order; a valuing of freedom of thought and expression and diversity of opinion in an Islamic civil society; and the condemnation of censorship and political repression as a reaction to dissent in Iran.

Khatami's concept of Islamic civil society was more firmly grounded in ethical precepts than material standards. Although it promoted a measured degree of separation of politics and capital alongside government intervention in public life to help the needy, ensure justice and implement the laws of Islam, ultimately it relied on moral force to win the day. Like many other religious-political thinkers, Khatami was keen to emphasise that a moral, virtuous and humane existence delivers a better standard of living in economic and social terms, rather than vice versa.

Together, Khatami's conception of 'Islamic democracy' and Khomeini's vision of a theocratic-pluralistic system of governance provided a meaningful blueprint for the gradual moderation and reform of Iranian governance that would assist in its reintegration into the international system. From 1997 until 2001, Khatami was able to set in motion a gradual process of reform that won the support of a large majority of Iranians. He was very comfortably elected for a second term, with his supporters also dominating the *Majlis*. Yet Khatami's programme did not proceed unimpeded. The obstacles to reform would become increasingly prohibitive after 2001 as a result of both domestic political factors and international developments. From within Iran, Khatami faced growing resistance from the Islamic conservative faction that had traditionally dominated the government structures. From without, Khatami was confronted by sustained US objection to the Iranian Islamic regime, which, along with many European states, gave little recognition to Khatami's reforms. US hostility to the Islamic regime in Iran achieved new heights following al-Qaeda's 11 September 2001 attacks on the United States and the declaration of the 'war on terror', due partly to US speculation on Iranian involvement in the attacks. Such an allegation, which was widely circulated by the US neoconservative right and media, caused considerable damage to US–Iran relations despite President Bush's 2002 public admission that the 9/11 Commission found no evidence of a connection. Neither Khatami's public expressions of sympathy for the victims and repeated outreach to the United States for concerted action against the perpetrators, nor Tehran's cooperation with the United States in making the Afghan Bonn Conference of November– December 2001 a success, were able to improve the situation. In his 2002 State of the Union speech, President George W. Bush condemned Iran, together with North Korea and Syria, as part of an 'axis of evil'. By 2005, continued *jihadi* pressure on the Khatami government, coupled with a lack of real Western goodwill towards the Iranian state, had reaped their toll. The conservatives re-emerged as the dominant cluster in the *Majlis*. The Iranian Revolutionary Guard (IRG) became the 'praetorian guard' for the conservatives, whose resurgence in Iranian politics culminated in the election of Mahmoud Ahmadinejad, former conservative and populist mayor of Tehran, to the presidency in 2005.

Dysfunctional Governance

Following Ahmadinejad's election, Iran was subjected to greater theocratic control and foreign policy pressures. Khomeini's mandate for a two-tiered Islamic polity and a pluralistic form of Shi'a *jihadi–ijtihadi* politics was left unfulfilled.[27] Instead, his vision was manipulated by the conservative factions of the ruling clerical elite, who proved themselves intent on securing their own political and economic fortunes at great cost to the Iranian people. This, in turn, opened the door to systems of wider patronage, nepotism and corruption on a similar scale to Iran's neighbours. Crippled by internal divisions and lacking any meaningful claim to represent the people, the Islamic regime increasingly proved ineffective, provoking a serious legitimacy crisis – no less serious, some might argue, than the one that had dogged the Shah's rule.

Fractured elite and political infighting

Prior to Ahmadinejad's political ascendancy, Khatami's election to the presidency provoked the first serious schism within the Iranian elite. The president's appeals for wider and more amiable foreign relations, including a possible rapprochement with the United States, were met with rejection by both the *jihadis* and their backer, Khamenei. For the conservatives, reconciliation with Western powers, along with Khatami's reforms more broadly, would only serve to unravel their ideological base and the fabric of the revolutionary Islamic Iran that Khomeini left behind, and provide an opening for the West, especially the United States, to restore its influence in Iran. As the reform process moved forward, the *jihadis* increasingly targeted one of the issues at the heart of the process – freedom of thought and expression.[28] While Khatami initially held the upper hand, considering his majestic popular mandate following the 1997 elections and the predominance of his supporters in the *Majlis*, the *jihadis'* entrenchment within other state bodies enabled them to impose an effective deadlock on reform. Ahmadinejad's election drastically altered the Iranian political scene. Facing accusations of 'sleeping with the enemy' – that is, the United States – the reformists found themselves with little choice but to give ground to their ascendant conservative opponents. Ahmadinejad presented himself as the true follower of Khomeini, and champion of the *mosta'zafin*. His supporters were drawn primarily from among the urban poor, rural dwellers (who comprise a majority of Iran's population) and some elements of the upper middle class (*bazaaris*) who had benefitted from the Islamic regime's economic policies.[29] Claiming that the United States and its allies, especially Israel, were determined to destroy the Islamic regime, Ahmadinejad focused on building Iran's military power and nuclear programme, as well as maintaining support for Iran's partners, including Syria, Lebanon's *Hezbollah* and some powerful Shi'a factions in Iraq.[30]

During his first term, Ahmadinejad worked in tandem with Khamenei to consolidate the *jihadis'* hold on power. This in turn prompted the effective merging of the reformist *ijtihadis* and pragmatic centralist factions, where both viewed the new president's over-assertive and in many cases ill-considered policies to be detrimental to the country. The June 2009 presidential election, in which Ahmadinejad secured a second term amidst widespread allegations of election-rigging and vote-buying, was a clear showdown between the *jihadi* forces and the pragmatist–*ijtihadi* coalition. Leading figures in both the *ijtihadi* and pragmatic clusters had publicly turned against the government. Khatami and Mir-Hossein Mousavi (the reformist candidate and prime minister from 1980 to 1989) sharply rebuked Ahmadinejad's election as 'illegitimate'.[31] Rafsanjani, who still held immense power and prestige as chairman of both the Assembly of Experts and the Expediency Council, berated the government for failing to recognise that 'large numbers of Iranians still doubted [the election] results', calling for the release of all those who had been jailed for protesting the outcome.[32] These criticisms amounted to a direct challenge to Khamenei, whose management of the post-election situation was considered to be very poor. While Khamenei had played a somewhat delicate balancing act in Ahmadinejad's early years, shifting more power to Rafsanjani's Expediency Council and constituting a new foreign policy advisory board,[33] his immediate declaration of support for Ahmadinejad's re-election as a 'blessing from God' without waiting for the customary announcement of the election results by the Guardian Council, his uncompromising position towards the opposition, and his punitive handling of the mass protests by supporters of Mousavi, made him appear to be no less of an autocrat than the Shah in the eyes of many Iranians.

The public split among the ruling clerical elite, along with an iron-fisted and bloody approach by the security forces (whose heads are appointed by the Supreme Leader and who hold allegiance to him) against those who protested against the election outcome, resulted in the killing of dozens of protestors, the placing of Mousavi and Karroubi under house arrest, and the trial and imprisonment of many more opposition figures, including former reformist Vice-President Mohammad Ali Abtahi and Deputy Foreign Minister Mohsen Aminzadeh. Although Abtahi was released in 2009 after publically confessing to charges of attempting to overthrow the Islamic government – a confession many Iranian reformists have argued was extracted under duress – Aminzadeh was transferred from jail to hospital detention in 2012.[34] These developments further blackened and diminished the domestic and international standing of the Iranian Islamic regime.

Meanwhile, the 2009 election and further consolidation of the *jihadis'* power highlighted a second schism in the elite, this time within the conservative faction itself. The Supreme Leader and several powerful elements, most notably the faction of the *Majlis* Speaker, Ali Larijani, had apparently decided that the time had come to make watertight their hold on the system as a whole. Having supported Ahmadinejad in the election dispute, they now wanted to ensure that both he and his supporters in the IRG remained subordinate to Khamenei's political authority and worldview. The president, growing aware of these machinations, became increasingly uncomfortable. Shortly after his re-election, he hinted at some changes in his approach. He promised to set up a more inclusive cabinet that could especially cater for the demands of youth and provide a better quality of life for all. He appointed one of his relatively young and moderate allies, Esfandiar Rahim Mashaei, as vice-president, to the disapproval of Khamenei and Larijani. Khamenei, in response, seized on a remark that Mashaei had made in 2008 about Iran's interest in having friendly relations with all countries, including Israel, to insist that Ahmadinejad should rescind Mashaei's appointment. The president initially resisted Khamenei's call to remove Mashaei but, under enormous pressure, eventually relented. Ahmadinejad made it clear, however, that he was acting for constitutional reasons, rather than out of deference to the Supreme Leader, and appointed Mashaei to another powerful post as his chief of staff. Moreover, eight days before he was sworn in for his new term on 6 August 2009, Ahmadinejad sacked two ministers believed to be close to the Supreme Leader who had opposed Mashaei's appointment as vice-president.[35]

This dispute broke into the open. While Ahmadinejad, ever the populist, increasingly referenced secular Iranian and Persian nationalism, Larijani presented his followers as the true adherents to the Revolution and Islamic system of governance.[36] Larijani, who boasted a list of Islamic credentials that included service in the IRG, a former position as Iran's chief nuclear negotiator and belonging to a family of ayatollahs, found himself in an increasingly prominent position, especially as his brother, Ayatollah Sadiq Larijani, was also head of the judiciary. Whilst a growing number of clerics – including Grand Ayatollah Ali Hossein Montazari – opposed Khamenei over his response to the management of the post-election situation, Ahmadinejad's position suffered even more as he enjoyed neither the support of the legislative nor of the religious 'branches' of government.[37] Khamenei's and the parliament's refusal to accept the forced resignation of Intelligence Minister Heydar Moslehi, a hardline cleric, Ahmadinejad's consequent brief absence from cabinet and council meetings, and Khamenei's proposal to abolish the position of president in October 2011, were all clear manifestations of an internal power struggle besetting the regime.[38] Gradually, the traditional conservatives, rallying behind Khamenei and Larijani, gained the upper hand. This was reflected in the results of the March 2012 parliamentary elections, where the ultra-conservatives expressed their shift from supporting Ahmadinejad to opposing him due to his nationalist Persian rhetoric, and where many of Ahmadinejad's candidates were disqualified by the Council of Guardians.[39]

The reformist cluster itself, united temporarily during the 2009 election, once again splintered into competing groups, three of which would emerge as prominent in the following years. The first and most liberal among them was the Participation Front Party (*Jebhe-ye Mosharekat*), led officially by Mohammad Reza Khatami (brother of the former president), and intellectually by Saeed Hajjarian and his associates. The second most influential and disciplined party was the Organization of Strivers of the Islamic Revolution (*Sazman-e Mojahedeen-e Enghelab-e Islami*). A third non-clerical group was the Solidarity Party (*Hezb-e Hambastegi*), whose leading figure was Ibrahim Asgharzadeh. Asgharzadeh was renowned for his role as one of the leaders in the 1979 hostage-taking fiasco, although he now admits that the action was detrimental to world peace and Iran's foreign relations. Indeed, many leading reformists are now critical of the radical conservatism that was on display in the first few years of the Revolution. The least modern group among the reformists remains the AAC, which is led by Mohammad Mousavi Khoeiniha and was mainly affiliated with Ayatollah Montazari until his death in December 2009.

The political crisis that enveloped Iran after June 2009 was a reflection of a process that was set in motion by the conservative ascendency in 2005. By and large, Iranian politics during the two terms of Ahmadinejad witnessed 'a progressive shift in the Iranian Revolution from popular republicanism to absolute theocratic sovereignty'.[40]

Without effective checks on their power, the conservative cluster in general, and Khamenei specifically, managed to increase their hold over the entire political system. In March 2011, they even managed to replace Rafsanjani with Mohammad Reza Mahdavi Kani, Khamenei's close associate, as head of the Assembly of Experts.[41] Rafsanjani's position became extremely precarious. On the one hand, his influence diminished to the point whereby the regime imprisoned his daughter and son in 2012 on allegations of activities against the regime. On the other hand, Rafsanjani surprisingly managed to keep himself afloat. Rafsanjani's children were released in early 2013, but the ruling conservative faction decided that he would not be able to make a political comeback – the Guardian Council rejected his application to stand for the 13 June 2013 presidential election. In turn, Rafsanjani accused Iranian leaders of 'incompetence and ignorance', claiming that 'I don't think the country could have been run worse.'[42] Along with Rafsanjani, the other prominent figure whose application was turned down by the Council of Guardians was Ahmadinejad's close ally, Mashaei, prompting Ahmadinejad to say that he would appeal the Council's decision to the Supreme Leader, despite the absence of any appeal process. These developments not only revealed deeper rifts within the ruling elite, but also demonstrated the extent to which Khamanei and his ruling clerical circle had been prepared to go in order to entrench their power, contributing to the intrinsic culture of nepotism and corruption that has evolved under the Islamic order.

Corruption and patronage politics

In many ways, the difficult governability of the state can be seen as a partial legacy of the 1978–79 Revolution itself. Like many inside and outside Iran, including the US government and its intelligence agencies,

Khomeini had not foreseen the coming of the Iranian Revolution. As a consequence, Khomeini had neither fully developed his vision, nor mapped out a strategy for its application. By the same token, neither he nor many of his close companions had much policy or administrative experience on which to draw in order to lead and to Islamise an Iran that had been subjected to a great deal of secularisation under the Shah. Yet this was also an Iran whose state apparatus had virtually disintegrated by the time Khomeini took over the helm. The collapse of government structures, the political inexperience of the new Islamic leadership, and the contradictory economic policies necessary to maintain the backing of the Revolution's two main supporting constituencies (traditional clergy and the merchant class, and the lower classes),[43] made post-revolutionary Iran an ideal environment for the entrenchment of patronage and corruption.

In the context of the war with Iraq, hostile relations with the United States, and an uncomfortable coexistence within the region, Khomeini set up the Iranian Revolutionary Guard (IRG) as the protector of the Islamic order. The IRG was closely linked to various paramilitary and security organisations, most importantly the *Basij*, whose full name (*Basij-e Mosta'zafin*) literally means 'Mobilization of the Oppressed'. The *Basij* is a paramilitary militia established in 1979 which numbers approximately half a million and is comprised of youth volunteers who obtain official benefits in exchange for their services. The IRG also retains ties with the revolutionary committees and quasi-state religious foundations (*bonyads*) that took over much of Iran's private and public assets in the wake of the establishment of Islamic rule, and which represented Khomeini's most potent forces to homogenise and monopolise power. As such, the IRG, along with other affiliated forces, rapidly emerged as the eyes, ears and rule enforcers of the post-January 1979 regime. Aside from their confirmed position as coercive instruments of the state, the IRG and security forces, with the initial acquiescence and support of Khamenei and later Ahmadinejad, have now assumed a prominent role within Iranian politics and society. Ahmadinejad appointed many governors and deputy governors from the ranks of the IRG, the *Basij* and prison heads – lately redubbed by the regime as 'corrective centre administrators' – all three of which are currently among the core pillars of the Islamic regime's strength.[44] In addition, former and current IRG members made up a substantial part of Ahmadinejad's cabinet. This also continues to be the case with the current *Majlis*.

With Khamenei's credibility shaken in the wake of the 2009 election, and Ahmadinejad's growing reputation, in the words of IRG Commander Ali Jafari, as a 'deviant current', the IRG became an increasingly powerful actor in Iranian politics.[45] It has achieved a capability to overshadow the government, should it desire to do so. In addition to its paramount security role, the IRG has become a central player in Iran's economic and cultural sectors. It appears to have left no aspect of the market untapped and holds important interests in the defence, technology, construction and oil sectors. In 2009, the IRG and its affiliates won over US$5 billion in no-bid contracts from the government.[46] This continued in 2010, with a special parliamentary commission singling out the sale to the IRG of the Telecommunication Company of Iran, worth US$7.8 billion, as another one-sided venture.[47] The IRG has also expanded far-reaching tentacles into Iran's cultural life. It has penetrated a number of educational institutions and established its own think tanks and a variety of cultural organisations. The economic and social privileges enjoyed by the IRG's commanding echelons, in addition, have placed them in a class of their own. It is no surprise that corruption nearly doubled on Ahmadinejad's watch, with Transparency International ranking Iran the 133rd country in the world in this category in 2012.[48]

The Economy

Inflation and unemployment

Along with state patronage of selected groups and institutions, Ahmadinejad pursued a policy of wealth redistribution through such measures as salary and subsidy increases, cash hand-outs and pet projects to win over his rural constituency. The redistribution of wealth, while consistent with the Revolution's initial ambitions to correct injustice and restore the downtrodden, occurred at the expense of policies that could have promoted sustainable national social and economic growth and development. Unlike Khatami and Rafsanjani, Ahmadinejad espoused a position of uncompromising isolationism that led him to shun all foreign investment in favour of a policy of Iranian self-sufficiency.[49] As such, he managed to stagnate the Iranian economy even in the context of high oil revenues and a focus on domestic investment. In 2012, Iran's official inflation rate was estimated at 23.6 per cent and its unemployment rate at 15.5 per cent. However, the real rates for both were probably around 30 to 50 per cent and increasing, especially as the Western sanctions accelerated into 2013. Unemployment became particularly acute among those aged 16–25, who comprise over 50 per cent of the population. The country's annual economic growth declined precipitously from 8 per cent in 2007 to 4.5 per cent the following year, 3.2 per cent in 2009, 2 per cent in 2011, and -0.9 per cent in 2012.[50] The rise in inflation and unemployment and decline in growth has been linked to the ongoing dispute surrounding Iran's nuclear programme and the related tightening of Western sanctions. Aggravating Iran's economic situation was also Ahmadinejad's depletion of the emergency oil reserve fund, established by Khatami, within the first few years of his presidency.

Inefficient taxation and state bureaucracy

Ahmadinejad's mismanagement of the economy became even more worrisome in the context of a broader social and economic impasse within Iran. Since the Revolution, the entrenchment of an oil-based rentier economy controlled by the clerical elite, and its subsidiary consequences – corruption and patronage politics – has impeded the development of an effective progressive tax system.[51] Taxes constitute only 7 per cent of Iran's gross domestic product (GDP), with 50 per cent of the population exempt from taxation and the remainder for the most part engaging in tax evasion.[52] Oil production, which comprises 80 per cent of foreign income for the state, declined by early 2013 to around 70 per cent below the 1979 levels, yet the oil industry today employs around 126,000 more workers than at that time.[53] This is reflective of the increasing inefficiency of Iran's public sector as a whole, and bodes ill in light of the fact that over 70 per cent of the economy is currently in the hands of the government and state-affiliated enterprises.[54] In addition, a 2006 International Monetary Fund report states that Iran has the highest rate of brain drain of 90 countries measured, at an estimated cost to Iran of US$90 billion a year, highlighting what is perceived, both by foreigners and local citizens, to be a lack of opportunities within the country.[55] This trend seems to have accelerated in the face of increased theocratic control and economic difficulties. The failure of Iran's Central

Bank to release its economic annual report for four consecutive years (2010–13) appeared as a sad confirmation of the country's continued poor economic situation.

Western sanctions and obstacles to reform

In early 2011, in an attempt to redress its economic failures, the Ahmadinejad government proposed a series of fiscal reforms that included income tax increases on traders and merchants and the cutting of food and fuel subsidies.[56] This raised the ire of *Majlis* parliamentarians and clerics, a number of whom represent the traditional merchant class. While the tax increase was put on hold, Iran's stagnating economy eventually convinced the majority of the conservative elite of the necessity of reform. After initiating a system for the handling of monthly payments to families, the government drastically cut subsidies. While this entailed higher costs for basic products – diesel prices increased up to 2,000 per cent – it also meant a higher level of disposable income for families, decreased domestic demand for oil (enabling a rise in exports) and decreased government expenditure.[57]

These tentative reforms were in no way capable of stemming Iran's economic slide in the face of increased UN- and US-led Western sanctions over the country's nuclear programme – an issue which will be explained later. Whilst calling on Tehran to halt its uranium enrichment, by 2012 the UN Security Council had slapped Iran with four rounds of economic sanctions. The United States and several European states had also tightened their own financial and economic sanctions against the country. On 1 July 2012, new sanctions against Iran went into effect in the European Union, putting a total halt to imports of Iranian oil. The ambiguous scope of the EU sanctions also impacted on Iran's exports of liquefied petroleum gas, starving the nation of even more revenue.[58] Furthermore, in conformity with the United States, the EU sanctions involved the expulsion of all Iranian banks from the Belgian-based consortium Swift, an electronic banking network through which passes all of Iran's monetary transactions with Europe.[59] The US and EU actions pushed the economic situation from bad to worse, with Iranian oil production plummeting from a height of 4 million barrels a day in 2009 to about 2.9 million a day in mid-2012.[60] This figure dropped even further in the following months, in spite of the Iranian oil minister's claims that the sanctions had not affected the country's oil production.

Iran's oil exports and revenue followed suit, causing a severe shortage of hard currency (dollars and euros), the collapse of the Iranian currency (the rial), and higher inflation and unemployment, with serious consequences for the cost of living, especially for ordinary citizens. Even in the absence of any credible public opinion survey and the regime's intolerance of all forms of dissent, anecdotal evidence pointed to greater public dissatisfaction with the regime than ever before.[61] In response to one of the first public protests among Iran's *bazaaris* since the widespread demonstrations over the disputed results of the 2009 election, the government retaliated with coercive measures rather than instigating appropriate domestic reforms and foreign policy changes.

The effective and lasting reform necessary to resolve Iran's economic impasse has desperately required a meaningful reorientation of the governing elite and political system as well as a negotiated settlement of the nuclear dispute between Iran and Washington – a dispute which is deeply entangled with other dimensions of the long-standing hostility between Iran and the United States and most of its allies, especially Israel. For as long as their entrenchment within existing political structures has allowed, the various Iranian conservative groups and other factions have used state instruments and wealth to further their interests to the cost of a majority of the populace. Civil society in general and universities specifically have been held captive to the aims and political policies of the government in question. As Ali Mirsepassi argues, 'Iranian higher educational institutions have neither accomplished much by way of serious research nor created *public dialogue and debate*.'[62] There has been a proliferation of semi-official and non-official bodies that have formed pressure groups to exert influence on the government. As such, the government has often made decisions that contradict other policies and that continue to undermine the efficiency of the economy.[63] The unhalting ascendency of the IRG has brought with it the risk of triggering a conflict with the clerical establishment's already entrenched patronage system – the *bonyads* – which provide social services under the auspices of religious guidance and which account for 10 to 20 per cent of the nation's GDP.[64] This battle for supremacy within the Iranian economic sphere between various patrons of the state has further entrenched a deeply established pattern of dysfunctionality.

International Relations and Foreign Interests

The United States' refusal to come to terms with the Islamic regime and constant efforts to demonise and threaten it have also played their part in the Iranian situation. Washington's hardline response to the radicalism of Iranian conservatives, especially during the two-term presidency of George W. Bush (2001–09), who operated under the strong influence of minority groups including evangelical Christians, neoconservatives and ultranationalists (all staunch supporters of Israel), paradoxically tightened the space in which the Iranian *ijtihadis* could operate. The more the United States and some of its allies, Israel in particular, threatened the overthrow of the Iranian regime, the more they forced the Iranian reformists to avoid appearing out of 'sync' with their conservative counterparts in the face of a foreign threat. This made it easier for the ruling conservatives to rally supporters, suppress dissent and invoke national unity in the context of greater tensions and hostility with the United States and Israel.[65] Indeed, in the face of persistent US and Israeli threats, any inclination towards reconciliation or liberalisation left individuals open to accusations of treason and pro-Western complicity from the conservative camp. It is not surprising, therefore, that the conservative factions proved so capable of expanding their political power in the wake of the tragic events of 11 September 2001.

Foreign policy

The Islamic regime's foreign policy outlook has been shaped by a long-standing fear and distrust of outsiders, a desire for strong independence and recognition, and ambitions for regional defensive measures. In this respect, the regime has remained within the framework established by Khomeini. Iranian foreign policy since the Revolution has combined both selective pragmatism and hardline ideology, which has in turn reflected the balance and fluctuation of power within the domestic political sphere. The policy behaviour of the United States and some of its allies helped generate favourable regional and international conditions for Khamenei and Ahmadinejad to adopt a more radical stand in Iranian foreign policy. The conservative cluster benefited enormously from the manner in which the United States has handled the Afghanistan, Iraq and Palestine problems, and the 'war on terror'. The management of these problems created massive strategic vulnerabilities for the United States, but favourable strategic opportunities for the Iranian regime and Shi'a Islam to become more defensively assertive than ever before. At the same time, developments in the Arab world since the beginning of the popular uprisings in December 2010, and particularly the crisis in Syria, engendered concerns regarding Iran's regional and international position. The result until recently was a continuing Iranian alienation from the United States and its Western allies, but widening Iranian relations with emerging Eastern power players, Russia, China and India in particular.

Khomeini's legacy: continuity in Iran's foreign policy posture

Following the Revolution, Khomeini had increasingly opted to diversify Iran's foreign relations in order to minimise the foreign policy consequences of his *jihadi* approach, which had resulted in Iran's international isolation. Despite his expressed contempt for the 'godless' ideology of communism, and his opposition to the December 1979 Soviet invasion of Afghanistan and subsequent backing of a number of Shi'a Afghan resistance groups, Khomeini backed a fostering of working relations with the Soviet Union that allowed Iran to purchase military hardware and expand trade. He similarly showed a growing inclination to improve ties with China and India. As such, Iranian foreign policy assumed a posture that on the one hand lambasted the United States and Israel as archenemies and sought counter-regional leverages, and on the other hand demonstrated a capacity for moderation and pragmatism when Tehran felt that there was no strategic threat to the country.

Tehran's well-known patronage of *Hezbollah* in Lebanon and, to some extent, support of Palestinian Hamas and the Islamic Jihad Movement is best understood within this context. *Hezbollah* has become both an effective Iranian proxy force against Israel (as demonstrated in its military confrontation with the Jewish state in 2006) and the most powerful actor in Lebanese politics as well as a regional player, as demonstrated by its combat involvement in support of the Bashar al-Assad government in the Syrian conflict – an issue which will be discussed later. All in all, the aftermath of the US-led invasions of Afghanistan and Iraq saw the emergence of what might be called a 'Shi'a strategic entity' stretching from Afghanistan to Lebanon, with the empowerment of the Iraqi Shi'a and the Iranian–Syrian strategic partnership significantly strengthening the links between the region's Shi'as.[66] The force with which Tehran has had little or no leverage in the relevant states is al-Qaeda, which, in Afghanistan, Iraq and, for that matter, the entire region, has pursued its own agenda. At any rate, al-Qaeda's double-edged pro-Sunni and anti-American operations cancel themselves out in terms of Iranian interests.[67] Tehran has upheld its Iraqi, Lebanese, Syrian and Afghan connections as a necessary defensive mechanism against outside intervention – a policy largely justified in view of Iran's historical experiences with external influence, invasion and threats. It should be noted that the expansion of Tehran's regional influence has not come about because of any major initiatives on its part, but rather due to the opportunities that have come its way largely as a result of US policy debacles in the region.

Iran's regional gains have caused deep concerns not only for the United States and Israel, but also for the Gulf Cooperation Council (GCC), a grouping of the Arab monarchies led by Saudi Arabia.[68] Most of the GCC members have historically seen Iran's posture as threatening, particularly in view of Iran's past efforts to export its revolution in the region and, recently, the state's nuclear ambitions. Saudi Arabia is home to around two million Shi'a, the majority of whom reside in the oases of Qatif and al-Hasa in the Eastern Province, home to the world's greatest concentration of oil assets and 90 per cent of Saudi production.[69] King Abdullah of Saudi Arabia has viewed Iran with increasing trepidation, imploring Washington in 2010 to 'cut off the head of the snake' while there was still time.[70] Bahrain, the third Shi'a majority country in the Gulf region after Iran and Iraq, is ruled by a Sunni Arab monarch and elite. Bahrain's Shi'a have been marginalised and politically disempowered, with only 13 per cent of important government posts held by Shi'as compared to a 70 per cent Shi'a population in the nation as a whole.[71] The Sunni monarchs of Saudi Arabia and Bahrain supported Saddam's war against Iran, and have stood in unison with the United States in containing the country.

A signatory to the Nuclear Non-Proliferation Treaty (NPT), Tehran has categorically refuted US, Israeli and Arab claims that it is developing nuclear weapons. It has insisted that its acquisition of nuclear technology and uranium enrichment up to a certain grade permissible under the NPT are solely for civilian objectives. Despite its failure to report on some aspects of its nuclear activities to the International Atomic Energy Agency (IAEA) for many years, Iran signed the 'additional protocol' in early 2004, enabling the agency to carry out vigorous inspections of Iranian nuclear facilities, and also temporarily halted its uranium enrichment. And the agency had not, until 2011, produced any evidence to support suspicions of an intended military nuclear programme in Iran.[72]

This, however, was apparently thrown into question by the IAEA Director General's report of November 2011, which indicated that:

> The [IAEA] has serious concerns regarding possible military dimensions to Iran's nuclear programme. After assessing carefully and critically the extensive information available to it, the Agency finds the information, overall, to be credible. The information indicates that Iran has carried out activities relevant to the development of a nuclear explosive device … and that some activities may still be ongoing.[73]

However, like previous reports, the IAEA relied primarily on information from one or two member states. The 2011 report was therefore far from a 'smoking gun', and the subject of Iran's nuclear programme remained, in reality, a bone of contention. Tehran has long maintained the need for a civil nuclear programme to provide for the country's growing energy needs and expanding population, while insisting that its oil reserves must remain free for export if the country's economy is to survive. Yet the cost, both political and economic, of such a programme in comparison with other possible energy sources (such as solar or wind) suggests somewhat more complex motivations. Iran's nuclear ambitions remain uncertain, but must be considered in the light of broader regional contexts, particularly where the United States and Israel are concerned.[74]

Iran's GCC neighbours and Israel, on the other hand, continue to view a nuclear Iran as an existential threat. External powers, especially the United States, have expressed fears that an Iranian nuclear military capability will create 'unstable bipolar nuclear competition in the Middle East', and view Iran's nuclear programme as likely to trigger additional nuclear proliferation in the region, despite the fact that the US nuclear umbrella covers the GCC countries.[75] The Stuxnet worm that targeted Iran's nuclear capacity in 2011–12 reflects this fear. The virus, which was designed to target the Siemens systems used by the computer controllers that operate in most Iranian nuclear plants, causes the centrifuges used in uranium enrichment to malfunction, thus interrupting the nuclear cycle.[76] In 2011, it was reported that over 60 per cent of systems infected with the virus were located in Iran, and suspicions of US–Israeli involvement swiftly mounted.[77] It is now clear that given its complexity, Stuxnet could only have been deployed by either Israel or the United States or both, and this falls in line with the US and Israeli publicly-stated commitment to do whatever possible to halt Iran's uranium enrichment, including using high-technology cyber warfare.[78] Although Iranian experts had reportedly succeeded in purging the virus from their computer systems by early 2012,[79] the incident may have delayed Iran's nuclear programme by some years, and certainly impeded the possibility of an early rapprochement between the United States and Iran.

Until early 2010, Iran had used its economic and political influence to garner some tepid international backing for its position in the nuclear dispute. America's European allies, especially Britain, France and Germany, had maintained a more constructive approach toward Iran, due to the volume of trade with the country that ran into billions of dollars annually. For instance, in May 2010, while the United States objected to a proposed Turkey–Brazil–Iran nuclear fuel swap deal, the Europeans were cautiously receptive to, albeit sceptical of, the idea.[80] While the deal was similar in essence to a 2009 October package offered by the United States and its allies, Iran felt more secure dealing with Turkey and Brazil, two states not aligned with the West on this issue.[81]

Nonetheless, from 2011, Iran's regional position came under increasing pressure not only from mounting Western sanctions, but also from the popular revolt against Iran's most critical and only strategic ally in the Arab world: Syria. The Syrian crisis, commencing in March 2011, placed Tehran in a grave quandary. On the one hand, Iran found it imperative to provide whatever support it could to ensure the survival of the Assad regime due to Syria's status as a strategic partner, whose existence has also been extremely important for Tehran's organic links with, and the survival of, *Hezbollah*.[82] On the other hand, the longer Iran has stood by the Assad government, the more it has put itself at odds with Turkey, with which Iran has developed lucrative economic and strong political ties since the rise to power of the Turkish moderate Islamist Justice and Development Party in 2002.[83] The Syrian crisis has also imperilled Iran's relations with most of the Arab countries, where Tehran over the years has gained some popular support due to its stiff opposition to Israel. Of course, Tehran has not been alone in its backing of the Assad regime. Moscow and Beijing have also firmly opposed any form of Western intervention in Syria largely due to regional power rivalry with the United States. Iraq, currently under the Shi'a-dominated government of Prime Minister Nouri al-Maliki, has also found it expedient to pursue close relations with the Iranian and Syrian regimes for both sectarian and political reasons.[84] The fall of the Assad government, coupled with crippling Western sanctions, has been viewed as a clear risk to Tehran's regional position, with serious domestic implications for the Iranian Islamic regime.

These developments increasingly prompted Tehran to return to its earlier foreign policy posture, that of 'looking East' toward the rapidly developing Asian economies, and of cementing relationships with other countries based on their natural resource and geopolitical needs and preferences. Russia and China, two emergent critical players on the world stage, have maintained lucrative relations with Iran, despite backing an IAEA resolution against it. Russia has reaped profits from building Iran's nuclear reactors and from arms exports to Iran. China, on the other hand, imports some 11 per cent of its oil from the country. India, another major power in the region, imports even more, with 16 per cent of its oil flowing from Iranian tankers.[85] And with their shared interest against US domination in the region, Iran and India have even taken to conducting joint naval exercises in the Indian Ocean basin.[86] As Iran has found itself increasingly straightjacketed by economic sanctions, it has entered barter trade arrangements with a number of countries, most importantly China and India, with goods from these countries consequently flooding the Iranian markets. To further circumvent sanctions, in 2012, Iran engaged in a large volume of currency trading of rials for US dollars in Afghanistan, which has been awash with the latter. The rials purchased by Afghan traders frequently flow back into the country in exchange for imported Iranian goods.[87]

US involvement in Afghanistan presented Iran not only with a much-needed economic opportunity, but also an important political opening. As discussed in Chapter 2, the mismanagement of the war in Afghanistan enabled the Pakistani-backed Taliban and their affiliates to regroup and re-equip. Yet it also opened the way for Tehran, which sees Shi'a resurgence as constituting the most powerful resistance and challenge to Pakistani-supported Sunni Islamism in the region, to build substantial political, economic and infrastructural influence in Afghanistan.[88] This is particularly the case in western Afghanistan, which has become increasingly linked to Iran. Tehran has pledged around US$1 billion in aid to Afghanistan, of which US$500 million had been provided as of 2012.[89] In addition, Tehran has been in a position to exploit its close sectarian ties with a number of notable elements among Afghanistan's 15 to 20 per cent Shi'a minority, and other non-Pashtun Sunni minorities. Some of these elements are important local power holders not only in the west, but also in Kabul and central Afghanistan. Many such figures have the potential not only to undermine the fragile Afghan government, but also to unravel what America has gained in the country.

Similarly, but to a greater extent, Tehran was able to benefit from the empowerment of the Shi'a majority under the impulse of the US push for democratisation in Iraq. A majority of Iraq's Shi'a population are of Arab origin, an ethnic identity which has historically formed the cornerstone of Iraqi nationalism. Nevertheless, Tehran has been able to develop close sectarian and non-sectarian ties with some of the most powerful Shi'a in Iraq, most notably Grand Ayatollah Ali al-Sistani, Muqtadar al-Sadr and Ammar al-Hakim. They have also been able to forge ties with a number of Iraqi Shi'a political organisations, such as the Islamic Supreme Council of Iraq (ISCI), the *Da'wa* Party, headed by Prime Minister al-Maliki, the Virtue Party and the Badr Organisation, as well as al-Sadr's Mahdi Army.[90] Tehran's policy approach to the Iraq conflict has all along been two-pronged. On the one hand, it has encouraged its Shi'a allies to act within a united alliance and to let the US-induced processes of democratisation deliver power to them in a peaceful manner. On the other hand, it has had an interest in seeing that the United States and its allies are denied a strategic foothold in Iraq that could be damaging to Iran's regional interests. Tehran's policy in Iraq appears to have paid off quite handsomely. Tehran has had good reason to provide its Iraqi Shi'a allies with assistance where such efforts are favoured by policy needs and regional contexts. The April 2011 Iraqi government's move against the People's *Mujahideen* Organisation of Iran, a dissident 'terrorist' group that aims to topple the Iranian Islamic regime, and permission of transfer of Iranian military assistance to the Assad regime through Iraq have been a clear indication of Iran's substantial influence in Iraq.[91] It has become increasingly difficult for the Iraqi government to function without taking Tehran's interests into account.

Meanwhile, Tehran has endeavoured to keep a close eye on Iraq's Kurdish minority, a group viewed with apprehension due to its alliance with the United States and receipt of Israeli intelligence assistance. Iran, like Iraq's other neighbours, Turkey and Syria, possesses its own Kurdish minority. These three states are therefore commonly concerned in making sure that the Iraqi Kurds do not go beyond enjoying anything more than autonomy, in the interests of maintaining peace and power among their own minority populations.

Oil and natural gas wealth will continue to play a vital role in Iran's foreign policy possibilities. Aside from building ties with critically important states, Iran has also managed to maintain links with non-aligned yet influential countries, such as Malaysia, South Africa and Turkey, despite the latter's stance on the Syrian crisis. These countries, along with the Europeans, will always try to walk the thin line between respecting US-backed sanctions and attempting to remain mindful of Iran's substantial resource wealth. In September 2009, only three months after Iran's disputed and controversial elections, Malaysia joined a number of key US allies – Japan, South Korea, the UK, Germany and the Netherlands – in attending the Iran gas forum.[92] Turkey and South Africa derive approximately 50 and 25 per cent of their crude oil from Iran respectively. Many of these countries, and at the very least Russia and China, which have grown increasingly uneasy with the US role in world politics, have not seen it in their interests to vote for any more UN sanctions, let alone support any military action.[93]

Conflict and Defence

As a pre-eminent rival of the United States, Israel and many regional Arab states, Iran found itself under significant threat of military attack following the US military engagements in Afghanistan and Iraq. While war fatigue has come to replace military fervour in most Western countries, the fear among the United States and its allies, along with some of Iran's Arab neighbours, of a strengthened and potentially aggressive Iran, is unlikely to mitigate the threat of future conflict in the region. As such, an understanding of both the capacity and military potential of the Iranian regime is critical in pressing the need for a diplomatic and non-confrontational approach to Iran.

In the face of repeated fears of foreign attempts to eliminate Iran's nuclear programme and degrade its military capability, Tehran has publically vowed to retaliate with devastating consequences. The gravity of these assertions must be considered in light of both the nature of the Iranian regime, which is far more resourceful, resilient and tenacious than that of Saddam Hussein, and the historical willingness of the Iranian leadership to accept the risk of a confrontation irrespective of the damage that might incur to Iran or its people.

Iran's assertive posturing in relation to its nuclear programme has rested not only on words, but on a very formidable range of viable non-military and military options in the event of foreign intervention. The first of these is Iran's ability to block the highly strategic Strait of Hormuz, through which the bulk of oil supplies from the Gulf countries is exported to the outside world. Located at the mouth of the Persian Gulf, the Strait touches Iran to the north, and the United Arab Emirates (more specifically its Ras al-Khaimah emirate) and the Sultanate of Oman to the south. The Strait is about 280km in length and 50km in width at its narrowest point, with shipping lanes of only 2x2 km, and it connects the Gulf to both the Gulf of Oman and the Indian Ocean. Iran has deployed considerable military and naval power to the north, with a capacity to carry out commando actions to mine or sink a number of ships in order to block the Strait. The readiness of the Iranian regime to undertake such action has been repeatedly emphasised by officials.[94]

Second, Iran's global importance in the oil industry has featured in its geopolitical calculations. Iran was the second largest producer within OPEC and fourth largest in the world in 2013, contributing just short of 5 per cent of the global oil supply. Iran's ability to completely halt its oil output in the present climate of growing global oil consumption endows it with the ability to generate a serious panic in the world market, prompting a dramatic rise in global oil prices and resulting in serious economic and therefore political consequences for the United States and its allies at a time when they are in the grip of ongoing financial and economic difficulties. Neither any of the oil-producing states (most importantly Saudi Arabia as the largest producer within OPEC) nor the United States, which possesses considerable strategic reserves and is moving increasingly toward energy independence, has the capacity to buffer the loss of Iranian oil in the global market, or to completely assuage the panic of an energy crisis. Of course, any drastic reduction in oil exports must cause considerable financial and economic harm to Iran itself. Yet the survival of the Islamic regime and therefore Iran can be expected to remain a priority for policymakers, whatever the economic, social or political costs.

Third, Tehran has fostered a growing influence in the region and has it within its power to make life much more difficult for the United States in the region. Tehran has historically acted with restraint with regard to US influence in the area, for two main reasons. First, it believes that the US-sponsored democratisation processes in Iraq and, to some extent, in Afghanistan have considerably empowered Iranian-backed forces. Second, its proxy in Lebanon, *Hezbollah*, has gained traction through its participation in the Lebanese democratic political process. This self-restraint, however, has hinged on the absence of a US or Israeli attack. Nevertheless, since the 2001 US invasion of Afghanistan, Tehran has placed itself in a very favourable position that has enabled it to count on the support of many Shi'a individuals and groups within its regional network of Islamic activists. Both the United States and Israel have been forced to take into account Iran's growing regional influence when considering their approaches to the country, and the potential outcomes of conflict with Tehran.

Tehran has also developed the potential to engage in serious retaliatory military action. It has built a very sizeable and highly devoted cadre and a strong military machine, equipped with both medium and long-range Shahab 1-3 missiles capable of carrying heavy payloads to hit targets as far away as 2,000km. Iranian missiles could therefore easily reach targets anywhere in the Gulf region and Israel. This has placed Iran in a position to exercise considerable military and political muscle in response to any acts of foreign aggression. An Iranian attack in Dubai, for example, could set off a massive financial crisis, given the city's importance as a regional financial and trading hub. Furthermore, in addition to the half a million troops and thousands of revolutionary guards already at its disposal, the Iranian regime has the capacity to mobilise one million men under arms. As was the case in the war with Iraq, Iran's human resources have the potential to compensate partly for the country's inability to match American firepower. Islamist and nationalist fanaticism, channelled by the unity of purpose, have also historically proved critical in bolstering Iran's ability to react against an external attack, and have provided Iran a very powerful force to be reckoned with. And while there have been simmering levels of discontent in the Kurdish and Baluchi regions of the country, no opposition group – unlike in Afghanistan, Iraq or Pakistan – has had the capacity to directly or openly challenge the regime.

It is against the backdrop of this panorama of issues and challenges that Iran held its tenth presidential election on 13 June 2013 to replace Ahmadinejad, who constitutionally could not run for a third term. Of the eight candidates (six conservative, one reformist and one moderate/ pragmatist) endorsed by the vetting and electoral watchdog, the Council of Guardians, one of the conservative and the reformist aspirants withdrew before the election date. Whilst the general expectation was that the Supreme Leader and his supporters would have preferred the election of one of the conservatives from their camp, the reformist- and pragmatist-backed moderate cleric, Hassan Rouhani, triumphed unexpectedly. This not only indicated a realisation on the part of the Supreme Leader that, in the wake of Ahmadinejad's debacles and the difficulties facing Iran, the time had come for some moderation, but also swung the pendulum back to a considerable extent to the reformist camp.

Rouhani was closely associated with the Iranian Islamic system, within the *jihadi/ijtihadi* framework laid down by Ayatollah Khomeini, from the beginning. Having served as secretary of the Supreme National Security Council for 16 years and as the country's top nuclear negotiator during the presidency of Mohammad Khatami, as well as a *Majlis* representative for several terms, Rouhani came to power as a very experienced and deft clerical political figure. He has had effective organisational ties with the Supreme Leader and good working relationships with all other factions in Iranian politics. As President, he promised to relax political and social controls, secure the release of political prisoners, improve social and economic conditions for a majority of the Iranian people, engage the West, the United States in particular, in the interests of better relations and reach a settlement of the nuclear dispute, without compromising Iran's right to uranium enrichment for peaceful purposes. Achieving these objectives within

Iran's highly complex domestic and foreign policy settings, in order to transform the country into what Khatami had earnestly desired as 'Islamic democracy', with a 'dialogue of civilisations' underpinning Iran's foreign relations, nevertheless promised to be a daunting task for the new president, as it had proved to be for Khatami.

Even so, by the end of 2013, Rouhani had managed to take some firm steps on all these fronts. His achievements had been crowned by a telephone conversation with President Obama – the first of its kind since the rise of the Islamic regime – on 27 September, and an interim agreement with 5+1 world powers (the United States and four other permanent members of the UN Security Council, and Germany) to limit Iran's uranium enrichment in return for the lifting of some sanctions on 24 November. The agreement, for which secret negotiations had begun between Washington and Tehran in Oman before Rouhani's election, inaugurated a thaw in US–Iranian relations. It was to be implemented within six months as a prelude to a possibly wider settlement of Iran's nuclear dispute and differences with the United States. As was to be expected, Israel opposed the agreement, called it a 'historical mistake' and vowed to combat it, and the GCC welcomed it but with a great of deal of trepidation. Meanwhile, the Rouhani leadership launched a diplomatic offensive to improve relations with the Arab world, Saudi Arabia and its GCC partners in particular.

The Way Forward

The Islamic Republic of Iran is a state wrapped in serious political and economic difficulties. It suffers from a deeply divided polity and international pressure and isolation – two factors that have unhappily overshadowed the country's potential for greatness. For over 30 years, Iran reaped some dividends from an anti-US and anti-Israeli posture, especially in the context of US regional policy debacles. In recent years, however, this era has come to a dead end. The Islamic regime's failure to engage in appropriate structural domestic reforms and foreign policy changes has placed it in an increasingly precarious position in a fast-moving and rapidly changing world. The results of the 2009 elections and persistent divisions within both the *jihadi* and *ijtihadi* clusters raised questions not only as to whether a rapprochement between the West and Iran is achievable under the prevailing circumstances, but also whether Khomeini's and Khatami's moderate vision of two-tiered Islamic governance would prove to be workable in the long run. President Rouhani faced many of the same issues upon his 2013 election, a fact that required him to take stock of Iran's domestic fragility and foreign policy difficulties in order to set a new course for Iran – one that would enable it to assume the greatness and the global pre-eminence it deserves.

A number of observable trends have impeded such developments in the past. The first has been the obstinacy and inflexible posturing of the *jihadis*, which has proved a serious obstacle to incorporating more plurality and leeway in the political arena, and to the implementation of the requisite political and economic reforms that are required to place the common interest before self-centred ideological and political dispositions. Whilst Ahmadinejad was a very polarising figure and an unguided ideologue, and Khamenei has remained elusive and self-preserving, Rouhani seems to hold the promise of being visionary, pragmatic and inclusive, with a commitment to good governance in order to lift Iran out of its existing state.

Washington's intransigence regarding the nuclear issue, combined with its historically single-minded and unaccommodating approach to the Iranian leadership, has provided a second serious obstacle to Iran's political development. Rouhani's election, like that of Khatami, has provided a window of opportunity for the US administration to effect a degree of reconciliation with the Iranian regime. The failure of the Bush administration to achieve such a rapprochement serves only as a reminder that the way out of the hostilities that have marred US–Iranian relations for too long can only occur if Washington shows itself willing to recognise Iran as a legitimate power and to engage in respectful and constructive dialogue. Threats and hardline approaches on the part of the United States have historically produced few gains with respect to Iranian nuclear policy, and have contributed only to the hardening of the Iranian regime's resolve. President Obama has shown some signs of taking these lessons to heart. He acknowledged Rouhani's inauguration as an opportunity for better relations between the two states, pronouncing that Iran would find a 'willing partner' in the United States if it were to move forward in meeting its international obligations.[95] Ultimately, the best way out of the nuclear dispute may well prove to be a negotiated resolution, especially if it is conducted within the framework of a region-wide regime of arms control that includes Israel. Israel's status as the only nuclear power in the region, however, has historically made it vehemently resistant to any development perceived as weakening its strategic supremacy in the Middle East.

Iran's predicament, as it has developed over the course of the past decade, is best understood in the context of two overriding features that have dominated its economic and political structures. On the one hand, the Iranian government has continued to exercise a centralised form of hold over resources – in this case mostly oil wealth. On the other hand, it has increasingly moved towards theocratic control, little different in substance from the Shah's autocracy. The persistence of these two features has contributed to Iran's potential instability and has severely restricted its foreign relations. A deep incongruity between the 'sovereignty of God' and the 'sovereignty of the people' in the Iranian Islamic system, and thus between state and society, has come to pervade the country's political arena. In light of this, Iran, as in the past, stands at a critical crossroads. The United States' withdrawal from Iraq and its drawdown from Afghanistan, as well as its declining influence in the Middle East since the events of the 'Arab Spring', have provided Iran's political elite with greater autonomy in their choice of paths in the long term.

One path is where the *jihadi* cluster maintains dominance over Iranian domestic politics and utilises Iran's strengthened regional position to further Iranian and Shi'a influence in the region. This has the potential to destabilise the region, deepen Sunni–Shi'a tensions and regional rivalry, and cement divisions within Iran's own political elite. Such a course would potentially not only exacerbate the *jihadi–ijtihadi* divisions and power struggle, but would also lend itself to in-fighting among the various *jihadi* factions.

Another path is where the Iranian polity moves in accordance with *ijtihadi* politics, providing the potential for reconciliation with the outside world and more pluralistic and open politics within the country. It would also create an opportunity to mitigate the internal security challenges of the state, especially in relation to the numerous minority ethnic and religious groups in the country such as the Sunni Baluchis, Kurds, Arabs and members of the Baha'i faith. Yet such a development seems contingent on a sense of security within Iran and is unlikely to take place in the context of a hostile international climate. And even if

Iran manages to move in this direction, numerous structural issues –
corruption, patronage and an undiversified economy – still constitute
a substantial obstacle to reform and progress within the state and
society. These, however, must be viewed simply as great challenges to
be overcome, and for that President Rouhani has had his work cut out
for him.

IRAQ

Divided and Threatened

Introduction

After the US-led intervention in Afghanistan, the George W. Bush administration and its supporters turned their gaze towards oil-rich Iraq. Iran's secular neighbour, under the dictatorial leadership of Saddam Hussein, was seen as 'primed' for change and democratisation. The view in Washington was that the toppling of Saddam's regime, which had weakened considerably since the 1991 Gulf War, could pave the way for the wider implementation of the neoconservative agenda for 'democratisation' in the Middle East. Armed with allegations of an Iraqi weapons of mass destruction (WMD) programme, which proved non-existent, and Saddam's links with al-Qaeda, which proved unfounded, the United States and three of its close allies, Britain, Australia and Poland, forming the so-called 'coalition of the willing', invaded Iraq in March 2003. The occupation, which lasted until the end of 2011, replicated many of the strategic failures that characterised the war in Afghanistan. The United States, as the leading occupying force, could neither fully grasp the complexity of the Iraqi situation, nor put in motion an appropriate and effective post-invasion strategy of political reform, governance and reconstruction for the country. It appeared to prefer to leave the treatment of the country's political ills to the supposedly curative effects of democracy. As in Afghanistan, the occupation failed to ensure Iraq's transition into a stable, secure and democratic state to underwrite the country's integrity and continuity in the long run. Since the US-led invasion, therefore, the country has remained in dire straights, struggling to hold itself together and to free itself from the grips of long-term structural disorder.

Iraq is caught between a rock and a hard place. On the one hand, it has been led down the path of embracing a type of pro-Western secular democratic transformation. On the other hand, a majority of its population remains under the strong influence of Islamic and ethnic traditions, which have played a determining role in shaping their psyche and behaviour. The US push for democratisation under the Bush administration widened the arena not only for disgruntled supporters of Saddam and some of their Sunni co-activists, but also for the radical forces of political Islam, including al-Qaeda, to resist any outside imposition. This, together with national divisions, regional power rivalry and the fragmentation of the governing elite, has been instrumental in sharpening a struggle in which various sectarian and ethnic factions continue to compete for the soul of Iraq. This has added a new dimension to the overall complexity of the country in a chronically volatile, oil-rich and strategically significant region of the world. Following strained negotiations over the formation of a new governing coalition after the March 2010 elections (as a result of which Iraq earned the unsavoury world record for the longest time taken to form a new government), and the US withdrawal from the country in December 2011, Iraq found itself in a more precarious and fragile position than at any time since its consolidation as a modern state under British tutelage in the 1920s.

Social Divisions

The modern state of Iraq, like so many others in the region, is a recent creation whose boundaries were determined by a colonialist power with little regard for existing social realities. Following the collapse of the Ottoman Empire in the wake of the First World War, Britain assumed a mandate to transform three former Ottoman provinces (Baghdad, Basra and Mosul) into a sovereign state, or states, in accordance with the League of Nation's vision of national self-determination.[1] The three *vilayets*, or provinces, had broadly different ethnic and sectarian populations: Baghdad was dominated by Sunni Arabs, Basra by Shi'a Arabs, and Mosul by Sunni Kurds and, to a lesser extent, Turkmen with affiliations with neighbouring Turkey. Furthermore, the end of the war witnessed the migration of approximately 20,000–30,000 Assyrian Christians from Anatolia into northern Iraq.[2]

Despite the clear divisions between the provinces of Baghdad, Basra and Mosul, the British administration elected to unify them into a single state of Iraq in 1921, under a constitutional monarchy headed by the Hashemite King Faisal I. The British, whose mandate required them to promote Iraqi national independence, were nevertheless concerned to ensure the situation in Iraq remained in favour of British interests, especially regarding the security of Britain's air routes, its communications with India and its access to Iraqi and Persian oilfields.[3] Faisal, a Saudi-born sheikh who aided the British against the Ottomans during the First World War, was Britain's top candidate for the Iraqi throne. A capable leader who was at the same time sufficiently vulnerable to ensure his continuing dependence on Britain, Faisal was also a Sunni. The British viewed his rule, dominated by Sunni Arab officers, as a counterbalance to the influence of Iraq's Shi'a majority.[4] His ascendency set the precedent for a pattern of Sunni Arab dominance in Iraqi politics and Iraq's traditionally close identification with the mostly Sunni Arab world – something that lasted until the US-led invasion of 2003.

Today, the Arabs constitute approximately 80 per cent of the country's 33 million people. The remainder of the population is primarily composed of ethnic Kurds, who represent just under 20 per cent of the population and are based in the mountainous north-east. Historically divided by internal tribal and political rivalries, the Kurds are even so a distinct people in their own right. Predominantly Sunni, they have nevertheless framed their discourse around their unwillingness to accommodate centralised Sunni Arab rule, fiercely agitating for the right to autonomy or even full independence. Until the US-led invasion, these demands often resulted in brutal suppression by the central Iraqi government, deepening the Kurds' sense of independent identity and hostility to Iraq's Arabs. Saddam's callous treatment of the Kurds, including his use of chemical and biological weapons on civilians and entire villages during the Iran–Iraq War, is a well-known but no less horrific legacy of modern Iraq.

The Arabs themselves have historically suffered from sectarian divisions between the minority Sunnis, who form a little less than 20 per cent of the population and are concentrated in the centre and the west of Iraq, and the majority Shi'as, who constitute some 60 per cent of Iraq's total population. The Shi'as, many of whom hold sectarian affiliations with the Iranians, are concentrated in the south-east of the country. Compounding these three distinct blocs (the Kurds, Sunni Arabs and Shi'a Arabs), tribal identity remains important as both a unifying and divisive factor. Additionally, a number of smaller minorities are present in modern Iraq. Some are religious, such as the ethnically Kurdish Yezidis; however, most, like the Mandeans, the Assyrians and the Armenians, are both religious and ethnic minorities, adding to the complexity of Iraq's social fabric.

This mosaic nature has long impeded the development of national unity within Iraq and given rise instead to a pattern of the political dominance of one group at the exclusion and suppression of others. Since the fall of Saddam Hussein's regime, Iraqis have not been able to shake off the deeply entrenched patterns of political authoritarianism and political–social divisions which have underpinned the operation of the modern Iraqi state since its creation. The twinned legacies of an authoritarian political culture and a highly divided society inform not only the calculations and perceptions of the Iraqi political elites, but also the culture within which they interact. Engrained dynamics of factionalism have plagued Iraq's fledgling process of democratisation, with the majority of Iraq's political parties grounding their claims to legitimacy in their opposition to Saddam Hussein's rule rather than in an inclusive vision of a new Iraq. As such, while keen to participate in elections, a majority of Iraqis have not been able to absorb the depth and breadth of what a democratic transformation of their country would involve and require. More than a decade after the invasion, the opportunity to rise above the struggle for daily survival still remains beyond the reach of many Iraqis.

Historical Legacy

Political authoritarianism

Like Afghanistan, and to a great extent Pakistan and Iran, Iraq has never had a tradition of democracy. The history of modern Iraq has been characterised by various species of authoritarian rule, and punctuated by extreme violence and bloodshed.[5] A majority of Iraqis have been denied the experience of anything but a dictatorial political culture, shaped very much by the state, or more specifically by the ruler. Iraq's various dictators, popular and unpopular, have sought to be seen as indispensable to Iraq's political operations, whilst frequently treating their subjects as dispensable. External intervention and pressure, in the form of a British policy of 'divide and rule' and the imposition of a Hashemite monarch on modern Iraq, formed one of the bases of this authoritarian culture and entrenched a pattern of Sunni Arab dominance over other religious and ethnic groups in the country.

The rule of Saddam, whose effective dictatorship, dominated by his Sunni Arab Tikriti clan, lasted for three and a half decades (1969–2003 – although during the first decade of this period President Hassan al-Bakr was nominally the head of state), proved little different from those of his predecessors. A member of the secular, pan-Arabist Ba'ath party, Saddam acquired increasing political stature following the successful Ba'athist coup d'état of 1968. Rather than promote the party line of pan-Arab political unity, Saddam used his growing influence to strengthen his personal ambitions for the national leadership, resulting ultimately in his takeover of the presidency in a 1979 coup. He reinforced and exploited Iraq's historical authoritarian settings to the maximum to create a personalised state, where he loomed large in every aspect of Iraqi politics and daily life.[6] The Iran–Iraq War (1980–88) marked the peak of power for Saddam's brutal regime.

While militarily and strategically a disaster – Iraq failed to achieve its objectives of capturing the oil-rich Iranian province of Khuzestan or overthrowing the Iranian Islamic regime – the war was presented on the domestic front by Saddam as a resounding success for his regime. Portraying Ba'athist Iraq as the bulwark against radical Islamism, he was able to gain the support of many Western, communist and Arab countries that feared an export of the Islamic revolution by Iran. Iraq not only received a considerable amount of help from a number of powerful Western countries, most importantly the United States, and Sunni Arab monarchies, Saudi Arabia and Kuwait in particular, but also managed to procure weaponry and supplies from the Soviet Union late in the war. For the Arab Shi'as and Kurds of Iraq, who were frequently the victims of the bombs and chemicals, which were partly used against them and against Iranian targets, the war created a lingering sense of mistrust toward foreign powers. The United States' and, for that matter, the international community's conspicuous silence over Saddam's gassing of thousands of Kurds in Halabja in 1988 could only encourage the Iraqi dictator to continue his repression at home and aggression in the region. To consolidate his rule in outlying areas during the war, Saddam had also referred back to the British policy of 'tribalisation', favouring certain hierarchies of cooperative sheikhs and giving tribal elders the authority to settle disputes and arbitrate between tribesmen.[7] However, the West's flirtation with Saddam came abruptly to an end when his forces invaded the oil-rich, pro-Western Kuwait in August 1990. The brief Gulf War of 1991 resulted in a decisive defeat for Saddam's forces by a coalition of US-led Western powers and Saudi-led Arab states, including Egypt and Syria. But the way the United States and its allies handled that war and its aftermath only served to assist the Iraqi leader in maintaining his rule within authoritarian settings.

Repression, exiles, connections and division

While the war with Iran permitted Saddam to consolidate his personal control over the Iraqi state, the 1980s nevertheless witnessed the persistence or resurgence of various secular and sectarian oppositional movements, domestically and from abroad. Any opposition, wherever it existed and in whatever form, was subject to a policy of uncompromising repression under Saddam. The Shi'a *ulama* in Iraq, the representatives of Iraq's oppressed majority, constituted the most potent threat to his rule. Grand Ayatollah Mohammad Baqr al-Sadr, founder of the Islamic Call Party (*Da'wa*), and Ayatollah Mohammad Bakr al-Hakim, later founder of the Supreme Council for Islamic Revolution in Iraq (SCIRI),[8] were the forefathers of the modern Islamic movement in Iraq, working in tandem for most of the 1970s. Following the 1977 Shi'a uprising in Najaf and the concurrent increasing popularity of the Islamists, Saddam had al-Sadr executed in April 1980. Soon after, al-Hakim fled to Iran, and in 1982, with the patronage and support of Ayatollah Ruhollah Khomeini, established SCIRI.

With the near dismantling of *Da'wa* in Iraq by Saddam's regime, SCIRI took the lead in establishing a robust Shi'a opposition in exile. Al-Hakim and his brother, Abdul Aziz al-Hakim, aimed for nothing less than the replacement of the Ba'athists with an Islamic regime modelled on Khomeini's Iran.[9] To this end, they collaborated with both the Iranian Revolutionary Guard (IRG) and some leading Iranian clerics, even to the point of providing military support for Iran's war effort against Iraq through the establishment of the Badr Brigade, a move that precipitated a divide within the Shi'a community in exile. Many *Da'wa* members, most notably Ibrahim al-Jaafari and the current prime minister, Nouri al-Maliki, took exception to SCIRI's strong pro-Iranian outlook and pushed for a more independent line. The first sought refuge in London after spending a period of time in Tehran, and the second settled in Damascus.

As a Shi'a opposition was taking shape abroad, a secularist challenge to Saddam's regime was emerging both in exile and within Iraq. Domestic opposition, following a brief period of quietism, was revitalised by Iyad Allawi, a Shi'a and former Ba'athist, who instigated efforts from within the Ba'athist hierarchy to overthrow Saddam and formed the Iraqi National Accord (INA) to further these efforts. Ahmed Chalabi, an American-educated Shi'a, built up close relationships with both the Kurds and neoconservatives within the US political establishment in order to facilitate his umbrella Iraqi opposition group, the Iraqi National Congress (INC). The INC had its heyday following the 1991 Gulf War, when all opposition groups, including the SCIRI and *Da'wa*, acted briefly under its direction. Its cooperation with the US government was also a key part of the planning for the 2003 invasion.

For Iraq's Shi'as, the systematic repression and expulsion of suspected *Da'wa* members and Islamists, coupled with the ongoing war with Iran, had generated a sense of futility. However, following in the footsteps of his elder cousin (Mohammad Baqr al-Sadr), Grand Ayatollah Mohammad Sadeq al-Sadr reinvigorated the Shi'a domestic opposition to Saddam in the late 1980s. Al-Sadr took aim not only against Saddam and the Sunnis, but also against those Iraqi Shi'as whom he viewed as either having abandoned Iraq to Iranian interests (such as SCIRI and the al-Hakims), or as having acquiesced to Saddam's regime (such as the quietist Najaf establishment under Grand Ayatollah Ali al-Husayni al-Sistani). Al-Sadr's message found wide resonance among the disenfranchised and impoverished Shi'as of the capital, Baghdad. Over time, 'Sadr II' proved to be just as threatening to Saddam's regime as his predecessor, especially after al-Sadr's support of the 1991 uprisings which threatened to topple the Ba'athist rule. In 1999, Saddam had him executed.[10]

The Iraqi Kurds, on the other hand, have historically been less concerned with questions of national politics than with the aim of securing autonomy within their territories in north-eastern Iraq. Following the collapse of negotiations for Kurdish autonomy with the central government in the early years of the Ba'athist regime, Mustafa Barzani, the leader of the Kurdistan Democratic Party (KDP), was forced to flee into permanent exile from Iraq in 1975. This created space for the ascendance of a rival political group in the Kurdish community: Jalal Talabani's Patriotic Union of Kurdistan (PUK). Whilst the Iran–Iraq War generated Iranian support for the Kurdish position in Iraq, it was only after the Gulf War that the movement experienced an effective turn in fortunes. Both Kurds and Shi'as overwhelmingly responded to Washington's call for a national uprising in the wake of Saddam's 1991 defeat. Yet unlike the Shi'as, whose contribution to the uprising was virtually ignored by the United States and its allies, the Kurds were rewarded with an autonomous region protected by US and British 'no fly zones' – a decision made for both humanitarian reasons and in order to clip Saddam's wings. Violence continued to plague the Kurds of Iraq, however, in the form of a destructive civil war over the region's resources that lasted until 1998. Foreign involvement exacerbated the conflict, with Turkey and Saddam's Iraq taking the side of the KDP, and Iran supporting the PUK.[11] Since then, however, both Massoud Barzani, the son of Mustafa Barzani, and Talabani have worked together with some success for the interests of the Kurdish community and reasoned relations with Baghdad.

These divisions and connections, forged and sustained under the authoritarian Ba'athist rule, provided the backdrop for the US-led invasion in 2003. Lacking a firm grasp on the inner dynamics of Iraq, the policies of occupying forces promoted structural disorder and dysfunctional governance underpinned by a highly fragmented political elite, to which we will return later.

The US and Coalition Approach

Washington's misreading and underestimation of Iraq's complexity boggles the mind. Military operations had been well planned by the Bush administration – Baghdad fell within three weeks of the invasion – but the war itself had been masterminded by an alliance of pro-Israel neoconservatives, evangelical Christians and ultra-nationalists. These groups believed in the 'doctrine of power reality' or the application of US economic and military power to change Iraq into a democracy, providing a base from which to reshape the Middle East and for that matter the world after the image desired by the United States.[12] Ironically, however, Washington went into Iraq without any serious notion of how to effect the nation's transformation into a stable democratic state after Saddam. As in Afghanistan, neither Iraq's domestic complexity nor the broader regional context figured adequately in US calculations, ensuring not only the failure of the state-building process but also the inflammation of pre-existing sectarian tensions which were further exacerbated by the involvement of various regional players seeking to manipulate the country's political situation. The fragmentation of state power and authority following the overthrow of Saddam opened up the space for a number of societal groups, ranging from radical Islamists to secularists to nationalists, to grapple for power with not only the United States, but also one another. Paradoxically, al-Qaeda, which had no presence in Iraq previously, was afforded a golden opportunity to secure a new front as well.

Unilateral invasion and isolation

Unlike military action in Afghanistan, the invasion of Iraq proceeded without the United Nations' sanction and against the wishes of a wide swathe of US allies both in the region and in the West. The failure of the United States to consider the regional implications of such an undertaking has been one of the more striking examples of political short-sightedness in the Iraq War. With the exception of Kuwait (where both state and society were largely in favour of invasion), and Afghanistan (whose government was totally dependent on the United States for survival), all Muslim governments publicly opposed the proposed military campaign, although to varying degrees. In 2006, these states were still calling for an immediate halt to hostilities and the withdrawal of foreign forces, and for an increased UN involvement in Iraq. Clearly, the United States' democratic rhetoric had failed to convince these states of the necessity of its invasion.

The Arab states in the region found Washington's democratic push confronting for various reasons. The autocratic Gulf Cooperation Council (GCC) monarchies, led by Saudi Arabia, silently embraced the US invasion of Iraq but remained wary of its democracy promotion efforts. They all remained highly vigilant in response to developments in Iraq, due to a common desire to protect and enhance their interests in the context of the changing Iraqi situation, for reasons explained in more detail later in this chapter. The Organisation of Islamic Cooperation (OIC)[13] and the Arab League adopted a similar line. In the March 2003 pre-war OIC summit, which also reflected the Arab League's position, 57 member countries declared their 'total rejection of any strike on Iraq and any threat to the security of any Islamic state', and called on Muslim countries 'to refrain from taking part in any military action targeting the security and territorial integrity of Iraq or any Muslim nation'. It also rejected the US vision for reshaping the Middle East and any US attempt to 'impose change in the region and interfere in its internal affairs'.[14] The OIC reiterated the need for a peaceful resolution of problems with Iraq. Both the OIC and the Arab League reinforced their assertions by stressing that the UN Security Council had not authorised military action against Iraq and that such action had to be justified under international law. The United States' archenemy in the region, the Iranian Islamic regime, pursued a position of its own regarding the invasion. Tehran adopted a dual policy of supporting the US overthrow of Saddam, but opposing its occupation of Iraq. It suspected that the United States' real target was Iran. Damascus shared Tehran's concerns, given President Bush's condemnation of Iran and Syria, together with North Korea, as an 'axis of evil' in his 2002 State of the Union address.[15]

Within the UN Security Council, France and Germany took the lead in condemning the proposed invasion and in questioning evidence of Saddam's ties with al-Qaeda, his alleged stockpile of chemical and biological agents, and his intentions to develop more WMDs. In spite of these all too prescient objections, and without the support of the UN, the US invasion went ahead, with the direct participation of primarily Britain, Australia and Poland. Paradoxically, the war succeeded in creating what it claimed it would destroy. Before the war, as was argued correctly by opponents of the US invasion, Iraq was not a theatre for operations by al-Qaeda and its sympathisers. It was the United States and its allies, through the mismanagement of the post-invasion Iraqi crisis, that managed to create the right conditions for such a development.[16] In addition, many moderate Islamists throughout the region, who in the past looked to the United States as a source of support for reforming and democratising their societies, became disillusioned with and alienated from the United States as a result of its conduct during the war. They found US behaviour in Iraq unjustifiable and took exception to what was perceived as the pointedly anti-Muslim conduct of the 'war on terror', with the two interactively being detrimental to Muslim causes. This perception prompted some Islamists to become amenable to the ideas of anti-US Islamic resistance groups. Important casualties of this development were, for instance, the reformist Islamists in Iran, who, until the start of the Iraq War, had succeeded in moderating some of the excesses of their conservative Islamist opponents and in restraining them from pursuing their anti-US foreign policy agenda. However, with the swing to the right with the election of Mahmoud Ahmadinejad, attributable at least in part to the Iraqi fiasco and the Bush administration's hostile attitude towards Iran, moderate Islamists increasingly became sidelined in the politics of their country, their voices drowned out by their radical counterparts, at least until the election of Hassan Rouhani to the Iranian presidency in June 2013.

Ostracised and unloved in the region in the wake of 'Operation Iraqi Freedom', the United States and their tepid coalition were soon confronted by the need to reconstruct the state whose political and administrative structures they had so rapidly dismantled. The policies that developed in the immediate aftermath of the invasion were formulated without consultation with informed actors, ensuring the continued influence of the same forces that had instigated the Iraqi invasion. Washington's initial approach to post-Saddam governance and the democratisation process in Iraq, which bore the mark of this influence, sowed the seeds of Iraq's subsequent political and security problems. From the outset, the US rhetoric of political freedom and autonomous governance clashed with the realities of repeated US interference in shaping Iraqi politics according to its preferences. The creation of the Coalition Provisional Authority (CPA), which encompassed a US administrator and an Iraqi Governing Council, reflected the United States' insistence on overseeing and regulating the 'democracy' that it wanted to create. Sanctioned under UN Resolution 1483 on 22 May 2003, the CPA operated in practice as an arm of the US federal government.[17] Its administrator reported to the US Secretary of Defense through the Secretary of the Army. Through the CPA, the US carried out a systematic programme of 'de-Ba'athification' in order to replace the former political elite under Saddam with figures chosen by Washington. These included both former Iraqi exiles who had cooperated with the US government against Saddam, and a number of local leaders viewed favourably by the administration. By the time Washington had become aware that the Governing Council was not the most effective mechanism with which to build a new Iraq, and of the necessity and value of engaging regional actors and the UN in the state-building process, all the conditions for political fragmentation, insecurity and regional interventions in Iraq had taken root.[18]

Military strategy

The US and Coalition military strategy in Iraq reflected a clear recognition of the enemy – the Ba'athists – but little more. In May 2003, soon after the successful capture of Baghdad and the capitulation of Iraqi forces, the US-backed CPA dissolved the Iraqi army of over 400,000 soldiers, producing not only a profound security vacuum, but also a substantial number of disenchanted and now unemployed individuals. The United States envisioned creating new Iraqi security forces from scratch by tapping into an undefined and untested source of Iraqi secular nationalism, which was to underpin the new state. In this aspiration, they failed to take into account both the historical legacy of the central state and the differing aspirations of the varied sectarian groups. For the Shi'a and Kurdish leadership, the bitter memory of US abandonment during the 1991 uprisings was firmly entrenched. The Shi'a population in particular felt a lingering sense of betrayal toward the United States, who had failed to come to their aid in the uprisings that the United States itself had encouraged, ensuring the failure of the insurrection and its brutal suppression by Saddam, resulting in the death of as many as 100,000 Iraqi Shi'as.[19] In the wake of the Ba'athist collapse, therefore, both the Shi'a and Kurd communities proved extremely anxious to prevent the recreation of an Arab Sunni-dominated state, and, as such, aimed to flood the security forces with loyalists at the expense of more experienced officials associated with Saddam's regime. This trend was exacerbated by the US policy of de-Ba'athification, which in its single-minded attempts to rid the Iraqi state of Saddam's supporters failed to distinguish between those who had been actively loyal to the regime, and those who had been driven into its fold by fear and the desire for self-preservation. Rather than calling on former Ba'athists to join the ranks of the government, the United States unilaterally excluded from political participation all those who had been associated with the ousted regime.

As a consequence, they succeeded not only in depriving themselves of valuable talent in the building of a new Iraq, but in alienating many potential and experienced advisors from the nation's reconstruction efforts. In short, in the process of toppling Saddam's regime, the United States also destroyed the Iraqi state, and created a massive political, administrative and security vacuum to be filled by various opposition societal groups.

As its occupation of Iraq continued to falter in the midst of a disjointed effort by the State department, the Pentagon and the CIA, Washington engaged in a number of pacification actions that in many ways paralleled those of Israel in the occupied Palestinian territories. Lacking sufficient manpower to achieve its security objectives, the Coalition not only enlisted the support of private security firms which were neither accountable nor reliable,[20] but also contracted a number of tactical alliances with several Shi'a militias. These groups, most notably the Sadrist Mahdi Army (*Jaysh al-Mahdi*) and SCIRI's Badr Brigade, discussed in depth later in this chapter, became tactically quiescent in these pacification activities and took part in what could amount to a vengeful campaign of ethnic cleansing against their former Sunni oppressors. This prompted many more Sunni Iraqis, now alienated from the establishment, to join the mushrooming resistance to the occupation, with some becoming increasingly amenable to al-Qaeda and its anti-American and anti-Israeli causes. As a result, average civilian casualties per month tripled between 2004 and 2006,[21] forcing a re-evaluation of US and Coalition efforts in the country both in Washington and Baghdad.

While maintaining its commitment to the Kurdish cause, the United States flip-flopped from supporting the Arab Shi'as to embracing the Arab Sunnis, for two main reasons. First, the Arab Sunnis, as had been the case under the British mandate in the 1920s, were seen as an important means of counterbalancing the influence of Iraq's Shi'as, whose perceived affinity with Iran was viewed with serious suspicion by the United States; and second, such a rapprochement was also viewed as necessary for the fight against al-Qaeda.[22] To achieve the second objective, General David Petraeus – Commanding General of the Multi-National Force, Iraq, from January 2007 to September 2008 – helped create a series of US-armed and paid local Sunni militias: the 'Awakening Councils', later known as the 'Sons of Iraq', intended as an opposition force to al-Qaeda. Petraeus also arranged for the deployment of an extra 21,500 US troops in Iraq with the aim of restoring order in Baghdad and its surrounding areas, bringing the total US military presence to 165,000 troops.

The noticeable reduction in civilian fatalities between 2007 and the US military withdrawal at the end of 2011, a fact confirmed by all available reports,[23] led some analysts to assert the success of both the US surge strategy and the creation of the Awakening Councils in promoting order and security in Iraq. Other reasons, however, were also influential in bringing about this development. One critical factor was Tehran's appeals to its Shi'a allies to hold their fire, both against the Sunnis and against the United States. The Sadrists, in response, eschewed their former policy of overt violent opposition to US forces in favour of an insistence on the total and unconditional withdrawal of US troops by December 2011 – a tactic which ultimately proved successful.[24] Tehran's approach was grounded in the expectation that the US push for democratisation would ultimately deliver power to Iraq's Shi'a majority, among whom the Iranian-backed groups were and remain the most prominent. Tehran was also concerned to signal its willingness to cooperate with Washington in the region, particularly in the context of heightened US and Israeli fears over Iran's nuclear programme.[25]

Meanwhile, the declining influence of al-Qaeda in Iraq was attributable not only to US strategy, but also to the group's own political miscalculations. In October 2006, al-Qaeda proclaimed the establishment of an Islamic state in Iraq and demanded not only that tribal leaders submit to their command, but also that they contribute the necessary resources to sustain the fight against occupation. Much of the Sunni tribal leadership, undermined by al-Qaeda and irritated by their increasingly authoritarian tendencies, switched sides once the United States promised to reward their allegiance. Al-Qaeda's arrogant attempt to assert its leadership in the insurgency thus produced a backlash among its former allies, who shifted their loyalty to the occupation they had previously opposed.

While the US approach of 'buying off' Sunni tribes, together with Iranian tactics, was successful in reducing violence in the short term, it also introduced a larger set of difficult problems into the Iraqi context. For one, the series of deals between the US military and Sunni tribes may have stoked the latter's revanchist fantasies against the Shi'a-dominated central government. The US approach did not merely succeed in creating an effective domestic force to combat al-Qaeda, but at the same time spawned an entrenched Sunni power to be reckoned with. Rather than attempting to unite the various segments of the Iraqi population in repulsing al-Qaeda, the United States, through its establishment of the Sunni-based Sons of Iraq, only created more divisions within the system. Meanwhile, the Iraqi government proved reluctant to integrate the Sons of Iraq units into the Iraqi armed forces, as there were disturbing hints of corruption within these units. Sunni sheikhs resisted attempts to reduce their slice of the takings as leaders of the Awakening Councils, which in 2008 had stood at around 20 per cent of the payment to each fighter under their command.[26] It was not until September 2010 that Iraq's National Security Council finally issued a directive allowing the army to incorporate Sons of Iraq units.[27] Although progress has been very slow ever since, the Iraqi government has nonetheless continued to pay monthly fees to the Sons of Iraq units following their assumption of control over the units from the United States.[28]

The Iraqi military environment also had an effect on the form and substance of training which US military instructors provided for the Iraqi army. Until 2007, with the insurgency at the forefront of US concerns, and defeating al-Qaeda in Iraq a priority, US training of Iraqi soldiers focused on combat and counter-insurgency. This produced a shortfall in 'enabling' functions within the Iraqi army, such as intelligence gathering and sharing, planning and logistics.[29] In addition, since the dismantling of Saddam Hussein's army in 2003, the recruitment of the security forces has focused on quantity rather than quality, and failed to instil in the troops any loyalty toward Iraqi institutions. In many respects, the army can be seen as a microcosm of Iraqi society as a whole. In both the armed forces and the nation, achieving reconciliation between various sectarian and ethnic groups and creating loyalty towards institutions that transcend social and cultural divisions remains extremely important but nevertheless highly evasive – a situation that in many ways resembles that of Afghanistan.

Reconstruction strategy

Washington's reconstruction strategy, or lack thereof, entirely overlooked the obstacles to state-building and democracy promotion that emerged from Iraq's authoritarian and fragmented historical legacy. As has been underscored, US and Coalition forces had no clear plan for creating stability out of the security vacuum they had so swiftly produced. Under the auspices of the United Nations Assistance Mission for Iraq (UNAMI), the United Nations, which was instrumental in legitimising and coordinating the Afghan civilian mission, was sidelined into a purely advisory role with regard to democratisation and reconstruction in Iraq.[30] In the interests of expediency and unimpeded decision-making, the United States embraced policies and strategies that proved both ineffective and incoherent.

The United States' initial focus on a military strategy to defeat al-Qaeda and remnants of Saddam's loyalists led it to disregard the potential role of another branch of the state security apparatus: the police. According to a British police advisor sent to Iraq, there was an assumption, indicative of policy approaches at the time, that an indigenous police force would simply 'rise like a phoenix'.[31] Efforts to build a viable police force were underfunded, even in light of the appalling conditions of police stations, courthouses and prisons following the US invasion. In this context, the police, like the army, easily became subject to sectarian patronage and division.

The fact that the entire security apparatus was in disarray boded ill for civilian reconstruction efforts. More often than not, completed and 'successful' civilian projects suffered from poor initial construction, lack of maintenance, petty looting, or simple neglect. In 2007, the US Special Inspector General for Iraqi Reconstruction, Stuart Bowen, found that of a sample of eight 'completed' projects, seven were no longer operational.[32] This was a sad reflection on the limitations of 'completion-minded' schemes and the disconnect between planned projects and the interests of the people they were intended to service, resulting from the fact that communities were rarely consulted on their local needs and concerns. Accountability has also been another serious issue. As early as 2005, the same Inspector General announced that the CPA had lost track of nearly US$9 billion in funds. In one case, Bowen's report suggested that thousands of 'ghost employees' – employees who do not actually exist – might have been on an Iraqi ministry's payroll.[33]

As they gradually came to appreciate the nature and extent of sectarian divisions and elite fragmentation, as discussed later, in Iraq, the United States sought to remedy many of the mistakes of earlier policies. It attempted to achieve this by reversing its initial policy of de-Ba'athification, and by instigating and supporting the creation of competing power centres in various political settings to prevent any single political or sectarian group taking control of institutions. For instance, from 2006, the United States threw its weight behind the National Intelligence Service (*Jihaz al-Mukhabarat al-Watani*), which employed a substantial number of intelligence officers of the former regime. This agency actively competes with the Ministry of State for National Security Affairs (*Wizarat al-Dawla li-Shuoun al-Amn al-Watani*), which is often seen as pro-Iranian.[34]

Crippled by sectarian divisions, the newly formed state, along with the US and Coalition forces, proved incapable of addressing the plight of many ordinary Iraqis. With more than 2,000 doctors killed since the invasion, it is no surprise that more than half of that profession – around 20,000 individuals – had fled the country by 2010.[35] The consequent lack of health services has continued to undermine the service capabilities of the state and foster discontent. The number of internally displaced persons (IDPs) in Iraq has also risen to extremely high levels. As of late 2010, they numbered around 2.7 million,[36] of whom 1.6 million had been displaced after February 2006.[37] These figures do not include the 1.5 million refugees who fled the country during the military occupation under the CPA from 2003 to 2004, mostly to either Syria or Jordan,[38] although most of those who sought refuge in Syria have found themselves with no choice but to return home in the wake of that country's turmoil since early 2011. Refugee camps and squatter settlements, cut off from state services, are often incubators of violence and radicalism in the region.

Civil society and democratisation

Parallel to the vacuum in state services has been the international community's failure to invigorate civil society in Iraq, weakened under Saddam's centralised and repressive state structure. The promotion of civil society in Iraq, as in Afghanistan, has often encouraged a dependence on international organisations, or Iraqi actors with strong international ties, at the expense of domestic groups, although the latter often have more support and influence and are more embedded within Iraqi society.[39] The relative feebleness of 'local' civil society leaves it vulnerable to becoming politicised, undermining the independence and effectiveness of civil society as a whole in the process. Notable examples in which political parties have sought to construct or co-opt faith-based organisations include al-Maliki's *Da'wa*'s 'Martyr Al-Hussaini Organisation' and the Islamic Supreme Council of Iraq's (ISCI, formerly SCIRI) 'Al-Mihrab Martyr Foundation'. The international community's reluctance to even provide basic funding to local groups has also driven many non-governmental organisations (NGOs) toward political factions.[40] By nurturing communal loyalties, these new 'civil' organisations may entrench cleavages in the system rather than overcome them. In this climate, the price of even nominal independence has proved extremely high: 85 per cent of Iraqi NGOs had stopped operating by the end of 2010.[41] In this context, the January 2010 liberal NGO law was promising, in so far as it provided for the establishment of an independent civil society delinked from politics through provisions eliminating fundraising restrictions and lowering start-up requirements.[42] However, this law may have proved to be a case of too little, too late.

US and Coalition military and reconstruction policies proved to be far from optimal in creating an effective and unified Iraqi state. More often than not, they served instead to harness a fragmented governing elite and to deepen sectarian divisions. In light of the political dynamics that produced the plans for invasion, this is not surprising. The INC, Iraq's opposition in exile in the United States, was as factionalised and riddled with internal animosities in 2003, as it had been a decade before. Allied with so schismatic a group, the United States was unlikely to come up with a viable alternative to Saddam's regime. Like so many squabbling children each offered a prize, the various factions of the INC were able to make a brief show of unity in the face of Washington's promise to secure power for the INC in Iraq. This image was shattered in the immediate aftermath of the invasion. In the eyes of many who have come to compete for power in Iraq, there is only one prize, and no possibility of sharing it. In the aftermath of the US withdrawal, what remained in Iraq was a dysfunctional elite operating under the guise of a limited democracy.

Dysfunctional Governance

If democracy is defined as a form of popular sovereignty, a method of governance, and public participation and contestation whereby power and authority can be transferred in an orderly and peaceful fashion from one popularly-mandated leader or party to another without the upheaval and bloodshed that often characterise such a transfer in non-democratic systems, then Iraq is far from it. What has transpired in the country since the invasion is at best a kind of foreign-imposed, minimalist and procedural democracy, which essentially denotes the institution of certain procedures such as regular elections, based on some kind of universal suffrage, and pluralist political participation and contestation, to produce an electorally legitimated government. Even in this very minimalist understanding of the concept, Iraq's process of democratisation has yet to reach a point where it can enjoy a genuine electorally legitimated government devoid of deep-seated sectarian dynamics. The country remains in the throes of political disarray and national disunity as it struggles with an ongoing security vacuum that continues to produce bloodshed and violence. In this respect, the situation in Iraq parallels that of Afghanistan, and to a considerable extent that of Pakistan.

Sectarian politics

Two cleavages have stood out in post-invasion Iraq: the Sunni–Shi'a Arab sectarian schism and the Arab–Kurdish ethnic divide. Having been effectively marginalised and repressed by Saddam's regime, Shi'a groups not only took advantage of the US invasion and their subsequent empowerment to exact revenge on the Sunni Arabs, but also displayed an impressive sense of solidarity and capacity for collective political mobilisation. In the first elections to the Iraqi Council of Representatives in 2005, the highest-ranking Shi'a cleric in Iraq, al-Sistani, managed to bring the majority of Shi'as, including all the main Shi'a parties, under the United Iraqi Alliance electoral list. At the same time, SCIRI's Abdul Aziz al-Hakim (Mohammad Bakr al-Hakim was assassinated by counter-systemic forces soon after the invasion) was bold enough to float the idea of a nine-governate, oil-rich, federal super region south of Baghdad dubbed 'Shiastan',[43] which would allow Shi'as to reap the majority of benefits from Iraq's oil.

Unlike the Shi'as, who have traditionally agitated for greater partici-pation and influence within the state, the Kurds have continued to push for increased autonomy and independence from Baghdad. Tensions between the central government in Baghdad and the Kurdistan Regional Government (KRG) in Erbil were on the rise after 2009, a year that witnessed the entry of Iraqi Security Force units into the Kurdish town of Altun Kupri.[44] Two critical and intertwined issues stand out in the contest between Baghdad and Erbil: territorial disputes and the fair allocation of oil wealth between both governments. The legacy of Saddam's Arabisation policy, which witnessed the state-sponsored migration of thousands of ethnic Arabs into Kurdish territory, has persistently plagued Iraqi–Kurdish relations and bedevilled territorial agreements. The Kurds have continuously called for 'normalisation', a process that would involve the removal of the tens of thousands of Iraqi Arabs settled in Kurdish areas under Arabisation.[45] Normalisation has been advanced in support of Kurdish territorial claims, with the assumption that the de-Arabised areas – particularly oil-rich Kirkuk – would vote to join the KRG if given the chance to exercise their constitutional right to such a referendum.[46] The Kurds have also been forthcoming in inviting international investment in oil fields in their region under different regulations to those of the central state.[47] These conflicting interests have continued to divide the two sides.

The US policy of de-Ba'athification also took on sectarian overtones due to the largely Arab Sunni character of the former Ba'athist regime. After the US recognition in 2006 of the Sunni tribes and community, de-Ba'athification ceased to be a pressing priority for the United States. However, the rhetoric of de-Ba'athification was transformed into an effective tool for the Shi'as and Kurds to marginalise the Sunni Arab minority. Reflecting this trend, the Accountability and Justice Commission, which at the time possessed uncertain legal standing, disqualified 499 candidates in the 2010 parliamentary elections for alleged ties to the banned Ba'ath Party, a substantive majority of whom were Sunni. Among the banned members was the serving Minister of Defence, which gave rise to further accusations of dogmatic politics.[48]

The US invasion served to introduce new cleavages into an already complex and multifaceted political arena. As US military forces withdrew, the façade of national unity rapidly disintegrated. In 2011, Shi'a Prime Minister al-Maliki provoked outrage in Iraq and the international community through his brazen treatment of the two most senior Sunni politicians in the country, Vice-President Tareq al-Hashimi and Deputy Prime Minister Saleh al-Mutlaq. After calling for the dismissal of al-Mutlaq for allegedly undermining his position, al-Maliki, in what was seen as a blatant power play, directed the Interior

Ministry to arrest al-Hashimi on charges of terrorism – allegations al-Hashimi has maintained, from exile in Qatar, to be a total fabrication for political gain. In response, the large *Iraqiya* bloc, led by secularist Allawi, boycotted the cabinet and threatened to withdraw from the fragile national coalition governing the country.[49] Al-Maliki's actions against the two most senior Sunni politicians in the country, whether justified or not, have unravelled whatever détente existed between the Sunni Arab and Shi'a blocs.

Elite fragmentation

Two further cleavages have superimposed themselves on Iraq's religious and ethnic divisions, compounding and confusing the differences and divisions within Iraq's political scene: a schism between secularists/semi-secularists and Islamists, and a split between centralists and regionalists, both of which have cut across sectarian lines. Combined with and underpinning deteriorating relationships between key policymakers, these splits have produced an elite so fractured that neither a national ideology of state-building nor an effective and non-partisan governance has seemed possible.

The secularist–Islamist split came about largely as a result of the brutal historical legacy of Saddam's rule. The secularists or semi-secularists, who were more than happy to sign up to the US policy of secularisation and democratisation, included those that either benefited from Saddam's rule – the Sunni Arabs – or framed their opposition to Saddam in ethnic or political terms – the Kurds and Shi'a exiles with links to the West. As such, they included the two key Kurdish leaders, Barzani and Talabani, who after years of rivalry finally signed a 'strategic agreement' in 2007 that joined their parties within the Kurdistan Alliance, although that alliance came under increasing strain from mid-2012. They also encompassed such Shi'a figures as Allawi and Chalabi, who both effectively transformed their respective US-backed exile groups, the INA and INC, into secular nationalist alliances in Iraq backed by large Sunni constituencies.

The Islamists, on the other hand, while initially considering it expedient to ride on the back of the US-led invasion, chose not to side with the occupying forces or to adhere to Washington's agenda of secularist democratisation. They strongly favoured an Islamist transformation of Iraq from within, grounded in their experience of religious opposition to Saddam and various ties with Iran's Islamic regime. The Islamists' major figures in the Shi'a camp in 2012 were the ISCI's Ammar al-Hakim, who succeeded his father Abdul Aziz al-Hakim in 2009; Da'wa's al-Maliki; and Muqtada al-Sadr, son of Grand Ayatollah Sadeq al-Sadr and heir to his legacy. A widespread belief that only a secular state would be capable of protecting Sunni interests from those of the Shi'a majority has contributed to a decline in the influence of Sunni Islamists, such as Mohsen Abd al-Hamid of the Iraqi Islamic Party and Adnan al-Dulaimi of the General Council for the People of Iraq.

In contrast to the sectarian and secularist–Islamist divisions, each faction's position on the centralist–regionalist cleavage has tended to reflect the changing balance of power between any group's regional influence and its dependence on the state structure. Hence, the Kurds and ISCI have been the most ardent supporters of increased regionalisation, due to their possession of a territorial stronghold in oil-rich areas – the Kurdish north-east and Shi'a south-east. Both groups also possess strong militias capable of defending their interests independent of the state – the Kurdish militia Peshmerga and ISCI's Badr Brigade. On the other hand, the Sunni Arabs, who are concentrated in the oil-poor region of central Iraq and who lack a unified militia (the Sons of Iraq units being under the control of tribal leaders), and al-Maliki's Da'wa, which also lacks an independent militia, have continued to invest in a strong centralised state structure. The Sadrists, led by Muqtada al-Sadr, have often found themselves sitting on the fence in this debate. Although they have a strong independent force in the form of the Mahdi Army, they lack strong regional backing, with the majority of their supporters drawn from Baghdad's Shi'a dispossessed.

The Shi'a factions have therefore proved fairly mobile within these various positions, in contrast to the Kurds or Sunni Arabs who have tended to display relative conformity in standing for or against any given issue.[50] Although all Iraq's Shi'a movements, in some form or another, have historical links to Baqr al-Sadr, developments since his death in 1980, both within and outside Iraq, have generated divisions. Even al-Sistani, whose quietist disposition ensured his survival through Saddam's years in power, and who is often recognised as a non-partisan mediator between various political groupings, ultimately fell prey to this internal Shi'a dissension, as evident in his undermining of Muqtada al-Sadr by often criticising his lack of formal religious teaching.

A lack of constitutional mechanisms to regulate disagreements between various factions has served to ingrain differences and impede cooperation. Parliamentarians have continued to grapple with pressing security issues, such as that of the 'Baghdad Brigade' – or US-supported counter-terrorism forces – whose nickname, the 'dirty brigades', reflects the extent to which this body has remained unregulated, unaccountable and in legal limbo.[51] Prime Minister al-Maliki, for his part, has seized on the ineffectiveness of parliament in order to circumvent and marginalise established institutions by running his own security forces and creating separate chains of command that report directly to his office.[52] The result has been an ineffectual and often exasperating relationship both between and within various branches of government. Various factions and political players have not only become increasingly concerned to limit al-Maliki's powers,[53] especially on security matters, but have also begun to accuse the prime minister of 'smelling like a dictator'.[54]

The March 2010 parliamentary elections provided a clear reflection of the extent of Iraq's political and national fragmentation. What was supposed to mark a turning point in Iraq's democratic development proved to be a charade. The elections produced inconclusive results, with none of the major political coalitions able to secure a majority in the 325-member Representative Council. The two major blocs were closely split, with the secularist yet Sunni-dominated *Iraqiya* Coalition winning 91 seats, and the predominantly Shi'a State of Law Coalition 89.[55] Faced with the possibility of losing office to *Iraqiya*'s leader, Allawi, al-Maliki immediately challenged the results, calling for a recount that delayed the election outcome by weeks. When the original results were confirmed and ratified by the Iraqi Supreme Court in June, al-Maliki and Allawi remained at loggerheads, unable to form a government of national unity or to agree on who should be prime minister. Despite US mediation efforts, led by Vice-President Joe Biden, the deadlock continued through to November 2010, all the while widening the political and strategic vacuum that has impaired Iraq's transition. Al-Maliki eventually managed to secure the premiership with the support of the United States' main Shi'a critic, Muqtada al-Sadr, at that time in self-exile in Iran, and the Kurdish Alliance, which managed to keep Talabani as president of Iraq.[56] The potential development of a Shi'a-dominated administration triggered concerns in Washington, forcing discussions on the creation of another 'national unity government' that ultimately produced a coalition inclusive of the Sunnis. Held together by an array of difficult promises made to various factions by al-Maliki and increased checks on his power, prospects for an effective and responsive administration proved dim.[57] Whatever potential this national coalition possessed has come unstuck. Al-Maliki has increasingly acted like a dictator, cementing patronage and nepotism as hallmarks of Iraqi governance. The entire fiasco has augured ill for Iraq's future political stability and national unity.

Corruption and patronage politics

According to Transparency International, Iraq ranked as the third most corrupt country in the world in 2006, 2007 and 2008; fifth in 2009; fourth in 2010; and eighth in 2011 and 2012.[58] This placed it close to Afghanistan, serving in a similar fashion to further elite fragmentation and to widen the distance between the ruling cluster and those they claim to represent. Corruption is pervasive throughout the entire system, ranging from hundreds of dollars at the lower levels to millions of dollars when ministers are involved. The case of the former trade minister, Abdul-Falah al-Sudani, stands as a clear example – he was accused of having been involved in the import of expired tea for US$50 million, which entailed an overvaluation of US$30 million.[59] In another case, Muqtada al-Sadr became so concerned about the level of corruption among his Sadrist ministers that he actually withdrew them from government in 2007. According to many, the ways in which Iraqi Members of Parliament (MPs) have used their democratic powers has given birth to corruption of another kind. In 2011, Iraqi MPs voted to convert the US$60,000 provided to them for the purchase of armoured cars and diplomatic passports for themselves and their families for ten years into a cash grant, despite two attempted presidential council vetoes and heavy criticism from the religious establishment.[60] Corruption has not only fuelled dysfunctional governance, it has become a major threat to the security and protection of the Iraqi people. It has led to ineffectual military procurement, where food and fuel allowances are often overstated, and the 'ghost soldiers' phenomenon, where a large proportion of those on the payroll of the security services either do not exist or fail to show up for work.[61]

Corruption is also rife within the various factions – Sunni Arab, Shi'a Arab and Kurd – who have used any means to further their own influence and personal position at the expense of national unity and development. After more than two decades of relative autonomy, the Kurdish leaders have stood out in this regard. Barzani has reportedly hoarded a fortune of US$2 billion, while Talabani has around US$400 million in his pocket.[62] Evoking Barzani's sizeable family, which includes his eight children, one analyst cynically remarked that the only difference between the two is that Talabani 'has only one wife and two children and so has less patronage to distribute'.[63] Since 2003, the Kurds have continued to take advantage of their unique position within the Iraqi state. According to Gorran, the main Kurdish opposition party to the PUK–KDP Kurdistan Alliance, Talabani's PUK unofficially siphoned off more than US$250 million a month from oil being exported to Iran in 2010.[64]

The Shi'a *Fadhila*, a smaller party based around Basra, and many other factions, have followed the Kurdish lead in smuggling oil out of the country. To compensate for his lack of a popular constituency, *Da'wa*'s al-Maliki has also utilised state funds to create and legitimise support councils (*majalis al-isnad*) among the southern tribes. Buoyed by state stipends of US$10,000 a month and answering directly to al-Maliki and the *Da'wa* inner circle,[65] the councils have worked to contain fellow Shi'a and Kurdish influence. In light of this, it is no surprise that a USAID report has stated that the majority of hiring and promotions in the Iraqi civil service are based on political connections rather than merit.[66]

Nepotism and corruption often breed crime, and Iraq is no exception. As Phil Williams has succinctly argued, 'the government monopoly over oil combined with a lack of transparency and an absence of accountability mechanisms have created multiple opportunities for theft, diversion, and smuggling'.[67] Theft of crude oil and refined products, not only by political actors but also by a range of militia and insurgent players, has run into billions of US dollars a year since 2003.

Reconstruction, whereby the United States and the Coalition attempted to promote an inclusive political order to avert control by a single political faction, has ironically fostered nepotism within the government. The US and Coalition push for the formation of a 'national unity government', instead of leading to unified governance, has led to the creation of ministries with overlapping jurisdictions that have been farmed out to various rival parties without significant oversight.[68] Factionalism, compounded by entrenched political patronage and corruption, has led to a major failure in servicing the needs of the Iraqi people.

The Economy

Iraq's economic situation, in view of these ongoing reconstruction issues, appears less than rosy. As of 2011, only 38 per cent of working age adults were employed. Seven per cent were unemployed and 57 per cent were 'not in the labour market', whatever that might entail.[69] Iraq's Public Distribution System (PDS), an instituted scheme that allocates rations and subsidies to Iraqi citizens, supports many middle-class families but represents a tremendous burden on the government. It stood at a cost of US$5.8 billion to the state in 2008, a figure that exceeds national expenditure on health or education. The PDS has also become increasingly wasteful, due to theft, corruption and inefficiency. A 2010 report by the World Bank estimated that around US$6 was spent to transfer every US$1 of benefits to the people.[70]

Natural resources and oil fields

In this troubled climate, both US and Iraqi authorities have pointed to Iraq's oil wealth as a potential source of economic salvation. By 2020, based on 2010 prices, Iraq's oil revenue could rise to about US$280 billion a year from a figure of around US$70 billion in 2010.[71] The 2009 oil-field auctions were encouraging in this respect, with some of the world's largest oil companies displaying interest in Iraq's long-closed oil fields. Twelve new contracts were awarded to international oil companies as a result of the auctions. The ownership and management of the southern Rumaila field, the country's largest oil producer, was given to British Petroleum and China National Petroleum, reflecting cross-sectional international interest in Iraq's oil fields. Considering oil exports, which accounts for 98 per cent of Iraqi exports and comprises 90 per cent of government revenue, a successful oil industry is critical for Iraq's economic stability and well-being.[72]

After the invasion, a temporary arrangement was provided for the deposit of Iraq's oil revenues into the UN-monitored Development Fund for Iraq at the Federal Reserve Bank of New York, theoretically entailing a high level of transparency for oil transactions. With the exception of 5 per cent of the proceeds, which were set aside as reparations for Kuwait because of Iraq's 1990 invasion of the country, the rest of these funds were supposedly allocated to the reconstruction of Iraq.[73] However, opacity within the Iraqi financial system itself was so great that the 'Open Budget Index gave Iraq a score of absolute zero for the transparency of its 2010 budget and budget process, [the] bottom of 94 countries surveyed'.[74] The transfer of oversight from the UN-created International Advisory and Monitoring Board to the Iraqi Committee of Financial Experts came into effect on 30 June 2011,[75] with uncertain outcomes for the nation's economic well-being.

Aside from the entrenched obstacles of corruption and a lack of transparency, state rentier theory (whereby a state drives all or a large portion of their national revenues from the rent of its resources to external clients or from foreign aid) suggests that oil wealth, often referred to as 'black gold', cannot be a panacea for all ills. The salient question for all involved is who will gain from the oil – the Iraqi people, the central government or individual political parties? In many ways, Iraq's oil may serve to be more divisive than unifying. Iraq's major oil deposits are concentrated in the Kurdish north-east and Shi'a south-east, ensuring conflict regarding the allocation and potential redistribution of oil wealth between various sectarian groups, with the most polarising dispute being that between the Kurds and Arabs over the status of Kirkuk and its surrounding oil-rich lands. As such, rent from oil can only fuel patronage politics and sectarian competition.

There is another theory that gives cause to refrain from optimism about Iraq's oil wealth. The 'resource curse' argument draws attention to the correlation between an abundance of natural resources and slow economic growth, and points out that nations rich in natural wealth tend to remain mired in poverty.[76] In light of both rentier theory and the resource curse argument, some scholars have suggested that Iraq should take a new path by distributing a significant oil dividend directly to Iraqi citizens.[77] This would theoretically offset state rentierism and the possibility of Iraq becoming a 'petro-state'. Whatever its potential benefits, this novel idea is unlikely to gain much traction. Aside from the US state of Alaska, no government has ever implemented such a programme, and the invested interests of various factions and individuals provide a very powerful obstacle to such a development.

Counter-systemic Actors

In contrast to Afghanistan, Iraq's complex and divided socio-political landscape has historically left the country with a weak society and fragile domestic structures reliant upon a strong state. National cohesion has been maintained under a series of absolute or semi-absolute rulers, who have held Iraq together in what has often been a very volatile regional climate. The 2003 invasion uprooted Iraq's legacy of a relatively strong state, with a largely weak society, not only by toppling Saddam's regime but also by demolishing the coercive capacity of the Iraqi state apparatus. The US and Iraqi failure either to reconstruct a strong central state or to build a robust civil society has generated a wide space for the strengthening of various societal groups and actors at the expense of the state. Historical trends have therefore been inverted: Iraq after the US invasion became a weak state locked in competition with strong micro-societies.

Various militias linked to political factions have successfully penetrated the state security apparatus. Following the infiltration of the Interior Ministry in 2005 by ISCI's Badr Brigade,[78] and that of the Sadrist Mahdi Army from 2006 to 2007, the police force, especially in the Shi'a-dominated provinces, became a tool for sectarian interests.[79] The army as well has undergone an increasingly evident process of 'balkanisation', with divisions and brigades entirely composed of certain ethnic or religious groups.[80] Within this context, suspicions regarding the loyalty of the armed service and its ability to act as a neutral party within Iraqi politics have abounded.

Outside the political system, violent opposition to the government and, until 2011, the occupying forces, has taken root among various Islamist and sectarian-induced groups. These groups have come to include elements from both Iraq's Sunni and Shi'a communities. Given the cross-sectarian nature of the groups, it is no longer possible to assume that they have necessarily hoisted the flag of radical political Islam in the hope of establishing a government similar to that of neighbouring Iran. The aims and motivations of counter-systemic actors in Iraq are in fact often different and conflicting. A significant component of the Sunni Islamist opposition, for example, has been drawn from the disgruntled Ba'athist, and even non-Ba'athist, secularist supporters of Saddam's regime. In light of such complexity, the extent to which religion provides a genuine motivation for opposition movements remains open to question. Regardless, however, certain elements from both sides of the Sunni–Shi'a divide have found it politically and ideologically desirable to make common cause in demanding an Islamist government for Iraq.[81]

Al-Qaeda has also been able to carve an important niche for itself within the ranks of counter-systemic actors, but largely as a spoiler in pursuit of broader ideological and political purposes. Its central objectives have been to block the United States and its Iraqi allies as well as various Shi'a groups from transforming Iraq according to their preferences. This is part of al-Qaeda's wider goal of driving the United States out of the Middle East and reshaping the region according to its own Islamic vision.[82] In light of the group's lack of support in both Iraq and the region, even among many of the Sunnis with whom al-Qaeda shares a sectarian allegiance, al-Qaeda's goals may prove unattainable. However, for as long as Iraq remains politically and nationally fragmented, there is a space for al-Qaeda and its supporters to remain active and assertive in the country. Al-Qaeda has already shown itself quick not only to take advantage of the US withdrawal to plunge Iraq into a similar cycle of domestic violence that marked the years between 2005 and 2008, but also to secure an operational niche for itself in neighbouring Syria in the wake of that country's crisis. Despite the upbeat assertions by the United States and its Iraqi allies, the Iraqi army was not ready to take over from the Americans for another decade – something the Iraqi army chief of staff, Lieutenant General Babakir Zebari, affirmed as late as 12 August 2010.[83] Meanwhile, the underlying ethnic, religious and political as well as regional causes of Iraq's conflict are, by and large, ignored. The failure to address the root causes of Iraq's political and social plight has damaged Iraq's ability to stand on its own feet, and has imperilled its prospects of national political and territorial unity in the long term.

International Relations and Regional Interests

With the fracturing of state power in Iraq and the resurgence of its micro-societies, the interests of its neighbours became ever more important, especially after the US withdrawal in 2011. While most of Iraq's major neighbours – Iran, Turkey, Saudi Arabia and Syria – took pleasure, in some form, in seeing the fall of Saddam's regime, they have subsequently found themselves grappling with a substantially altered regional balance of power. Situated precariously at the crossroads of a mosaic of religions and ethnicities, Iraq has become a geopolitical battleground, with all of its neighbours struggling to come to grips with the political dynamics of post-Saddam Iraq.

As mentioned earlier, Iran's approach to Iraq until the US withdrawal was two-pronged. On the one hand, it encouraged its Shi'a allies to come together to allow the US-induced processes of democratisation to deliver power to them peacefully. On the other hand, it had an interest in tying up the United States in Iraq for whatever length of time necessary to prevent Washington from acting against it, and to avoid being eclipsed by the Iraqi regime in terms of regional influence. Following the US pull-out, while it has become increasingly clear that no Iraqi government can afford to function without heeding Tehran's interests, Iran and the Iraqi Shi'a factions have also come to recognise the usefulness of diversifying their relationships with other parties. In particular, after its losses in the January 2009 provincial elections, ISCI moved to a more nationalist line and shelved much of its Islamist rhetoric.[84] The nationalist shift had already been foreshadowed in 2007, when the group decided to abandon 'SCIRI' in favour of its current name, reflecting a self-conscious move away from Iran and Khomeini's vision. Tehran, for its part, began to branch out in Iraq's Shi'a political community by inviting Muqtada al-Sadr to study in the country and by building links with al-Maliki.[85]

Until the start of its own troubles, Iran's strategic ally, Syria, with ties both to former Iraqi Ba'athists and many former non-Iranian Shi'a exile groups, such as al-Malaki's *Da'wa*, had the potential to be a pivotal actor in Iraq. Home to the largest number of Iraqi refugees outside the country, Syrian policy had been based on balancing its Iranian strategic relationship with its interest in a stable Iraq not dominated by any one faction. Recognising Allawi's inability to form a government, Syria joined Iran in throwing their support behind al-Maliki.[86] This seems to have paid off for the Syrian regime, as even in the context of the ongoing conflict in Syria, the al-Assad regime has enjoyed the tepid backing of the al-Maliki administration as well as that of Iran,[87] with the latter providing arms and logistic support to the Assad government through Iraq.

Turkey, Iraq's northernmost neighbour, aims to preserve the territorial integrity of Iraq, both in order to contain the influence of Iran and to limit the possibilities for Kurdish subversive action within its own borders. Since 1984, it has waged an intermittent war against the Kurdistan Workers' Party (PKK), a militant group seeking independence from Turkey. While initially adopting a confrontational approach toward the Iraqi Kurds, the ruling Turkish Justice and Development Party has increasingly advocated a deeper engagement with the Kurdistan Regional Government and pluralism within Iraq's major cities.[88] In April 2013, Ankara and the PKK agreed to settle their differences peacefully, with the PKK's jailed leader, Abdullah Ocalan, calling on his fighters to lay down their arms as part of a negotiated settlement. In this context, Turkey's pressing concern with regard to Iraq has been to ensure that the Iraqi Kurds do not reach a point where they are capable of demanding more than just autonomy. An independent Kurdistan in Iraq's north-east, with its own oil wealth, could become a source of effective support for Turkey's Kurdish population to secede from the Turkish state. This is an anxiety that Tehran shares with Ankara, given the historical wish of some of Iran's Kurdish minority to become autonomous. With Iraqi–Turkish trade standing at US$11 billion in 2011, Turkey is also Iraq's biggest economic partner.

Relations with the Gulf Arab states have been somewhat more tenuous. Saudi Arabia, as the Sunni Islamist counter to Shiʻa Iran in the region, stands vehemently opposed to the possibility of Shiʻa hegemony within Iraq. Along with the other Gulf monarchies, it has remained very watchful of developments there, and has provided verbal and material support for Allawi's *Iraqiya* bloc and the Sunnis where possible.[89] Iraqi relations with Kuwait have also been strained in light of continuing Kuwaiti demands for war reparations and the al-Maliki government's close ties with Tehran. As of 2010, Iraq still owed the tiny sheikhdom US$25 billion and has had to set aside 5 per cent of its oil revenue, every year, for reparations, as imposed under Chapter 7 of the UN Charter.[90] However, Iraq announced in early 2013 that it expected the reparation payments to be completed by 2015.

A weaker Iraq, with its political factions remaining highly responsive to external patronage and influence, has created both a new set of possibilities and potential problems for its neighbours. Whilst Saddam's Iraq was a threat – militarily, ideologically or politically – to the majority of them, it was neither unstable nor politically fragmented. The influence and actions of Iraq's neighbours, whether through cooperation or conflict, may very well have a determining effect on the fate of the Iraqi people.

The prevailing Iraqi situation is one of fragility after the departure of foreign forces, which generated a substantial increase in instability in the country. A majority of the Iraqi people have continued to suffer from frequent sectarian and ethnic violence and conflict, and have come to fear the present and future. Many of them, along with most serious scholars of the region, believe that Iraq may not recover from its post-invasion traumas for at least a generation, provided that the country proves capable of holding itself together. Iraq has become a hotbed of sectarian and ethnic conflict, and a zone of proxy conflict between various regional actors, with the United States reaping little benefit for all the blood and money that it invested in the country. Apart from getting rid of Saddam and his murderous clique, Washington must ask if it was worth the extraordinary price that the Iraqis, Americans and their allies, especially the British, paid. Hundreds of thousands of Iraqis are dead, more than 4,000 US and Coalition soldiers killed (95 per cent of these are American), and many more thousands injured and diseased in the war. Yet none of this appears to have been successful in freeing Iraq from the grip of long-term structural disorder, with its integrity remaining in serious danger. In 2013, the level of sectarian and criminal killings peaked once again, with close to 10,000 Iraqis losing their lives, and with a majority of Iraqis feeling insecure and fearing the future.

The Way Forward

Following the collapse of Saddam Hussein's rule, the Iraqi state became subject to the fragmentation of its political elite, resulting in a pulverisation of power and authority that substantially contributed to the rise of counter-systemic actors and regional interventionism. These developments have not only driven the consolidation of a dysfunctional system of governance, but have also undermined the possibility of moving beyond this legacy. The most urgent need for Iraq in this climate has been to secure a regional consensus, especially involving Iran, Saudi Arabia and its GCC partners and Turkey, in order to find a common interest in supporting the processes of national unity, reconstruction and stability in Iraq. A stable Iraq is in the interests of all regional players for two important reasons. First, all of Iraq's neighbours have demonstrated their common opposition to al-Qaeda and would like to see it deprived of any opportunity that could enable it to maintain and expand its influence. Second, a secure and functioning Iraq of any kind – provided it does not threaten the interests of its neighbours – would be far less costly to its neighbours in the long term than a volatile Iraq. A formal policy of neutrality in world politics appears to be a sensible option for Iraq.

In tandem with these regional efforts, Iraq's leaders have a key role to play in developing a new constitutional framework in which differences are mitigated and cooperation enhanced. An established system of checks and balances and effective mechanisms of public scrutiny are required to transcend Iraq's entrenched problems of factionalism, nepotism and corruption. On the other hand, incentives must be provided for the various factional groups to work with one another. The common perception that the politics of Iraq is a 'zero-sum' game, where the privileges of those in prominent and powerful positions far exceed those in opposition, provides a serious obstacle to the democratisation process. Iraq does not need a 'grand coalition' government. Instead, it hungers for a ruling regime that is inclusive and responsive to all the various parties while remaining efficient in its aims to reform and establish a viable state structure.

A national ideology of state-building which is culturally relevant and inclusive has long evaded the Iraqi leadership. Even in the aftermath of the foreign troop withdrawal, no vision for Iraq's national future was clearly articulated. Is it to be an Iraq with a secular political system shaped by Western-type democratic preferences? Or is it to be an Islamic Iraq with a political system that conforms to its cultural and religious traditions? Like Hamid Karzai's government in Afghanistan, the Iraqi government's various factions have vacillated between religiosity and secularism on the basis of convenience as much as conviction. State promotion of a national platform which stresses the compatibility of Sunni and Shi'a Islam with democracy might provide a timely solution to this impasse. This might include the institution of a political system akin to what the former Iranian president, Mohammad Khatami, sought to promote as 'Islamic democracy', rather than a replica of

Western traditions. An Islamic democracy can be as effective as many of its Western variants if it is conducted within an *ijtihadi*, or creatively reformist, approach to the interpretation and application of Islam. Such an approach is entirely capable of providing political legitimacy, public participation, human freedoms, individual rights and duties, the rule of law, separation of powers, and immunity of citizens against the state's arbitrary actions and violation of its powers.[91]

One model of a power structure that the Iraqi leaders may find appealing is a consociational structure, whereby the varying numerical strength of the three major communities – the Shi'a Arabs, the Sunni Arabs and the Kurds – is proportionally represented in the state, without any of the communities having the right of veto. Within this structure, sufficient internal mechanisms can be incorporated to be able to accommodate changes in the demographic size of each community. The consociational power structure was successful for a long time in Lebanon, before collapsing in the mid-1970s (largely because it lacked these internal mechanisms of adjustment and because it came under strain from Lebanon's rival neighbours), only to be reinvented from 1989. Such a model could prove effective in Iraq, if implemented in the context of a regional consensus.

CONCLUSION

Despite their manifold and complex differences, Afghanistan, Pakistan, Iran and Iraq may in many ways be understood as part of a continuous geostrategic zone, which has been an arena of change and conflict from ancient times until the present day. Throughout its long history, this region has rarely seen long periods of peace, stability and security. In modern times, and with the dawn of the nation state and rise of world hegemonic powers, the difficulties that have beset the region have assumed new forms and acquired new patterns, and transitional or transformative events in one of the zone's constituent states have had rippling effects on the rest of the zone and beyond. Domestically, within the borders acquired relatively recently, these four states have shared a number of critical underlying problems, which have persisted at two levels. At the social level, the fragmented, mosaic character of their populations, a factor compounded by cross-border alliances and affiliations, has posed a serious impediment to national unity. At the political level, the ethnic, linguistic and sectarian divisions are reflected in the persisting elite fragmentation, dysfunctional and factionalist government, corruption and nepotism. This fact, compounded by an ongoing split between secularists and Islamists, and several other kinds of activists in between, and foreign interventions, has given rise to inappropriate and ineffective political systems, modes of social and economic change and processes of state-building.

With regional and international actors each seeking to implement their own vision within the zone of conflict, local actors have found themselves increasingly caught up in a larger game, which may ultimately determine the fate of the region. This has been true both of trans-state and regional developments, and major power interventions and invasions, for much of the region's modern history. One of the legacies of this influence may be seen in the deepening divide between secularist and religious sectarian groups, with many of them seeking to garner favour among powerful regional and international backers, who compete amongst themselves to implement their desired agenda in each of the four states.

Although each state has also had their dividing national character-istics that in various ways have set them apart, it is by and large these two sets of variables – one domestic, and one regional and international – that have interacted to shape the landscape of each of the states and their region into a volatile, uncertain and unpredictable zone, with serious implications for changing world order. In modern times, this has been no more pronounced than since the Iranian revolution of 1978–79, the Soviet occupation of Afghanistan in the 1980s, and the US-led intervention in Afghanistan from 2001 to 2014 and occupation of Iraq from 2003 to 2011 – the period that has been the main focus of analysis in this book.

It was on 7 October 2001 that US President George W. Bush addressed the nation, announcing the beginning of Operation Enduring Freedom against the Afghan Taliban and al-Qaeda, with a wider aim that included realignment with Pakistan, containment of Iran and invasion of Iraq. In relation to Afghanistan, Bush declared: 'We will not waver; we will not tire; we will not falter; and we will not fail. Peace and freedom will prevail.'[1] This, together with the invasion of Iraq shortly thereafter, was to be part of an expansive agenda to transform the whole West Asian and Middle Eastern domain in accordance with American ideological and geopolitical preferences, as largely dictated by three minority groups – the neoconservatives, the evangelical right-wing Christians and the ultra-nationalists who came to dominate the Bush administration's foreign policy. However, after over a decade of US interventionism, the prospect of freedom, peace and democracy remains a distant vision for Afghanistan and Iraq; Iran is not successfully contained, and Pakistan is more volatile than ever before. The region as whole is desperate for stability and security.

The American people and their armed forces, along with the international community, have indeed faltered and grown tired. Declining public support for the United States' misadventures and growing doubts about the value of an international presence in Iraq or Afghanistan have forced changes in foreign policy. By December

2011, the last American soldier had left Iraq, despite worrying signs of impending long-term structural unrest and instability. Having left Iraq, a nation 'neither sovereign, stable nor self-reliant',[2] the United States and its allies also committed themselves to withdrawing most of their troops from an equally volatile Afghanistan by the end of 2014, even while grave concerns over a return to Taliban rule loomed large.[3] President Barack Obama kept emphasising America's success in achieving its goals in the region, but he could not declare a victory in the 'war on terror'[4] – a war that Washington no longer speaks of, yet whose legacy remains a major challenge to the United States and its allies.

That such uncertainty and instability should be the product of more than a decade of US military involvement in the region should not be surprising. The very framing of the 'war on terror' itself, from the outset conceived as a battle between the forces of civilisation and barbarism, reveals a poverty of understanding that has plagued US policy in the region for far too long. The 'war on terror', coupled with the US-led invasions of Afghanistan and Iraq, and policy of containing Iran and helping to stabilise Pakistan, has added another layer of complexity to an already complex region. This, in turn, has greatly increased the difficulties for foreign policymakers in Washington, compounding and frustrating political calculations.

Whatever the immediate consequences, the American and international withdrawal from the region may eventually allow regional dynamics to take precedence once again and some kind of equilibrium to be restored. This will undoubtedly prove a slow and painful process, but one that is ultimately necessary to the long-term stability of the region. The threat to peace and security posed by extremism, as the American experience has made all too clear, is not eliminated with the deaths of the terrorists themselves. Terrorism, like any other form of radicalism, is a consequence of the situation on the ground. The 'war on terror' has provided fertile soil for the seeds of radicalism to take root, and its continuation will only serve to breed support for counter-systemic actors and further instability.

Sectarian divisions and ideological fault lines continue to cut across the entire region, demanding both understanding and sensitivity on the part of international actors. The empowerment of Iraq's Shi'as has provoked concerns among Arab Sunni-dominated countries, particularly in the Gulf. There are brewing fears over the development of an Iran-centred 'Shi'a crescent' stretching from Afghanistan through Iraq and Syria to Lebanon. Increased dialogue, with the participation of moderate actors, could provide the foundations on which some elements of trust may slowly be built between Sunni and Shi'a nations in the region. This cannot occur in the presence of offensive-minded states in the area. Aggressive postures and harsh rhetoric both from states within the region and outside actors trigger defensive reactions and prohibit constructive dialogue. Neutrality and openness are required of all involved parties if progress is to be made.

The democratisation project so dear to America's original agenda has had mixed outcomes in the region. Whilst Iran remained in a class of its own by claiming to have a theo-democratic order, with its June 2013 presidential election producing a moderate-reformist government for the second time since the advent of the country's Islamic regime, Pakistan managed to take a step forward with its May 2013 general elections in a quest for building a democratic order, and Afghanistan and Iraq remained subject to externally induced processes of democratisation. However, these processes failed to progress beyond a merely electoral form. Implementing electoral democracies through representative governments and voting procedures has done little to produce the positive changes associated with substantive democracies – improvements in human rights, civil liberties, the rule of law with justice, separation of powers and freedom from oppression and violence. Democracy comes in many shapes and forms; it is not a universal medicine to be administered alike and to all. The most stable democracies, and the most enduring, are those that arise organically. Civil society and substantive democracy cannot therefore be imposed in the same way as electoral democracies have been; they must develop from within.

In the mosaic contexts of each of these countries, the search for a clear consensus is necessary, but not easily achievable. In light of this, political systems must be created to allow for and promote plurality, compromise, moderation and the acceptance of dissent. The centralisation of power not only breeds nepotism and authoritarianism, but also threatens to deepen sectarian divides by potentially concentrating authority in the hands of a single group. In view of the currently widespread acceptance of Islam as a source of political legitimacy, it appears sensible to revisit the possibility of a reformist or *ijtihadi* Islamist democracy, as envisioned by Iran's former President

Mohammad Khatami (1997–2005) and echoed by the country's current President Hassan Rouhani.

The long-term stability and security of these countries and their region will be linked to the success of state-building processes, including the mobilisation of national ideologies. In relation to Afghanistan and Iraq, state-building and reconstruction efforts have so far remained stunted. Whether in the context of a multifaceted approach, as in the NATO/UN involvement in Afghanistan, or a unilateral one, such as the US invasion of Iraq, prospects for failure appear equally high. The international community has neither the will nor the resources to fix these disrupted states. Pakistan and Iran, too, have remained historically constricted in their creation of viable state structures and national ideologies. Both have fallen drastically short of producing a manifesto of statehood capable of transcending the ethnic, sectarian and political divides that cut across their own societies.

The creation of a national ideology of state-building is essential for all of these countries in order to mobilise and unite their respective states. This ideology must be flexible, pluralistic and all-inclusive if it is to succeed in fostering a widespread sense of national belonging. When constricted to a single framework, it may entrench conservatism, impeding change and obstructing progress. Furthermore, national ideologies of state-building must develop locally and at the grass-roots level. They cannot be externally constructed or imposed. Their successes or failures must also be evaluated in light of prevailing social conditions within each individual state. For historical, demographic and sectarian reasons, the concept of statehood in Afghanistan, Pakistan and Iraq cannot be expected to resonate as strongly as in Iran. Nevertheless, the possibility remains of fostering a wider identification with and loyalty to the Afghan, Pakistani or Iraqi state.

The persistence of dysfunctional and factional elites has been a clear and prominent obstacle to the development of national unity and state-belonging. The national good often appears to be far from the minds of present elites, who frequently prefer to appropriate power and authority to further their own interests and those of their faction. Rentier income, whether from foreign aid or oil, has often been used for the benefit of dysfunctional elites rather than the nation as a whole. Continued reliance on international aid or a single source of income, coupled with a redistributive economic structure, will ensure that largesse and corruption remain the hallmarks of the political systems of these four states, although to varying degrees. To counter this, a gradual diversification of economies and the implementation of an effective national framework of taxation are necessary. Rentier income must be streamlined so as to cohere with government policies, while ensuring these policies themselves are in tune with local needs and in support of wider regional cooperation.

Finally, it is impossible to reflect on the problems that bedevil this region without pausing to consider the broader and shifting strategic environment in which they exist. Several external variables have the capacity to seriously disrupt the dynamics of this region. The Arab uprisings of 2011–12 have called into question the legitimacy of all Arab political establishments in North Africa and the Middle East, and have overthrown some of the dictatorial rulers. The influx of new political systems and governments, whose futures remain uncertain, has destabilised the entire region, and it is difficult to say how the balance of power will appear when the dust has settled. Of all the nations that have experienced unrest in the course of the Arab uprisings, Syria has been the most affected. Whereas a majority of Arab revolts ended either in revolution or in suppression, Syria fell into the grips of a bloody deadlock. The sectarian dynamics of the Syrian conflict, where the Alawite regime of Bashar al-Assad, backed materially by Iran and the Lebanese Hezbollah and protected politically by Russia and China, but opposed by most Arab countries and Turkey (which have sided with Syria's very divided opposition), clung fiercely to power in spite of a 70 per cent Sunni majority in the country. The Syrian crisis has already resulted in a spillover effect into neighbouring countries, Lebanon and Iraq in particular. This trend has clearly demonstrated the potentially destabilising effects of any internal, armed conflict in the region. The interconnected character of this part of the world indicates the urgent need for regional dialogue, stability and consensus, if any of its constituent states are to stand a chance of peace and prosperity in the long run.

Any long-term solution for peace and stability in the region must also provide for the resolution of the Israeli–Palestinian dispute, a conflict which has for too long been the source of antagonism and hostility towards Israel and the country's stalwart ally, the United States. The perceived existential threat of Israel has made it easier for authoritarian forces to justify oppressive measures and militant postures. This factor has played a role in the animosity that Israel and Iran have towards one another. The United States has not succeeded in alleviating tensions in the region through retrenching its unconditional support for the Israeli government, however reproachable its actions. The United States must take a stronger stance toward Israel, particularly in the context of the ongoing and internationally condemned process of settlement building in East Jerusalem and the West Bank, and blockade of the Gaza Strip.

Like the Israeli–Palestinian dispute, the Indo-Pakistani contestation over Kashmir has long complicated the regional situation. It has not only affected bilateral relations, but has also had an impact on the region. The Indian–Pakistani competition in Afghanistan, coupled with Afghanistan's strategic agreements with India and Iran to shore up its position against Pakistan's support of the Taliban, and the appearance of a Kabul–New Delhi–Tehran axis, favoured by Moscow but feared by China and not favoured by Washington, has become part of a very complicated regional architecture. This has made the search for a viable resolution of the Afghan conflict a more complex process. Islamabad and New Delhi need to take active steps towards resolving their dispute if they are to have any hope of alleviating the threat of extremism within even their own borders, let alone the region.

The question of Iran's nuclear programme finally took a turn in late 2013 towards dialogue, compromise and negotiation. Hardline postures have produced no positive outcomes and are likely to impede the development of an effective and acceptable solution. A US–Arab–Iranian rapprochement, with the participation of regional mediators such as Turkey, is critical for all countries to move towards constructive interaction and cooperation in Iraq and the Gulf. A final nuclear deal must be part of any such package and should be approached with a view to making the region, including Israel, nuclear-free. One way to achieve a Middle East nuclear-free zone is to institute a region-wide regime of arms control that could include Israel.

As the international community drew down from Afghanistan and has moved on from Iraq, the need for ongoing support and involvement remained prominent. Even within a limited framework, outside actors have a critical role to play in these two countries if they are to emerge as viable and stable states. Instability and sectarianism will continue to breed violence and extremism, posing a threat to security both in the region and the world. International actors can positively influence these dynamics by continuing to provide support for indigenous governments while ensuring that their efforts remain pluralistic and inclusive.

What emerges as the most important lesson of this study is the interconnectedness of the West Asian region. Every political decision ripples across the landscape to surrounding nations, with destabilising effects that often create zones of conflict. Policymakers in the area must constantly balance their international and domestic constituents, especially in a region so subject to external influence and intervention. Only through a deep understanding of historical and contemporary features that fuse and divide the mosaic but strategically important constituent states of West Asia can constructive and long-term policies be designed to promote and support regional stability and security as part of building a tranquil world order. Tragically, such an understanding has so far largely eluded both the actors from inside and outside the area. No wonder the region has become a zone of perpetual tension, conflict and major power intervention more than any other part of the world in recent times.

NOTES

Chapter 1: Introduction

1 For a discussion of *jihadi* and *ijtihadi* Islamists, see Amin Saikal, *Islam and the West: Conflict or Cooperation?* London: Palgrave Macmillan, 2003, pp. 26–29.

Chapter 2: Afghanistan

1 Amin Saikal, *Modern Afghanistan: A History of Struggle and Survival* (London: I.B.Tauris, 2006), pp. 18–19.

2 For a figure of about 40 per cent in the 1990s, see Ralph H. Magnus and Eden Naby, *Afghanistan: Mullah, Marx and Mujahid* (Boulder, CO: Westview Press, 2002), p. 93, and Alfred Janata, 'Afghanistan: the ethnic dimension', in Ewan W. Anderson et al. (eds), *The Cultural Basis of Afghan Nationalism* (London: Pinter Publishers, 1990), p. 64.

3 For a detailed discussion, see Saikal, *Modern Afghanistan*, ch. 1; Magnus and Naby, *Afghanistan*, ch. 1; Louis Dupree, *Afghanistan* (Princeton, NJ: Princeton University Press, 1980), Part II; William Maley, *The Afghanistan Wars* (London: Palgrave Macmillan, 2002), ch. 1; Barnett R. Rubin, *Fragmentation of Afghanistan*, 2nd edn (New Haven, CT: Yale University Press, 2002), chs 2–3.

4 See M. Nazif Shahrani, 'State Building and Social Fragmentation in Afghanistan: A Historical Perspective', in A. Banuazizi and M. Weiner (eds), *The State, Religion, and Ethnic Politics: Afghanistan, Iran, and Pakistan* (Syracuse, NY: Syracuse University Press, 1986), pp. 23–74.

5 See Amin Saikal, 'Afghanistan's ethnic conflict', *Survival* 40/2 (1998): 115–26.

6 Declan Walsh, 'US had "frighteningly simplistic" view of Afghanistan, says McChrystal', *Guardian*, 7 October 2011.

7 For failures of US and NATO strategy, see Seth G. Jones, 'Averting failure in Afghanistan', *Survival* 48/1 (2006): 111–27; Barnett R. Rubin and Ahmed Rashid, 'From the great game to grand bargain', *Foreign Affairs* 87/6 (2008): 30–44.

8 See the comments at the time by US envoy Zalmay Khalilzad, *Afghanistan Online Press*, 15 June 2002, www.afghan-web.com/aop (accessed 10 May 2013).

9   See Amin Saikal, 'The role of sub-national actors in Afghanistan', in Klejda Mulaj (ed.), *Violent Non-State Actors in World Politics* (London: Hurst & Co., 2010), pp. 239–56.

10 Moshe Schwartz, *Department of Defense Contractors in Iraq and Afghanistan: Background and Analysis*, Congressional Research Service, 2 July 2010, p. 10.

11 Antonio Giustozzi, *Empires of Mud: War and Warlords in Afghanistan* (London: Hurst & Co., 2009), p. 91.

12 For a discussion on the prevalence of warlordism today in Afghanistan, see Roger Mac Ginty, 'Warlords and the liberal peace: state-building in Afghanistan', *Conflict, Security & Development* 10/4 (2010): 577–98. For a history of warlordism in Afghanistan, see Giustozzi, *Empires of Mud*.

13 Michael Hastings, 'The runaway general', *Rolling Stone*, 8–22 July 2010.

14 Elisabeth Bumiller, 'Pentagon says Afghan forces still need assistance', *New York Times*, 10 December 2012.

15 'NATO-backed local police terrorising Afghans', *Reuters*, 12 September 2012.

16 World Bank, *Afghanistan Economic Update*, Policy and Poverty Team – South Asia Region, April 2010, p. 2.

17 Rich Clabaugh and Ben Arnoldy, 'Can Afghanistan economy thrive without poppy?', *Christian Science Monitor*, 5 March 2010.

18 'Highlights of US–Afghanistan strategic partnership deal signed by Obama and Karzai', *Washington Post*, 1 May 2012.

19 Nicole Ball and Yoichiro Ishihara, *Afghanistan – Security Sector: Afghanistan Public Expenditure Review 2010 Working Paper* (Washington, DC: World Bank, 2010), p. 2.

20 Thom Shanker, 'General Allen testifies on Afghan troop strength', *New York Times*, 22 March 2012.

21 Steve Chapman, 'Myths of Iraq and Afghanistan: Obama and Romney falsely claim success', *Chicago Tribune*, 21 October 2012.

22 Patrick Wintour, 'Afghanistan withdrawal before 2015', *Guardian*, 26 June 2010.

23 Max Fisher, 'Afghanistan optimism at the presidential foreign policy debate', *Washington Post*, 23 October 2012.

24 Joshuah Bearman, 'George, meet George: It's time for a real Marshall Plan', *LA Weekly*, 17 October 2001.

25 Remarks by Secretary of State Colin Powell, reported in *Al Bawaba News*, 22 October 2001.

26 Bearman, 'George, meet George'.

27 International Crisis Group, *Aid and Conflict in Afghanistan*, Asia Report No. 210, 4 August 2011.

28 Dexter Filkins and Mark Mazzetti, 'Karzai aide in corruption inquiry is tied to CIA', *New York Times*, 25 August 2010.

29 Alastair Leithead, 'Donors accused of failing Afghans', *BBC News*, 25 March 2008, news.bbc.co.uk/2/hi/south_asia/7311972.stm (accessed 12 May 2013).

30 Beth Eggleston, 'The Afghan people: forgotten and frustrated', in Amin Saikal (ed.), *The Afghanistan Conflict and Australia's Role* (Melbourne: Melbourne University Press, 2011), pp. 115–29.

31 See *The Afghanistan Compact*, The London Conference on Afghanistan, 31 January–1 February 2006.

32   See 'Declaration of the International Conference in Support of Afghanistan', Paris Conference on Afghanistan, 12 June 2008.

33   The core budget is the government's budget system. The external budget is expenditures independent of and outside the government's fiscal control. See World Bank, *Afghanistan Public Expenditure Review 2010: Second Generation of Public Expenditure Reforms*.

34   For an evaluation of US foreign assistance to Afghanistan, see US Committee on Foreign Relations, *Evaluating US Foreign Assistance to Afghanistan*, United States Senate, 8 June 2011.

35   World Bank, *Afghanistan Economic Update*, p. 6; World Bank, *Afghanistan Public Expenditure Review 2010*, p. iii.

36   Pamela Constable, 'A weary Afghanistan sighs at Obama's second term', *Washington Post*, 7 November 2012.

37   Curt Tarnoff, *Afghanistan: U.S. Foreign Assistance*, Congressional Research Service, 12 August 2010, p. 12.

38   Jude Howell, 'The global war on terror, development and civil society', *Journal of International Development* 18/1 (2006): 126.

39   Ibid., p. 129.

40   Eggleston, 'The Afghan people'.

41   William Maley, *Rescuing Afghanistan* (Sydney: University of New South Wales Press, 2006), p. 54.

42   UNODC (United Nations Office on Drugs and Crime), *Corruption in Afghanistan: Bribery as Reported by the Victims*, UNODC Statistics and Surveys Section, January 2010, p. 5, www.unodc.org/unodc/en/data-and-analysis/statistics/surveys. html (accessed 13 May 2013).

43   Rhoda Margesson, *United Nations Assistance Mission in Afghanistan: Background and Policy Issues*, Congressional Research Service, 14 December 2009.

44   For more information on recent political and social changes, see World Bank, *Afghanistan Economic Update*, and Jon Boone, 'Hamid Karzai takes control of Afghanistan election watchdog', *Guardian*, 22 February 2010.

45   See UNHCR, 2013 UNHCR Country Operations Profile – Afghanistan, www. unhcr.org/cgi-bin/texis/vtx/page?page=49e486eb6 (accessed 10 July 2013).

46   Eggleston, 'The Afghan people'.

47   Donn Bobb, 'Funding shortfalls undermine fragile gains made in Afghanistan: Ging', United Nations Radio, 6 June 2012.

48   James Gerstenzang and Lisa Getter, 'Laura Bush addresses state of Afghan women', *Los Angeles Times*, 18 November 2001.

49   Thomas Carothers, *Aiding Democracy Abroad: The Learning Curve* (Washington, DC: Carnegie Endowment for International Peace, 1999), pp. 211–15.

50   Amnesty International, *Afghanistan: Women's Human Rights Defenders Continue to Struggle for Women's Rights*, 7 March 2008, www.amnesty.org/en/ library/asset/ASA11/003/2008/en/ASA110032008en.html (accessed 7 January 2013). See also Virginia Haussegger, 'Gender and social justice in Afghanistan', in Amin Saikal (ed.), *The Afghanistan Conflict and Australia's Role* (Melbourne: Melbourne University Press, 2011), pp. 129–54.

51   Diya Nijhowne and Lauren Oates, 'Living with Violence: A National Report on Domestic Abuse in Afghanistan', PLACE?: Global Rights: Partners for Justice, March 2008.

52   'More women jailed for "moral crimes", says HRW', *BBC News*, 21 May 2013.

53   'Afghan parliament halts debate on women's rights law', *BBC News*, 18 May 2013.

54   Heidi Vogt, 'Karzai backs strict guidelines for Afghan women', *Washington Times*, 6 March 2012.

55   See Amin Saikal and William Maley, 'The president who would be king', *New York Times*, 6 February 2008.

56   See Carlotta Gall, 'New Afghan constitution juggles Koran and democracy', *New York Times*, 19 October 2003; Victoria Burnett, 'Afghan constitution ready for public debate: draft would establish an Islamic republic', *Boston Globe*, 2 October 2003.

57   In order: the Islamic Society of Afghanistan, the National Islamic Movement, the National Alliance Party and the National Unity Movement.

58   See International Crisis Group, *Afghanistan: The Constitutional Loya Jirga*, Asia Briefing No. 29, 12 December 2003.

59   Barnett R. Rubin, 'Crafting a constitution for Afghanistan', *Journal of Democracy* 15/3 (2004): 4.

60   For details, see Maley, *Rescuing Afghanistan*, pp. 48–49.

61   Andrew Reynolds, 'The curious case of Afghanistan', *Journal of Democracy* 17/2 (2006): 114. See also Hamish Nixon and Richard Ponzio, 'Building democracy in Afghanistan: the statebuilding agenda and international engagement', *International Peacekeeping* 14/1 (2007): 26–40.

62   M. Hussain, 'Afghanistan parliamentary elections, immmunity and prosecution of parliamentarians', *Heinrich Böll Stiftung*, 27 March 2011, www.boell-afghanistan.org/web/52-323/html (accessed 10 January 2013).

63   For a discussion of the 2010 parliamentary elections, see International Crisis Group, *Afghanistan's Elections Stalemate*, Asia Briefing No. 117, 23 February 2011.

64   'September election has distanced people from govt. study', *TOLOnews*, 23 March 2011.

65   Alissa J. Rubin and Abdul Waheed Wafa, 'Karzai annuls Afghan court reviewing 2010 polls', *New York Times*, 8 October 2011.

66   For allegations of corruption on the part of some members of Karzai's family, see James Risen, 'Reports link Karzai's brother to heroin trade', *New York Times*, 4 October 2008.

67   For the status of Shah Shuja, see Amin Saikal, *Modern Afghanistan: A History of Struggle and Survival* , 2nd edn (London: I.B.Tauris, 2012), pp. 32–34.

68   For details, see Ahmed Rashid, *Taliban, Militant Islam, Oil and Fundamentalism in Central Asia* (London: I.B.Tauris, 2000).

69   See Michael Hughes, 'Afghan in exile: taking a stand against the Karzai cartel', *Huffington Post*, 12 May 2011.

70   James Risen, 'Intrigue in Karzai family as an Afghan era closes', *New York Times*, 3 June 2012.

71   For evidence of fraud, see Ghaith Abdul-Ahad, 'New evidence of widespread fraud in Afghanistan election uncovered', *Guardian*, 19 September 2009.

72   Following this ECC decision, Karzai moved toward substantially curtailing its independence. See 'Afghanistan: President Karzai modifying election law in his favor', interview with Grant Kippen, *EurasiaNet*, 4 March 2010, www.unhcr.org/refworld/docid/4b966e768.html (accessed 15 July 2013).

73   'Obama breaks up with Karzai? US considers total Afghanistan pullout', *Reuters*, 9 July 2013.

74   See Alissa J. Rubin, 'Afghan leader forces out top 2 security officials', *New York Times*, 6 June 2010.

75   'Wikileaks cables say Afghan President Karzai "paranoid"', *BBC News*, 3 December 2010.

76   Gregg Carlstrom, 'Afghanistan's governance problem: new US research concludes corruption and inefficiency still hallmarks of Afghan state', *Al Jazeera*, 13 May 2010, english.aljazeera.net/focus/2010/05/2010513105357535985.html (accessed 12 May 2013).

77   See Quentin Sommerville, 'Afghan corruption has doubled since 2007, survey says', *BBC News*, 8 July 2010.

78   UNODC, *Corruption in Afghanistan*, p. 10.

79   Ibid., pp. 4–5.

80   Ibid., p. 9.

81   See World Bank, *Afghanistan Economic Update*.

82   UNODC, *Corruption in Afghanistan*, p. 4.

83   World Bank, *Afghanistan Public Expenditure Review 2010: Second Generation of Public Expenditure Reforms*, Report No. 53892-AF, in consultation with the UK Department for International Development, April 2010, p. 4.

84   Many bribes demanded exceed US$1,000, which is double the average Afghan annual salary. See UNODC, *Corruption in Afghanistan*, p. 5.

85   Rod Nordland and Dexter Filkins, 'Antigraft units, backed by US, draw Karzai's ire', *New York Times*, 6 August 2010.

86   Filkins and Mazzetti, 'Karzai aide in corruption inquiry is tied to CIA'.

87   *Agence France Presse*, 13 December 2013.

88   Indeed, this estimate has been questioned by geologists and mining experts who argue that it was based on old and possibly Soviet-era data. See Tom A. Peter, 'What could $1 trillion in mineral wealth mean for Afghanistan?', *Christian Science Monitor*, 14 June 2010.

89   'Karzai: Japan gets priority in Afghan mining', *msnbc.com*, 20 June 2010, www.msnbc.msn.com/id/37803781 (accessed 16 July 2013).

90   Jeremy Page and Michael Evans, 'Taleban zone's mineral riches may rival Saudi Arabia, says Pentagon', *The Times*, 15 June 2010.

91   Clabaugh and Arnoldy, 'Can Afghanistan economy thrive without poppy?'

92   Ron Synovitz, 'Afghanistan: China's winning bid for copper rights includes power plant, railroad', *Radio Free Europe/Radio Liberty*, 24 November 2007, www.rferl.org/content/article/1079190.html (accessed 10 July 2013).

93   Devon Maylie, 'Weak response likely for Afghan minerals auction', *Wall Street Journal*, 28 July 2010.

94   For a discussion of 'rentierism' and the resource curse, see Michael Herb, 'No representation without taxation? Rents, development, and democracy', *Comparative Politics* 37/3 (2005): 297–316.

95   Rod Nordland, 'Production of opium by Afghans is up again', *New York Times*, 15 April 2013.

96   Ben Farmer, 'Opium crop in Afghanistan heading for records levels', *The Telegraph*, 15 April 2013.

97 Ibid.
98 See Barnett R. Rubin and Jake Sherman, *Counter-Narcotics to Stabilise Afghanistan: The False Promise of Crop Eradication*, Center on International Cooperation, New York University, February 2008. For an optimistic view of the situation, see Joanna Wright, 'Poppy purge – Afghanistan's acting minister of counter-narcotics General Khodaidad', *Jane's Intelligence Review* 20/2 (2008): 58.
99 UNODC (United Nations Office on Drugs and Crime), *Afghanistan Opium Risk Assessment 2013*, April 2013, pp. 1–2.
100 UNODC, *Drug Use in Afghanistan: 2009 Survey: Executive Summary*, pp. 5–6, www.unodc.org/unodc/en/frontpage/2010/June/around-one-million-afghans-suffer-from-drug-addiction-unodc-survey-shows.html (accessed 15 July 2013).
101 See Meena Singh Roy, 'Role of the Shanghai Cooperation Organisation in Afghanistan: scope and limitations', *Strategic Analysis* 34/4 (2010): 545–61.
102 Ted G. Carpenter, 'Afghanistan's drug problem', *The National Interest*, 5 December 2008, nationalinterest.org/article/afghanistans-drug-problem-2936.
103 Thomas Schweich, 'Is Afghanistan a narco-state?', *International Herald Tribune*, 24 July 2008.
104 Ibid.
105 William Maley, 'Reconstruction: a critical assessment', in Amin Saikal (ed.), *The Afghanistan Conflict and Australia's Role* (Melbourne: Melbourne University Press, 2011), pp. 77–98.
106 For more on counter-narcotics strategies in Afghanistan, see Schweich, 'Is Afghanistan a narco-state?'
107 See Vanda Felbab-Brown: 'Peacekeepers among poppies: Afghanistan, illicit economies and intervention', *International Peacekeeping* 16/1 (2009): 100–14.
108 Carlstrom: 'Afghanistan's governance problem'.
109 Matt Robinson, 'Targeted civilian killings spiral in Afghan war: UN', *Reuters*, 9 March 2011.
110 See Joshua Partlow, 'Karzai to seek Obama's approval for peace deals with insurgents', *Washington Post*, 3 May 2010.
111 William Maley, 'Afghanistan in 2010', *Asian Survey* 51/1 (2011): 85–96 at p. 87.
112 Ben Farmer, 'Taliban diplomats arrive in Qatar', *The Telegraph*, 26 January 2012.
113 'Obama issues apology for Quran burning as Taliban calls for revenge killings', *Al Arabiya*, 23 February 2012.
114 'Afghanistan's Taliban suspend peace talks with US', *BBC News*, 15 March 2012.
115 *Daily Outlook Afghanistan*, 1 January 2013.
116 'Taliban reject Afghan elections, vow to fight until troops leave', *Reuters*, 6 August 2013.
117 *New York Times*, 2 July 2013.
118 Synovitz, 'Afghanistan: China's winning bid'.
119 'China, Afghanistan forge closer economic ties as new agreements are signed', *People's Daily*, 24 March 2010.
120 For a detailed discussion, see Jeffrey Mankoff, *Russian Foreign Policy: The Return of Great Power Politics* (Lanham, MD: Rowman & Littlefield, 2009).
121 S. G. Luzianin, *Vostochnaya Politika Vladimira Putina* (Moscow: Vostok-Zapad, 2007), p. 143.

122 See Harsh V. Pant, 'India in Afghanistan: a test case for a rising power', *Contemporary South Asia* 18/2 (2010): 133–53.

123 *Development Cooperation Report*, Islamic Republic of Afghanistan, 2010, p. 95.

124 Eltaf Najafizada, 'Indian group wins rights to mine in Afghanistan's Hajigak', *Businessweek*, 6 December 2011.

125 See Manu Pubby, 'How ISI paid Taliban to hit Indians in Kabul', *Indian Express*, 27 July 2010.

126 Roy, 'Role of the Shanghai Cooperation Organisation in Afghanistan'.

127 See Amin Saikal, 'Afghanistan's attitudes towards the region', in Aglaya Snetkov and Aris Steven (eds), *The Regional Dimension to Security in Afghanistan: Other Sides of Afghanistan* (London: Palgrave Macmillan, 2013).

128 Pant, 'India in Afghanistan'.

129 See Thomas Barfield and Neamatollah Nojumi, 'Bringing more effective governance to Afghanistan: 10 pathways to stability', *Middle East Policy* 17/4 (2010): 40–52; M. Nazif Shahrani, *Afghanistan's Alternatives for Peace, Governance and Development: Transforming Subjects to Citizens and Rulers to Civil Servants*, Afghanistan Papers No. 2 (Waterloo, Canada: CIGI & CIPS joint publication, 2009).

130 See Chris Johnson and Jolyon Leslie, *Afghanistan: The Mirage of Peace* (London: Zed Books, 2008), ch. 5.

131 UNODC, *The Global Afghan Opium Trade: A Threat Assessment*, July 2011, p. 30.

132 Clabaugh and Arnoldy, 'Can Afghanistan economy thrive without poppy?'.

133 World Bank, *Afghanistan Economic Update*, pp. 3–5.

Chapter 3: Pakistan

1   Pervez Musharraf, *In the Line of Fire* (London: Simon & Schuster, 2006), p. 201.

2   'Fatalities in terrorist violence in Pakistan 2003–2012', *South Asia Terrorism Portal*, www.satp.org/satporgtp/countries/pakistan/database/casualties.htm (accessed 27 June 2013).

3   Lawrence Wright, 'The double game: The unintended consequences of American funding in Pakistan', *The New Yorker*, 16 May 2011.

4   'Fatalities in terrorist violence in Pakistan 2003–2012', *South Asia Terrorism Portal*.

5   Zaheerul Hassan, 'Repercussions of Osama bin Laden killing', *Asian Tribune*, 8 May 2011.

6   Wasif Khan, 'Pakistan's looming crises: Increasing population, dwindling resources', *The Dawn*, 27 September 2012.

7   Abdul Sattar Khan, 'Population shoots up by 47 per cent since 1998', *The News*, 29 March 2012.

8   Christophe Jaffrelot (ed.), *A History of Pakistan and its Origins*, trans. Gillian Beaumont (London: Anthem Press, 2004), p. 253.

9   Ibid.

10   Simon Rogers, 'Muslim populations by country: how big will each Muslim population be by 2030?', *Guardian*, 28 January 2011.

11   Andrew Wilder, 'The politics of civil service reform in Pakistan', *Journal of International Affairs* 63/1 (2009): 29. For an overview of the nationalist

insurgency against the Pakistani state, see also Owen Bennett Jones, *Pakistan: Eye of the Storm* (New Haven, CT: Yale University Press, 2009), pp. 63–73.

12   R. S. N. Singh, *The Military Factor in Pakistan* (New Delhi: Lancer, 2008), p. 190.

13   Kamal Hyder, 'More trouble along the Afghan border', *Al Jazeera*, 20 August 2012.

14   For a discussion on the partition, see Joya Chatterji, *The Spoils of Partition: Bengal and India, 1947–1967* (Cambridge: Cambridge University Press, 2007), and Yasmin Khan, *The Great Partition: The Making of India and Pakistan* (New Haven, CT: Yale University Press, 2007).

15   Khan, *The Great Partition*.

16   See Tai Yong Tan and Gyanesh Kudaisya, *The Aftermath of the Partition in South Asia* (London: Routledge, 2000), ch. 6.

17   For more on the conflict in Kashmir, see Victoria Schofield, *Kashmir in Conflict* (London: I.B.Tauris, 2003).

18   For more on the evolution of Bengali nationalism, and the 1971 war, see Badruddin Umar, *The Emergence of Bangladesh* (Oxford: Oxford University Press, 2006).

19   Hassan Abbas, *Pakistan's Drift into Extremism: Allah, the Army, and America's War on Terror* (New York: East Gate, 2005), p. 94.

20   Hasan Askari Rizvi, 'Democracy in Pakistan', *A Future for Democracy (Panorama: Insights into Asian and European Affairs)*, Occasional Papers (Singapore: Konrad-Adenauer-Stiftung, 2011), p. 131.

21   Vali Nasr, 'Military rule, Islamism and democracy in Pakistan', *Middle East Journal* 58/2 (2004): 196.

22   For a discussion on the 'Islamisation' and militarisation of Pakistan, see Afzal Iqbal, *Islamization of Pakistan* (Lahore: Vanguard Books, 1986); Abbas, *Pakistan's Drift into Extremism*; and Lawrence Ziring, 'From Islamic republic to Islamic state in Pakistan', *Asian Survey* 24/9 (1984): 931–46.

23   Sharif Shuja, 'Pakistan: Islam, radicalism and the army', *International Journal on World Peace* 24/2 (2007): 29.

24   For a detailed discussion, see Stephen Cohen, *The Idea of Pakistan* (Washington, DC: Brookings Institution Press, 2004), ch. 5.

25   Nasr, 'Military rule, Islamism and democracy in Pakistan', pp. 197–98.

26   William Maley, *The Afghanistan Wars* (London: Palgrave Macmillan, 2002), ch. 10.

27   Nasr, 'Military rule, Islamism and democracy in Pakistan', p. 199.

28   See Bennett Jones, *Pakistan: Eye of the Storm*.

29   See Ryan Clarke, 'Lashkar-e-Taiba: Roots, logistics, partnerships, and the fallacy of subservient proxies', *Terrorism and Political Violence* 22/3 (2010): 394–417.

30   Rizvi, 'Democracy in Pakistan', p. 128.

31   For background analysis, see Mary A.Weaver, *Pakistan: In the Shadow of Jihad and Afghanistan* (New York: Farrar, Straus and Giroux, 2003), ch. 1.

32   'Pakistan's National Assembly passes key constitutional reforms', *Sunday Telegraph*, 8 April 2010; 'Pakistan politics: Power shift', EIU ViewsWire, Economic Intelligence Unit, 9 April 2010.

33   Ahmed Rashid, 'Increasingly isolated, Karzai turns to Pakistan', *The Spectator*, 31 July 2010.

34   'Zaheerul Islam succeeds Pasha as ISI chief', *Associated Press*, 10 March 2012.

35   Zeeshan Haider, 'Analysis – Pakistan's Gilani walks a political tight-rope', *Reuters*, 12 July 2010.

36   Issam Ahmed, 'Pakistan extends term of army chief amid applause – and doubt', *Christian Science Monitor*, 23 July 2010.

37   Policy Research Group, *Future Uncertain for Zardari, Bright for Gilani*, 2 February 2010, policyresearchgroup.com/terror_updates/pakistan_terror_updates/553.html (accessed 13 May 2013).

38   Waseem Ahmad Shah, 'General Kayani's statement continues to make waves', *The Dawn*, 12 November 2012.

39   'Pakistan Supreme Court bars Gilani from office', *BBC News*, 19 June 2012, www.bbc.co.uk/news/world-asia-18506728 (accessed 12 May 2013).

40   See Massoud Ansari, 'The militarisation of Pakistan', *Newsline*, 15 October 2004, www.newslinemagazine.com/2004/10/the-militarisation-of-pakistan (accessed 27 June 2013).

41   Mohammad Mohabbat Khan, 'Resistance to administrative reform in South Asian civil bureaucracies', in Ali Farazmand (ed.), *Administrative Reforms in Developing Nations* (Westport, CT: Greenwood, 2002), p. 80.

42   Craig Baxter, 'Historical setting', in Peter R. Blood (ed.), *Pakistan: A Country Study* (Washington, DC: Federal Research Division, 1995), p. 62.

43   Wilder, 'The politics of civil service reform in Pakistan', p. 22.

44   Sohail Khan, 'Civil servants shouldn't act as govt slaves: SC', *News International*, 13 November 2012, www.thenews.com.pk/Todays-News-13-18794-Civil-servants-shouldnt-act-as-govt-slaves-SC (accessed 12 May 2013).

45   Nasir Islam, '*Sifarish*, sycophants, power and collectivism: Administrative culture in Pakistan', *International Review of Administrative Sciences* 70/2 (2004): 316.

46   United Nations Development Programme, *Pakistan National Report: Social Audit of Local Governance and Delivery of Public Services* (Islamabad: UNDP Pakistan, 2010), pp. 14–15.

47   Wajahat S. Khan, 'Sharif to hold Pakistan's top job for third time as voters defy Taliban threats', *NBC News*, worldnews.nbcnews.com/_news/2013/05/13/18222427-sharif-to-hold-pakistans-top-job-for-third-time-as-voters-defy-taliban-threats?lite (accessed 15 July 2013).

48   Wilder, 'The politics of civil service reform in Pakistan', p. 20.

49   See Hamza Alavi (ed.), *Sociology of Developing Countries: South Asia* (New York: Monthly Review Press, 1989); Islam, '*Sifarish*, sycophants, power and collectivism', p. 322.

50   Islam, '*Sifarish*, sycophants, power and collectivism', p. 323.

51   Sabrina Tavernise, 'Upstarts chip away at power of Pakistani elite', *New York Times*, 28 August 2010.

52   For Bhutto family corruption, see John F. Burns, 'House of graft: Tracing the Bhutto millions: A special report; Bhutto clan leaves trail of corruption', *New York Times*, 9 January 1998.

53   In an ironic twist, the Swiss agency bribed the Bhutto family in order to win this contract. See Burns, 'House of graft'.

54   See Islam, '*Sifarish*, sycophants, power and collectivism'.

55   Wilder, 'The politics of civil service reform in Pakistan', p. 26.

56   Islam, '*Sifarish*, sycophants, power and collectivism', pp. 315–16.

57   Wilder, 'The politics of civil service reform in Pakistan', p. 30.

58   United Nations Development Programme, *Pakistan National Report*, p. 7.

59   'Hard-line Islam fills void in flooded Pakistan', *New York Times*, 6 August 2010.

60   International Monetary Fund, www.imf.org/external/pubs/ft/weo/2006/01/ data/dbcoutm.cfm?SD=1997&ED=2001&R1=1&R2=1&CS=3&SS=2&OS=C &DD=0&OUT=1&C=564&S=NGDP_RPCH-NGDP_R&CMP=0&x=57&y=7 (accessed 26 June 2013).

61   Pakistan Government, *Accelerating Economic Growth and Reducing Poverty: The Road Ahead (Poverty Reduction Strategy Paper)* (Islamabad: PRSP Secretariat and Pakistan Ministry of Finance, 2003), p. 1.

62   Nathaniel Heller et al., *Pakistan's $4.2 Billion 'Blank Check' for US Military Aid*, The Center for Public Integrity, 27 March 2007, www.publicintegrity.org/news/ entry/218 (accessed 26 June 2013).

63   Susan B. Epstein and K. Alan Kronstadt, 'Pakistan: US foreign assistance', *Congressional Research Service*, 4 October 2012.

64   K. Alan Kronstadt, 'Direct overt US aid and military reimbursements to Pakistan', FY2002-FY2012, *Congressional Research Service*, 6 May 2011.

65   See Pakistan Government, *Accelerating Economic Growth and Reducing Poverty*.

66   Imran Ali Kundi, 'Trade deficit widens by 36 per cent', *The Nation*, 11 July 2012.

67   Erum Zaidi, 'Current account deficit touches $4.517 billion in FY12', *The News*, 18 July 2012.

68   Ismat Sabir, 'Pakistan sinking in debt', *Daily Times*, 4 August 2010.

69   Pakistan Government, *Accelerating Economic Growth and Reducing Poverty*, p. 21. For a detailed background analysis, see Jaffrelot, *A History of Pakistan and Its Origins*, ch. 8; Syed Mubashir Ali and Faisal Bari, 'At the millennium: Macro economic performance and prospects', in Charles H. Kennedy and Craig Baxter (eds), *Pakistan 2000* (New York: Lexington Books, 2000), pp. 25–44; Sabir, 'Pakistan sinking in debt'.

70   Jones, *Pakistan: Eye of the Storm*, p. 271.

71   Qaiser Butt, 'Health and education: Pakistan aims high but wouldn't pay for the flight', *Express Tribune*, 15 November 2012.

72   United Nations Development Programme, *Pakistan National Report*, p. 3.

73   World Bank, 'Pakistan at a glance', 12 September 2009, devdata.worldbank.org/ AAG/pak_aag.pdf (accessed 15 July 2013); 'Pakistan balance of trade', *Trading Economics*, and Shahid Iqbal, 'Economy may face more jolts in 2012', *The Dawn*, 1 January 2012, www.dawn.com/2012/01/01/economy-may-face-more- jolts-in-2012.html (accessed 10 September 2012).

74   Paul Jonathan Martin, *Pakistan Strategic Country Environmental Assessment* (Washington, DC: World Bank, 2007), p. 61, www.environment.gov.pk/new- pdf/PK-SCE-FText-Oct-2006%20.pdf (accessed 15 July 2013). See also Asian Development Bank, *Islamic Republic of Pakistan: Country Environment Analysis*, December 2008, www.adb.org/documents/assessments/country-environmental/ pak/country-environment-analysis.pdf (accessed 15 July 2013).

75   Cathy Alexander, 'Freeze Pakistan's debt: UN summit', *Sydney Morning Herald*, 1 September 2010.

76   For a shift in Pakistan's 'army doctrine', see *The Nation*, 3 January 2013.

77   See Vipin Narang, 'Posturing for peace? Pakistan's nuclear postures and South Asian stability', *International Security* 34/3 (2009/2010): 38–78.

78   Andrew Small, 'China's caution on Afghanistan–Pakistan', *Washington Quarterly* 33/3 (2010): 81–97.

79   Amin Saikal, *The Rise and Fall of the Shah: Iran from Autocracy to Religious Rule*, p. 165.

80   For background, see Amin Saikal, *The Rise and Fall of the Shah* (Princeton, NJ: Princeton University Press, 1980), part II.

81   Amin Saikal, 'The role of outside actors in Afghanistan', *Middle East Policy* 7/4 (2000): 50–57.

82   Musharraf, *In the Line of Fire*, p. 19.

83   Peter Tomsen, *The Wars of Afghanistan: Messianic Terrorism, Tribal Conflicts, and the Failures of Great Powers* (New York: Perseus, 2011), pp. 591–95.

84   C. Christine Fair, *The Counterterror Coalitions: Cooperation with Pakistan and India* (Santa Monica, CA: Rand Corporation, 2004), pp. 17–21.

85   For instance, Islamabad hosted the third Regional Economic Cooperation Conference on Afghanistan in May 2009.

86   See Amin Saikal, 'Musharraf and Pakistan's crisis', in Rajshree Jetly (ed.), *Pakistan in Regional and Global Politics* (New Delhi: Routledge, 2009), pp. 1–19.

87   'A conversation with Pervez Musharraf', Transcript, Council on Foreign Relations, New York, 25 September 2006, www.cfr.org/publication/11540/conversation_with_pervez_musharraf_rush_transcript_federal_news_service.html (accessed 25 June 2013).

88   Rashid, 'Increasingly isolated'.

89   Najam Sethi, 'The road to Kabul runs through Islamabad', *Wall Street Journal*, 30 June 2010.

90   Carin Zissis, 'Judgment time for Musharraf', Analysis Brief, Council on Foreign Relations, 19 March 2007, www.cfr.org/publication/12890/judgment_time_for_musharraf.html (accessed 13 May 2013).

91   Carlotta Gall, 'Ragtag Taliban show tenacity in Afghanistan', *New York Times*, 4 August 2008.

92   See Matt Waldman, *The Sun in the Sky: The Relationship Between Pakistan's ISI and Afghan Insurgents*, Discussion Paper 18 (London: Crisis States Research Centre, London School of Economics, 2010).

93   See 'Pakistan: Islamabad picks its enemies in FATA', Country Report, OxResearch Daily Brief Service (Oxford: Analytica, 2010).

94   Greg Miller, 'US officials say Pakistani spy agency released Afghan Taliban insurgents', *Washington Post*, 10 April 2010.

95   See Ron Moreau, 'With friends like these …', *Newsweek*, 9 August 2010.

96   Anthony D. Smith, *The Nation in History: Historiographical Debates about Ethnicity and Nationalism* (Hanover, NH: University Press of New England, 2000), p. 65.

97   Louis Dupree, *Afghanistan* (Princeton, NJ: Princeton University Press, 1980), pp. 126–27.

98   Arnold Fletcher, *Afghanistan: Highway of Conquest* (Westport, CT: Greenwood Press, 1982), pp. 20–21.

99   'Afghanistan', *The World Factbook*, Central Intelligence Agency, https://www.cia.gov/library/publications/the-world-factbook/geos/af.html (accessed 12 May 2013).

100   'Pakistan', *The World Factbook*, Central Intelligence Agency, https://www.cia.gov/library/publications/the-world-factbook/geos/pk.html (accessed 12 May 2013).

101 OxResearch Daily Brief Service, 'Pakistan: Violence stalks renamed Khyber-Pakhtunkhwa', Country Report (Oxford: Analytica, 2010).
102 Robert D. Crews and Amin Tarzi, 'Introduction', in Robert D. Crews and Amin Tarzi (eds), *The Taliban and the Crisis of Afghanistan* (Cambridge, MA: Harvard University Press, 2008), pp. 1–58, at pp. 29–32.
103 Nasr, 'Military rule, Islamism and democracy in Pakistan', p. 205.
104 See Nasreen Ghufran, 'Pushtun ethnonationalism and the Taliban insurgency in the North West Frontier Province of Pakistan', *Asian Survey* 49/6 (2009): 1092–114; Nasr, 'Military rule, Islamism and democracy in Pakistan', p. 205.
105 See Ghufran, 'Pushtun ethnonationalism', p. 1107.
106 Ibid.
107 'Afghan–Pakistan border clashes probed', *BBC News*, 29 July 2003.
108 'Pakistan lodges protest with Afghan envoy over cross border shelling', *The Dawn*, 12 November 2012.
109 Hamid Shalizi, 'Afghanistan's Karzai accepts dismissal of top security leaders', *Reuters*, 5 August 2012.
110 Scott Atran, 'A question of honour: Why the Taliban fight and what to do about it', *Asian Journal of Social Sciences* 38 (2010): 351.
111 Ibid., p. 362.
112 Ibid., p. 355.
113 See Bennett Jones, *Pakistan: Eye of the Storm*.
114 Ghufran, 'Pushtun ethnonationalism', p. 1103.
115 Karin Brulliard, 'Pakistan conflicted over fighting extremists in its heartland; groups with terrorist ties sometimes have support from officials', *Washington Post*, 22 June 2010.
116 'Asia: Into the heartland; The Punjabi Taliban', *Economist* 395/8685 (5 June 2010): 50.
117 'Pakistan suicide bomber kills 43 in Shia parade backing Palestinians', *Guardian*, 3 September 2010.
118 Anatol Lieven, *Pakistan: A Hard Country* (London: Penguin Books, 2011), pp. 329–38.
119 See ibid., ch. 9.
120 Narang, 'Posturing for peace?', pp. 38–78.
121 See International Institute for Strategic Studies, 'Northern route eases supplies to US forces in Afghanistan', *Strategic Comments* 16 (August 2010), www.iiss.org/publications/strategic-comments/past-issues/volume-16-2010/august/northern-route-eases-supplies-to-us-forces-in-afghanistan (accessed 9 January 2013).
122 World Bank, *North-West Frontier Province Public Financial Management Assessment*, May 2007, http://siteresources.worldbank.org/SOUTHASIAEXT/rces/223546-1192413140459/4281804-1209417227555/4945415-1209417263990/NWFP.pdf (accessed 12 May 2013).
123 Simon Cameron-Moore, 'US aims to turn hostile Pakistan tribes friendly', *Reuters*, 30 January 2008.
124 Harrison, *Pakistan*, p. 19.
125 C. Christine Fair, 'Why the Pakistan army is here to stay: Prospects for civilian governance', *International Affairs* 87/3 (2011): 575.
126 See Small, 'China's caution on Afghanistan–Pakistan'.

127   Islam, *'Sifarish*, sycophants, power and collectivism', p. 318.
128   Rajiv Chandrasekaran, 'Neighboring nations wary of thaw in Afghan–Pakistan relations', *Washington Post*, 25 July 2010.
129   See Wilder, 'The politics of civil service reform in Pakistan', pp. 19–37.
130   Ben Doherty, 'Angry Pakistan goes to UN over air strike', *Sydney Morning Herald*, 30 November 2011.
131   Ramesh Thakur, 'Death from above', *Ottawa Citizen*, 17 November 2012.
132   The former head of the ISI, Ahmed Shuja Pasha (2008–12), admitted to an understanding with the US over the drone attacks in leaked comments reported in *The Dawn*, 9 July 2013.
133   Mustapha Ajbaili, 'Pakistan's Imran Khan: A rising national hero or hypocrite?', *Al-Arabiya*, 2 November 2012, english.alarabiya.net/articles/2012/11/02/247315.html [Accessed 12 May 2013].
134   Ahmed Rashid, 'Can Pakistan make peace next door?', *New York Times*, 5 June 2013.
135   Sikander Shaheen, 'UN ranks Pakistan 145 out of 187 in human development', *The Nation*, 30 November 2011.

Chapter 4: Iran

1   *Ijtihadi* Islamists are those who creatively interpret and apply Islam as an ideology of political and social transformation based on independent human reasoning according to the changing times and conditions. For a discussion of the *jihadi* and *ijtihadi* concepts, as used in this book, see Amin Saikal, *Islam and the West: Conflict or Cooperation?* (London: Palgrave Macmillan, 2003), pp. 26–29.
2   Eliz Sanasarian, *Religious Minorities in Iran* (Cambridge: Cambridge University Press, 2000), p. 53.
3   For a detailed discussion of Iran under the Shah, see Amin Saikal, *The Rise and Fall of the Shah: Iran from Autocracy to Religious Rule*, 2nd edn (Princeton, NJ: Princeton University Press, 2009).
4   For a detailed discussion, see Stephen Kinzer, *All the Shah's Men: An American Coup and the Roots of Middle East Terror* (New York: John Wiley & Sons, 2003).
5   For the Shah's perspective on the White Revolution, see Mohammad Reza Shah Pahlavi, *Answer to History* (Toronto: Irwin & Co., 1980), ch. 9.
6   Marvin Zonis, *The Political Elite of Iran* (Princeton, NJ: Princeton University Press, 1971), p. 13.
7   For a comprehensive discussion of the Shah's accelerated modernisation programme, see Saikal, *The Rise and Fall of the Shah*, part two.
8   For a discussion of Khomeini's early views, see Ervand Abrahamian, *Khomeinism: Essays on the Islamic Republic* (London: I.B.Taurus, 1993).
9   Ruhollah Khomeyni, *Islamic Government* (Springfield, VA: National Technical Information Service, 1979).
10   'Iran sword of a relentless revolution', *Time*, 12 June 1989; for different figures, see Shaul Bakhash, *The Reign of the Ayatollahs: Iran and the Islamic Revolution* (London: I.B.Tauris, 1985), pp. 59–64.
11   See Elaine Sciolino, 'Montazari, Khomeini's designated successor in Iran, quits under pressure', *New York Times*, 29 March 1989.

12   Odd Arne Westad, *The Global Cold War* (Cambridge: Cambridge University Press, 2005), p. 298.

13   Saikal, *Islam and the West: Conflict or Cooperation?*, pp. 69–88.

14   See Augustus Richard Norton, *Hezbollah: A Short History* (Princeton, NJ: Princeton University Press, 2007).

15   For a detailed discussion, see David Farber, *Taken Hostage: The Iran Hostage Crisis and America's First Encounter with Radical Islam* (Princeton, NJ: Princeton University Press, 2005).

16   For a discussion on the Iran–Iraq War, see Dilip Hiro, *The Longest War: The Iran–Iraq Military Conflict* (London: Grafton, 1989); Efraim Karsh, *The Iran–Iraq War: 1980–1988* (Oxford: Osprey Publishing, 2002).

17   For an example of American far-right support for Saddam, see Daniel Pipes and Laurie Mylroie, 'Back Iraq: It's time for a US "tilt"', *New Republic*, 27 April 1987, pp. 14–15.

18   For a detailed discussion, see Amin Saikal, 'Democracy and peace in Iran and Iraq', in Amin Saikal et al. (eds), *Democratization in the Middle East: Experiences, Struggles, Challenges* (New York: United Nations University Press, 2003), pp. 166–82.

19   See International Crisis Group, *Iran: The Struggle for the Revolution's Soul*, Middle East Report No. 5, 5 August 2002, pp. 16–19.

20   For a discussion of Saroush's early writings, see Ali Mirsepassi, *Democracy in Modern Iran: Islam, Culture, and Political Change* (New York: New York University Press, 2010), pp. 87–90.

21   For a discussion of reformism in Iran, see Shireen T. Hunter, 'Islamic reformist discourse in Iran', in Shireen T. Hunter (ed.), *Reformist Voices of Islam* (New York: M.E. Sharpe, 2009), pp. 33–97.

22   See Ray Takeyh, *Hidden Iran: Paradox and Power in the Islamic Republic* (New York: Times Books, 2006), ch. 1.

23   Ali M. Ansari, 'Chapter 1: The Rafsanjani and Khatami presidencies', *Adelphi Papers* 47/393 (London: International Institute for Strategic Studies, 2007), pp. 11–22, at p. 16.

24   Mohammad Khatami, *Dialogue and the New Millennium*, Address Delivered to the Thirtieth General Conference of the United Nations Educational Scientific and Cultural Organisation (UNESCO), Paris, 29 October 1999, p. 2.

25   Mohammad Khatami, *Islam, Dialogue and Civil Society* (Canberra: Australian National University, 2000), p. 2.

26   Ibid., pp. 17–18.

27   For a discussion of pre- and post-Khomeini factional politics, see Mehdi Moslem, *Factional Politics in Post-Khomeini Iran* (Syracuse, NY: Syracuse University Press, 2002), chs 2–3.

28   For a detailed discussion, see Moslem, *Factional Politics in Post-Khomeini Iran*, ch. 6.

29   Christopher de Bellaigue, 'New Man in Iran', *New York Review of Books* (11 August 2005): 19–22.

30   For an evaluation of Ahmadinejad's first presidency, see Michael Axworthy, *Iran: Empire of the Mind: A History from Zoroaster to the Present Day* (London: Penguin, 2008), ch. 9.

31   Michael Slackman and Nazila Fathi, 'Leading clerics defy ayatollah on disputed Iran election', *New York Times*, 5 July 2009.

32   *BBC News*, 17 July 2009.

33   Mehran Kamrava, 'Iranian national-security debates: Factionalism and lost opportunities', *Middle East Policy* 14/2 (2007): 84–100.

34   Jenny Percival, 'Former vice president of Iran sentenced over election protests', *Guardian*, 22 November 2009.

35·   *BBC News*, 7 August 2009.

36   Jamsheed K. Choksy, 'Is this really the end for Ahmadinejad?', *Foreign Policy* (26 November 2010).

37   For a discussion of the dispute between the various conservative branches, see Geneive Abdo, 'Iran's standoff: Khamenei vs Ahmadinejad', *Al Jazeera English*, 12 May 2011.

38   William Yong, 'Iranian leader asserts power over president', *New York Times*, 23 April 2011; Arash Aramesh, 'An angry Ahmadinejad absent from cabinet meetings in sign of protest', *insideIRAN.org*, 27 April 2011; Robert F. Worth, 'Iran's power struggle goes beyond personalities to future of the presidency itself', *New York Times*, 26 October 2011.

39   Hooshang Amirahmadi and Shahir Shahidsaless, 'The ninth Iranian parliamentary elections', The American Iranian Council, 13 February 2012.

40   Ramin Jahanbegloo, 'The two sovereignties and the legitimacy crisis in Iran', *Constellations* 17/1 (2010): 28.

41   Alan Cowell, 'Hard-liners ruling Iran gain ally in key post', *New York Times*, 8 March 2011.

42   *BBC News*, 23 May 2013.

43   Shireen T. Hunter, *Iran After Khomeini* (New York: Praeger, 1992), p. 163.

44   Ali Alfoneh, 'The revolutionary guards' role in Iranian politics', *Middle East Quarterly* 15/4 (2008): 3–14.

45   Amin Tarzi, 'Iran's internal dynamics', *MES Insights* 2/5 (November 2011).

46   For more on the IRG, see Jerrold D. Green, Frederic Wehrey and Charles Wolf Jr, *Understanding Iran* (Santa Monica, CA: RAND Corporation, 2009), pp. 2–15.

47   For a detailed discussion, see Sanja Kelly and Sarah Cook (eds), *Freedom on the Net 2011: A Global Assessment of Internet and Digital Media* (New York: Freedom House, 2011); Babak Dehghanpisheh, 'Iran's creeping corruption', *Newsweek*, 24 November 2009.

48   *Transparency International*, www.transparency.org/country#IRN (accessed 16 July 2013).

49   Ali M. Ansari, 'Iran under Ahmadinejad: The politics of confrontation', *Adelphi Papers*, No. 393 (London: International Institute for Strategic Studies, 2007), p. 81.

50   Robert F. Worth, 'Economy dominates Iran's presidential race', *New York Times*, 10 June 2009; *Index Mundi*, www.indexmundi.com/iran/gdp_real_growth_rate. html (accessed 16 July 2013).

51   See Hossein Askari, 'Iran's slide to the bottom', *Asia Times Online*, 15 September 2010, www.atimes.com/atimes/Middle_East/LI15Ak01.html (accessed 16 July 2013); and World Bank, 'Iran Country Brief' (Washington, DC: World Bank, 2010), siteresources.worldbank.org/INTIRAN/Resources/Iran_Web_brief.pdf (accessed 17 July 2013).

52 Jahangir Amuzegar, *Iran's Economy in Turmoil*, Carnegie Endowment for International Peace, March 2010, carnegieendowment.org/publications/ ?fa=view&id=40354 (accessed 10 January 2013).

53 For a discussion of Iran's dependence on oil and its political ramifications, see Massoud Karshenas and Hassan Hakimian, 'Managing oil resources and economic diversification in Iran', in Homa Katouzian et al. (eds), *Iran in the 21st Century* (Abingdon: Routledge, 2008); Elliot Hen-Tov, 'Understanding Iran's new authoritarianism', *Washington Quarterly* 30/1 (2006-07): 163-79.

54 Amuzegar, *Iran's Economy in Turmoil*.

55 Frances Harrison, 'Huge cost of Iranian brain drain', *BBC News*, 8 January 2007.

56 Farnaz Fassihi, 'Iran's economy feels sting of sanctions', *Wall Street Journal*, 12 October 2010. A household of four usually receives US$4,000 in annual fuel subsidies.

57 'Economic jihad: Iran's bold economic reform', *Economist*, 23 June 2011. For an in-depth discussion of the subsidy reform, see Dominique Guillaume, Roman Zytek and Mohammad Reza Farzin, *Iran: The Chronicles of the Subsidy Reform*, Working Paper WP/11/167 (International Monetary Fund, July 2011).

58 Julia Payne and Meeyoung Cho, 'EU sanctions strangle Iranian exports to Asia', *Reuters*, 31 October 2012.

59 Rick Gladstone and Stephen Castle, 'Global network expels as many as 30 of Iran's banks in move to isolate its economy', *New York Times*, 15 March 2012.

60 Heidi Moore, 'Sanctions are pushing Iran towards nuclear talks, just not US sanctions', *Guardian*, 24 October 2012; Steve Hargreaves, 'Iraq oil surpasses Iran', *CNN Money*, 10 August 2012.

61 Thomas Erdbrink and Rick Gladstone, 'Violence and protest in Iran as currency drops value', *New York Times*, 3 October 2012.

62 Mirsepassi, *Democracy in Modern Iran*, p. 171, emphasis added.

63 Green et al., *Understanding Iran*, p. 23.

64 For more on the wealth of the clerical elite, see Paul Klebnikov, 'Millionaire mullahs', *Forbes*, 21 July 2003.

65 International Crisis Group, *US–Iranian Engagement: The View from Tehran*, Middle East Briefing No. 28, 2 June 2009.

66 Amin Saikal, 'America is making conflict more likely', *The Age*, 13 January 2007.

67 For more on Iran's position in the region, see Amin Saikal, 'Iran's new strategic entity', *Australian Journal of International Affairs* 61/3 (2007): 296-305.

68 The GCC is comprised of Bahrain, Kuwait, Oman, Qatar, Saudi Arabia and the United Arab Emirates.

69 For a discussion of Saudi oil, see Matthew R. Simmons, *Twilight in the Desert* (Hoboken, NJ: John Wiley & Sons, 2005).

70 David E. Sanger, James Glanz and Jo Becker, 'Around the world, distress over Iran', *New York Times*, 28 November 2010.

71 'Bahrain's Shiites push for rights, equality', *Associated Press*, 29 May 2009.

72 For more on Iran's nuclear capability, see Amin Saikal, 'The Iran nuclear dispute', *Australian Journal of International Affairs* 60/2 (2006): 193-99.

73 *Implementation of the NPT Safeguards Agreement and Relevant Provisions of Security Council Resolutions in the Islamic Republic of Iran*, Report by the Director General, GOV/2011/65, International Atomic Energy Agency, 8 November 2011, p. 10.

74   For a recent and in-depth discussion of these issues, see David Patrikarakos, *Nuclear Iran: The Birth of an Atomic State* (London: I.B.Tauris, 2012).

75   The GCC and Egypt are unlikely to stand idly by if Iran develops a military nuclear capability. See Eric S. Edelman, Andrew F. Krepinevich and Evan Braden Montgomery, 'The dangers of a nuclear Iran: The limits of containment', *Foreign Affairs* 90/1 (2011): 66–81.

76   William J. Broad, John Markoff and David E. Sanger, 'Israeli test on worm called crucial in Iranian nuclear delay', *New York Times*, 15 January 2011.

77   'Update 2 – Cyber attack appears to target Iran-tech firms', *Reuters*, 24 September 2010.

78   See Sagar Meghani and Nasser Karimi, 'Anti-Iran computer bug had powerful backers', *Guardian*, 26 September 2010.

79   Mark Hosenball, 'Iran "neutralized" Stuxnet virus, experts say', *Reuters*, 15 February 2012.

80   'European powers skeptical over Iran–Turkey–Brazil nuke deal', *Agence France-Presse*, 17 May 2010.

81   Trita Parsi, 'The Turkey–Brazil–Iran deal: Can Washington take "yes" for an answer?', *Foreign Policy*, 17 May 2010.

82   Thomas Erdbrink and Rod Nordland, 'As chaos grows in Syria, worries grow on the sidelines', *New York Times*, 19 July 2012, www.nytimes.com/2012/07/20/world/middleeast/if-syria-collapses-iran-faces-loss-of-valued-ally.html?_r=0 (accessed 10 January 2013).

83   Dorian Jones, 'Turkey, Iran show signs of deep division over Syria', *Voice of America*, 10 August 2012.

84   'Iraq shares Iran's views on Syria', *Asia News Monitor*, 12 August 2012.

85   Farhand Morady, 'Iran ambitious for regional supremacy: The great powers, geopolitics and energy resources', *Journal of the Indian Ocean Region* 7/1 (2011): 81.

86   See M. Chansoria, 'India–Iran defence cooperation', *Indian Defence Review* 25/1 (2010): 125–58.

87   Matthew Rosenberg and Annie Lowrey, 'Iranian currency traders find a haven in Afghanistan', *New York Times*, 18 August 2012.

88   See Vali Nasr, *The Shia Revival* (New York: W. W. Norton & Company, 2006), p. 251 and ch. 5.

89   Kenneth Katzman, *Afghanistan: Post-Taliban Governance, Security, and US Policy*, Congressional Research Service, 3 May 2012, pp. 53–54.

90   Before 2007, the ISCI was known as the Supreme Council for Islamic Revolution in Iraq.

91   David Jolly, 'Iranian group seeks US shield after Iraqi raid', *New York Times*, 13 April 2011.

92   'Third Iran gas forum: September 26–27 in Tehran', *Payvand News*, 23 September 2009.

93   For more on China's complex relationship with Iran, see John W. Garver, 'Is China playing a dual game in Iran?', *Washington Quarterly* 34/1 (2011): 75–88.

94   For a discussion on Iranian military capabilities in the Strait of Hormuz, see Caitlin Talmadge, 'Closing time: Assessing the Iranian threat to the Strait of Hormuz', *International Security* 33/1 (2008): 82–117, and Anthony H. Cordesman,

'Iran, oil, and the Strait of Hormuz', Discussion Paper (Washington, DC: Center for Strategic and International Studies, 2007).

95 'White House extends olive branch as Iran president Rouhani inaugurated', *Guardian*, 5 August 2013.

Chapter 5: Iraq

1 Adeed Dawisha, *Iraq: A Political History from Independence to Occupation* (Princeton, NJ: Princeton University Press, 2009), p. 69.

2 Ibid., p. 38.

3 Peter Sluglett, *Britain in Iraq: Contriving King and Country, 1914–1932* (New York: Columbia University Press, 2007), p. 6.

4 Eric Davis, *Memories of State: Politics, History, and Collective Identity in Modern Iraq* (Berkeley: University of California Press, 2005), p. 49.

5 For more on contemporary Iraqi history, see Charles Tripp, *A History of Iraq* (Cambridge: Cambridge University Press, 2000), chs 5 and 6.

6 For a detailed discussion, see Efraim Karsh and Inari Rautsi, *Saddam Hussein: A Political Biography* (New York: Macmillan, 1991), chs 4 and 8.

7 Tripp, *A History of Iraq*, pp. 265–66.

8 The SCIRI became the Islamic Supreme Council of Iraq in 2007.

9 For more on Iran's Islamic regime, see Chapter 4 in this book.

10 For more on Shi'a repression in Iraq under Saddam, see Faleh Jabar, *The Shi'ite Movement in Iraq* (London: Saqi Books, 2004), pp. 159–276.

11 For an analysis of the Kurdish civil war, see Michael M. Gunter, *The Kurdish Predicament in Iraq* (New York: St Martin's Press, 1999), ch. 4.

12 For more on the neoconservative post-11 September 2001 perspective, see Stefan A. Halper and Jonathan Clarke, *America Alone: The Neo-Conservatives and the Global Order* (Cambridge: Cambridge University Press, 2005), ch. 1.

13 Until 2011, the OIC was known as the Organisation of the Islamic Conference.

14 'Islamic nations totally reject Iraq war', *Al Jazeera*, 20 March 2003.

15 See 'State of the Union Address', speech by President George W. Bush, Congress, Washington, DC, 29 January 2002, www.johnstonsarchive.net/policy/bushstun2002.html (accessed 10 January 2013).

16 See Amin Saikal, 'Struggle for the global soul: Afghanistan, Iran and the "war" on terror', *The World Today* 60/8–9 (2004): 7–10.

17 Ali A. Allawi, *The Occupation of Iraq: Winning the War, Losing the Peace* (New Haven, CT: Yale University Press, 2007), p. 106.

18 Tony Karon, 'Bush's big Iraq "to-do" list', *Time*, 27 April 2004; Steven R. Weisman and David E. Sanger, 'Bush supports replacement for Iraqi governing council', *The Tech*, 16 April 2004.

19 For a reflection on the 1991 uprising, see Peter W. Galbraith, 'The ghosts of 1991', *Washington Post*, 12 April 2003.

20 James Glanz and Andrew W. Lehren, 'Use of contractors added to war's chaos in Iraq', *New York Times*, 23 October 2010.

21 'Documented civilian deaths from violence', *Iraq Body Count*, www.iraqbodycount.org/database/ (accessed 10 January 2013).

22   Roel Meijer, 'Sunni factions and the "political process"', in Marcus E. Bouillon et al. (eds), *Iraq: Preventing a New Generation of Conflict* (Boulder, CO: Lynne Rienner, 2007), pp. 89–108.

23   See Brookings Institution, *Iraq Index: Tracking Variables of Reconstruction & Security in Post-Saddam Iraq*, Saban Center for Middle East Policy, 30 September 2010, p. 3, www.brookings.edu/saban/iraq-index.aspx (accessed 10 January 2013); 'Documented civilian deaths from violence'.

24   Steven L. Myers, 'Accords pave way for re-election of Iraq premier', *New York Times*, 1 October 2010.

25   For more details, see Chapter 4 in this book, and Amin Saikal, 'The Iran nuclear dispute', *Australian Journal of International Affairs* 60/2 (2006): 193–99.

26   Steven Simon, 'The price of the surge: How US strategy is hastening Iraq's demise', *Foreign Affairs* 87/3 (2008): 57–76.

27   International Crisis Group, *Loose Ends: Iraq's Security Forces Between US Drawdown and Withdrawal*, Middle East Report No. 99, 26 October 2010, p. 28.

28   See Martin Chulov, 'Sons of Iraq turned the tide for the US: Now they pay the price', *Guardian*, 13 May 2010; Brookings Institution: *Iraq Index*, p. 9.

29   ICG, *Loose Ends*, p. 4.

30   See UNAMI's mandate at United Nations Security Council, *Resolution 1770 (2007)*, S/RES/1770, 10 August 2007.

31   Sam Marsden, 'Efforts to rebuild Iraq police service "under-funded"', *Independent*, 29 June 2010.

32   For these projects, see James Glanz, 'Major problems found in Iraqi rebuilding effort', *New York Times*, 29 April 2007.

33   'Audit: US lost track of US$9 billion in Iraq funds', *CNN Online*, 30 January 2005.

34   For more on divisions within the intelligence branches, see ICG, *Loose Ends*, pp. 8–12.

35   Ibid., p. 35.

36   Ibid., p. 21.

37   World Bank, 'Iraq Country Brief', September 2010, go.worldbank. org/45E7BO8KQ0 (accessed 10 January 2013).

38   Christopher M. Blanchard et al., *Iraq: Regional Perspectives and US Policy*, Congressional Research Service, 6 October 2009, p. 22.

39   See Juliet Kerr, *Party Oppressions of Civil Society in the 'New' Iraq*, Discussion Papers, DP45 (London: Centre for the Study of Global Governance, London School of Economics and Political Science, 2009).

40   See Kerr, *Party Oppressions of Civil Society in the 'New' Iraq*.

41   Samah Samad, 'Iraq's dwindling NGO sector', *Environment News Service*, 9 September 2010, www.ens-newswire.com/ens/sep2010/2010-09-09-01.html (accessed 10 January 2013).

42   See Michael Allen, 'Iraq's NGO law: Rare victory for Arab civil society', *Democracy Digest*, 26 January 2010, www.demdigest.net/blog/regions/mena/iraqs-ngo-law-rare-victory-for-arab-civil-society.html.

43   International Crisis Group, *Shiite Politics in Iraq: The Role of the Supreme Council*, Middle East Report No. 70, 15 November 2007, pp. 17–18.

44   Michael Gunter, 'Kurdish–Arab tensions and Irbil–Baghdad relations', *Terrorism Monitor* 8/12 (2010), www.jamestown.org/programs/gta/single/?tx_

ttnews[tt_news]=36197&tx_ttnews[backPid]=457&no_cache=1 [Accessed 12 January 2013].

45 Andrew Lee Butters, 'Iraq elections set, but Kurdish tensions remain', *Time*, 10 November 2009.

46 See International Crisis Group, *Iraq and the Kurds: The Brewing Battle over Kirkuk*, Middle East Report No. 56, 18 July 2006.

47 For a Western business perspective on the oil and gas industry in Iraq and its preference for investing in the Kurdistan Regional Government, see Caron Howard, 'Iraq in context: An overview of the oil and gas industry', Presentation, Doing Business in Iraq, Deloitte LLP, 26 May 2010.

48 See Anthony Shadid, 'Iraqi commission bars nearly 500 candidates', *New York Times*, 14 January 2010.

49 Agence France-Presse, 'Iraq's unity government teeters amid US pull-out', *The Australian*, 20 December 2011.

50 For more on the Shi'a religious parties and their differences, see Matthew Duss and Peter Juul, *The Fractured Shia of Iraq*, Center for American Progress, January 2009, www.americanprogress.org/issues/military/report/2009/01/28/5496/the-fractured-shia-of-iraq/ (accessed 12 January 2013).

51 See ICG, *Loose Ends*, pp. 12–13.

52 See ibid., p. 6, and Duss and Juul, *The Fractured Shia of Iraq*, p. 14.

53 ICG, *Loose Ends*, p. 8.

54 KRG President Massoud Barzani in 'Is it really coming right?', *Economist*, 27 November 2008.

55 Timothy Williams and Rod Nordland, 'Allawi victory in Iraq sets up period of uncertainty', *New York Times*, 26 March 2010.

56 See Amin Saikal, 'Iraq: elite fragmentation, Islam and democracy', in Shahram Akbarzadeh et al. (eds), *American Democracy Promotion in the Changing Middle East: From Bush to Obama* (London: Routledge, 2013), pp. 104–06.

57 See Jim Muir, 'End to Iraq's epic journey in sight?', *BBC News*, 2 October 2010; John Leland and Steven Lee Myers, 'Tentative deal in Iraq keeps Maliki in power', *New York Times*, 11 November 2010.

58 Ahmed Rasheed, 'Corruption-plagued Iraq joins oil transparency group', *Reuters*, 10 January 2010, www.reuters.com/article/idUSTRE60917C20100110 (accessed 10 January 2013); 'Corruption Index 2011 from Transparency International: Find out how countries compare', *Guardian*, 1 December 2011; and Transparency International, 'Corruption Perceptions Index 2012', December 2012.

59 See Abbas Kadhim, 'Iraq's quest for democracy amid massive corruption', Arab Reform Bulletin, Carnegie Endowment for International Peace, 3 March 2010, www.carnegieendowment.org/arb/?fa=show&article=40278 (accessed 12 January 2013).

60 See Hassan Abdul Zahra, 'Religious outrage over Iraqi MP expenses', *Middle East Online*, 6 November 2011, www.middle-east-online.com/English?id=35554 (accessed 12 January 2013); Kadhim, 'Iraq's quest for democracy'.

61 For more on corruption in the armed forces, see ICG, *Loose Ends*, pp. 32–34.

62 Michael Rubin, 'The Middle East's real bane: Corruption', *Daily Star*, 18 November 2005.

63 Kamal Said Qadir, 'Iraqi Kurdistan's downward spiral', *Middle East Quarterly* 14/3 (2007): 19.

64 See International Crisis Group, *Where is Iraq Heading? Lessons from Basra*, Middle East Report No. 67, 25 June 2007, pp. 11–12; 'KDP to Sue Change Movement's Paper', *Rudaw*, 1 August 2010, rudaw.net/english/kurds/3070.html (accessed 12 January 2013).

65 See International Crisis Group, *Iraq's Provincial Elections: The Stakes*, Middle East Report No. 82, 27 January 2009, pp. 25–27; Duss and Juul, *The Fractured Shia of Iraq*, p. 3; Anthony Shadid, 'The political dance in Iraq's south', *Washington Post*, 19 January 2009; Gareth Stansfield and Liam Anderson, 'Kurds in Iraq: The struggle between Baghdad and Erbil', *Middle East Policy* 14/1 (2009): 134.

66 Walter Pincus, 'US targets reform of Iraq's civil service', *Washington Post*, 5 October 2010.

67 Phil Williams, *Criminals, Militias, and Insurgents: Organized Crime in Iraq* (Carlisle, PA: Strategic Studies Institute, 2009), p. 65.

68 Kadhim, 'Iraq's quest for democracy'.

69 Johnny West, *Iraq's Last Window: Diffusing the Risks of a Petro-State*, Working Paper 266 (Washington, DC: Center for Global Development, 2011), p. 8.

70 World Bank, *Iraq: First Programmatic Fiscal Sustainability Development Policy Loan Program*, Report No. 51528 (Washington, DC: World Bank, 2010), p. 22.

71 Hassan Hafidh, 'A shaky advance led by oil money', *Wall Street Journal*, 27 August 2010; 'Iraq: The awakening of an economic giant', *Financial Times*, 15 September 2010.

72 World Bank, 'Iraq country brief'.

73 United Nations Security Council, *Resolution 1483 (2003)*, S/RES/1483, 22 May 2003.

74 West, *Iraq's Last Window*, p. 12.

75 International Advisory and Monitoring Board of the Development Fund for Iraq, Press Release, 30 June 2011, www.iraq-businessnews.com/tag/iamb/ (accessed 10 January 2013).

76 For a discussion of the resource curse, see Jeffrey Sachs and Andrew Warner, *Natural Resource Abundance and Economic Growth*, Working Paper (Cambridge, MA: Center for International Development and Harvard Institute for International Development, Harvard University, 1997).

77 See, for instance, Nancy Birdsall and Arvind Subramanian, 'Saving Iraq from its oil', *Foreign Affairs* 83/4 (2004): 77–89.

78 For more on the ISCI and the Badr Brigade, see International Crisis Group, *Shiite Politics in Iraq*.

79 See International Crisis Group, *Iraq's Civil War, The Sadrists and the Surge*, Middle East Report No. 72, 7 February 2008, pp. 4–6.

80 See, for instance, the 15th and 16th Brigades, which are almost entirely composed of Kurds.

81 Abdel Salam Sidahmed, 'Islamism, nationalism, and sectarianism', in Marcus E. Bouillon et al. (eds), *Iraq: Preventing a New Generation of Conflict* (Boulder, CO: Lynne Rienner, 2007), pp. 71–88, at pp. 80–83.

82 For more on al-Qaeda's goals and objectives, see Karen J. Greenberg (ed.), *Al Qaeda Now: Understanding Today's Terrorists* (Cambridge: Cambridge University Press, 2005).

83   Matthew Weaver, 'Iraqi army not ready to take over until 2020, says country's top general', *Guardian*, 12 August 2010.

84   See ICG, *Iraq's Uncertain Future*, pp. 9–10.

85   See 'Iraqi PM Maliki seeks Iran's help in reconstruction', *BBC News*, 18 October 2010.

86   For more on Syrian relations with al-Maliki, see Sami Moubayed, 'Syrian–Iraqi relations start to thaw', *Asia Times Online*, 21 September 2010, www.atimes.com/atimes/Middle_East/LI21Ak02.html (accessed on 10 January 2013).

87   Adrian Blomfield, 'Syria: Fall of Bashar Al-Assad will bring war to Middle East, warns Iraq', *Telegraph*, 13 December 2011.

88   See International Crisis Group, *Turkey and Iraq's Kurds: Conflict or Cooperation?* Middle East Report No. 81, 13 November 2008.

89   See 'Saudi King offers talks to break Iraq deadlock', *BBC News*, 30 October 2010; Haider Ibrahim, 'SLC rejects Saudi invitation, Iraqiya accuses it of complying with Iran pressures', *AKnews*, 31 October 2010, www.aknews.com/en/aknews/4/192220/ (accessed 12 January 2013).

90   Zahraa Alkhalisi and Caroline Alexander, 'Iraq to push UN for end to payment of war reparations to Kuwait', *Bloomberg Businessweek*, 29 April 2010, www.businessweek.com/news/2010-04-29/iraq-to-push-un-for-end-to-payment-of-war-reparations-to-kuwait.html (accessed 12 January 2013).

91   Abolhassan Bani-Sadr, 'An Islamic solution', *New York Times*, 9 October 2009.

Chapter 6: Conclusion

1   George W. Bush, 'Address to the nation 7 October 2001', http://www.press.uchicago.edu/Misc/Chicago/481921texts.html (accessed 31 December 2012).

2   Bernhard Zand, 'Iraq is neither sovereign, stable nor self-reliant', *Spiegel Online International*, 27 March 2012, http://www.spiegel.de/international/world/iraq-hosts-arab-league-summit-a-823838.html (accessed 31 December 2012).

3   Arthur Bright, 'Afghanistan: 5 areas of concern after the US leaves', *Christian Science Monitor*, 6 April 2012, http://www.csmonitor.com/World/Asia-South-Central/2012/0406/Afghanistan-5-areas-of-concern-after-the-US-leaves/Security-and-the-Taliban (accessed 31 December 2012).

4   'Obama: '"Victory" not right word for Afghanistan', *Associated Press*, 23 July 2009.

BIBLIOGRAPHY

Government and Official Publications

Asian Development Bank, *Islamic Republic of Pakistan: Country Environment Analysis*, December 2008.

Khatami, Mohammad, *Dialogue and the New Millennium*, Address Delivered to the Thirtieth General Conference of the United Nations Educational Scientific and Cultural Organisation (UNESCO), Paris, 29 October 1999.

Organization for Economic Co-Operation and Development, *Development Co-Operation Report*, Development Assistance Committee, 2010.

Pakistan Government, *Accelerating Economic Growth and Reducing Poverty: The Road Ahead (Poverty Reduction Strategy Paper)*, PRSP Secretariat and Pakistan Ministry of Finance, Islamabad, 2003.

United Nations Development Programme, *Pakistan National Report: Social Audit of Local Governance and Delivery of Public Services*, UNDP Pakistan, Islamabad, April 2010.

United Nations Office for the Coordination of Humanitarian Affairs, *Afghanistan Humanitarian Action Plan 2010: Mid Year Review*, 14 July 2010.

United Nations Office on Drugs and Crime, *Afghanistan: Opium Poppy Free Roadmap and Provincial Profiles*, work-in-progress document, June 2008.

——, *Corruption in Afghanistan: Bribery as Reported by the Victims*, UNODC Statistics and Surveys Section, January 2010.

——, *The Global Afghan Opium Trade: A Threat Assessment*, July 2011.

——, *Afghanistan Opium Risk Assessment 2013*, April 2013.

United Nations Security Council, *Resolution 1770 (2007)*, S/RES/1770, 10 August 2007.

World Bank, *Iraq: First Programmatic Fiscal Sustainability Development Policy Loan Program*, Report No. 51528, World Bank, Washington, DC, 12 February 2010.

——, *Afghanistan Economic Update*, Policy and Poverty Team – South Asia Region, April 2010.

——, *Afghanistan Public Expenditure Review 2010: Second Generation of Public Expenditure Reforms*, Report No. 53892-AF, in consultation with the UK Department for International Development, April 2010.

Reports

Akram, Muhammad, *Health Care Services and Government Spending in Pakistan*, Pakistan Institute of Development Economics, Islamabad, 2007.

Amnesty International, *Afghanistan: Women's Human Rights Defenders Continue to Struggle for Women's Rights*, 7 March 2008, http://195.234.175.160/en/library/asset/ASA11/003/2008/en/05e378a0-ec98-11dc-9a27-819d7db3035f/asa110032008eng.html (accessed 7 January 2013).

Amuzegar, Jahangir, *Iran's Economy in Turmoil*, Carnegie Endowment for International Peace, March 2010.

Ball, Nicole, and Yoichiro Ishihara, *Afghanistan – Security Sector: Afghanistan Public Expenditure Review 2010 Working Paper* (Washington, DC: World Bank, 2010).

Blanchard, Christopher M., Kenneth Katzman, Carol Migdalovitz and Jeremy M. Sharp, *Iraq: Regional Perspectives and U.S. Policy*, Congressional Research Service, 6 October 2009.

Brookings Institution, *Iraq Index: Tracking Variables of Reconstruction & Security in Post-Saddam Iraq*, Saban Center for Middle East Policy, 30 September 2010.

Committee on Foreign Relations, *Evaluating U.S. Foreign Assistance to Afghanistan*, United States Senate, 8 June 2011.

Cordesman, Anthony H., 'Iran, Oil, and the Strait of Hormuz', Discussion Paper, Center for Strategic and International Studies, 26 March 2007.

Development Cooperation Report, Islamic Republic of Afghanistan, 2010.

Duss, Matthew, and Peter Juul, *The Fractured Shia of Iraq*, Center for American Progress, January 2009.

Guillaume, Dominique, Roman Zytek and Mohammad Reza Farzin, *Iran: The Chronicles of the Subsidy Reform*, Working Paper, WP/11/167, International Monetary Fund, July 2011.

Harrison, Selig S., *Pakistan: The State of the Union*, Special Report. Center for International Policy, Washington, DC, 2009.

Heller, Nathaniel, Sarah Fort and Marina Walker Guevara, *Pakistan's $4.2 Billion 'Blank Check' for U.S. Military Aid*, Center for Public Integrity, 27 March 2007.

Implementation of the NPT Safeguards Agreement and Relevant Provisions of Security Council Resolutions in the Islamic Republic of Iran. Report by the Director General, GOV/2011/65, International Atomic Energy Agency, 8 November 2011.

International Advisory and Monitoring Board of the Development Fund for Iraq, Press Release, 30 June 2011, http://www.iraq-businessnews.com/tag/iamb/ (accessed 17 December 2012).

International Crisis Group, *Iran: The Struggle for the Revolution's Soul*, Middle East Report No. 5, 5 August 2002.

——, *Afghanistan: The Constitutional Loya Jirga*, Asia Briefing No. 29, 12 December 2003.

——, *Iraq and the Kurds: The Brewing Battle over Kirkuk*, Middle East Report No. 56, 18 July 2006.

——, *Where is Iraq Heading? Lessons from Basra*, Middle East Report No. 67, 25 June 2007.

——, *Shiite Politics in Iraq: The Role of the Supreme Council*, Middle East Report No. 70, 15 November 2007.

——, *Iraq's Civil War, the Sadrists and the Surge*, Middle East Report No. 72, 7 February 2008.

——, *Turkey and Iraq's Kurds: Conflict or Cooperation?* Middle East Report No. 81, 13 November 2008.

——, *Iraq's Provincial Elections: The Stakes*, Middle East Report No. 82, 27 January 2009.

——, *US–Iranian Engagement: The View from Tehran*, Middle East Briefing No. 28, 2 June 2009.

——, *Iraq's Uncertain Future: Elections and Beyond.* Middle East Report No. 94, International Crisis Group, 25 February 2010.

——, *Loose Ends: Iraq's Security Forces Between US Drawdown and Withdrawal*, Middle East Report No. 99, 26 October 2010.

——, *Afghanistan's Elections Stalemate*, Asia Briefing No. 117, 23 February 2011.

——, *Aid and Conflict in Afghanistan*, Asia Report No. 210, 4 August 2011.

International Institute for Strategic Studies, 'Northern Route Eases Supplies to US Forces in Afghanistan', *Strategic Comments* 16 (August 2010), http://www.iiss.org/publications/strategic-comments/past-issues/volume-16-2010/august/northern-route-eases-supplies-to-us-forces-in-afghanistan/ (accessed 9 January 2013).

Katzman, Kenneth, *Afghanistan: Post-Taliban Governance, Security, and U.S. Policy*, Congressional Research Service, 3 May 2012.

Kerr, Juliet, *Party Oppressions of Civil Society in the 'New' Iraq*, Discussion Papers, DP45, Centre for the Study of Global Governance, London School of Economics and Political Science, 2009.

Kronstadt, K. Alan, *Direct Overt U.S. Aid and Military Reimbursements to Pakistan, FY2002–FY2012*, Congressional Research Service, 6 May 2011.

Margesson, Rhoda, *United Nations Assistance Mission in Afghanistan: Background and Policy Issues*, Congressional Research Service, 14 December 2009.

Martin, Paul Jonathan, *Pakistan Strategic Country Environmental Assessment*, World Bank, 3 September 2007.

OxResearch Daily Brief Service, 'Pakistan: Violence Stalks Renamed Khyber-Pakhtunkhwa', Country Report, Oxford Analytica, 27 April 2010.

Policy Research Group, *Future Uncertain for Zardari, Bright for Gilani*, 2 February 2010.

Price, Gareth, *After Osama*, Chatham House, London, June 2011.

Rubin, Barnett R., and Jake Sherman, *Counter-Narcotics to Stabilise Afghanistan: The False Promise of Crop Eradication*, Center on International Cooperation, New York University, February 2008.

Sachs, Jeffrey, and Andrew Warner, *Natural Resource Abundance and Economic Growth*, Working Paper, Center for International Development and Harvard Institute for International Development, Harvard University, November 1997.

Schwartz, Moshe, *Department of Defense Contractors in Iraq and Afghanistan: Background and Analysis*, Congressional Research Service, 2 July 2010.

Suzuki, Hitoshi, *Preliminary Discussions on the Urbanization of Rural Areas in Modern Iran*, Discussion Paper No. 284, Chiba Institute of Developing Economies, March 2011.

Tarnoff, Curt, *Afghanistan: U.S. Foreign Assistance*, Congressional Research Service, 12 August 2010.

Waldman, Matt, *The Sun in the Sky: The Relationship Between Pakistan's ISI and Afghan Insurgents*, Discussion Paper 18, Crisis States Research Centre, London School of Economics, June 2010.

West, Johnny, *Iraq's Last Window: Diffusing the Risks of a Petro-State*, Working Paper 266, Center for Global Development, September 2011.

Articles and Book Chapters

Albright, David, and Corey Hinderstein, 'Unraveling the A. Q. Khan and Future Proliferation Networks', *Washington Quarterly* 28/2 (2005): 109–28.

Alfoneh, Ali, 'The Revolutionary Guards' Role in Iranian Politics', *Middle East Quarterly* 15/4 (Fall 2008): 3–14.

Ali, Syed Mubashir, and Faisal Bari, 'At the Millennium: Macro Economic Performance and Prospects', in Charles H. Kennedy and Craig Baxter (eds), *Pakistan 2000* (New York: Lexington Books, 2000), pp. 25–44.

Allen, Michael, 'Iraq's NGO Law: Rare Victory for Arab Civil Society', *Democracy Digest*, 26 January 2010.

Amirahmadi, Hooshang, and Shahir Shahidsaless, 'The Ninth Iranian Parliamentary Elections', *American Iranian Council*, 13 February 2012.

Ansari, Ali M., 'Chapter 1: The Rafsanjani and Khatami Presidencies', *Adelphi Papers* 47/393, International Institute for Strategic Studies (2007), pp. 11–22.

——, 'Iran Under Ahmadinejad: The Politics of Confrontation', *Adelphi Papers* 47/393, International Institute for Strategic Studies (2007).

Atran, Scott, 'A Question of Honour: Why the Taliban Fight and What to Do about It', *Asian Journal of Social Sciences* 38 (2010): 343–63.

Barfield, Thomas, and Neamatollah Nojumi, 'Bringing More Effective Governance to Afghanistan: 10 Pathways to Stability', *Middle East Policy* 17/4 (Winter 2010): 40–52.

Baxter, Craig, 'Historical Setting', in Peter R. Blood (ed.), *Pakistan: A Country Study* (Washington, DC: Federal Research Division, 1995), pp. 1–74.

Behuria, Ashok K., 'Sunni–Shia Relations in Pakistan: The Widening Divide', *Strategic Analysis* 28/1, (2004): 157–76.

Bellaigue, Christopher de, 'New Man in Iran', *New York Review of Books*, 11 August 2005.

Birdsall, Nancy, and Arvind Subramanian, 'Saving Iraq from Its Oil', *Foreign Affairs* 83/4 (July/August 2004): 77–89.

Chansoria, M., 'India–Iran Defence Cooperation', *Indian Defence Review* 25/1 (2010).

Choksy, Jamsheed K., 'Is This Really The End for Ahmadinejad?', *Foreign Policy*, 26 November 2010.

Clarke, Ryan, 'Lashkar-e-Taiba: Roots, Logistics, Partnerships, and the Fallacy of Subservient Proxies', *Terrorism and Political Violence* 22/3 (June 2010): 394–417.

Edelman, Eric S., Andrew F. Krepinevich and Evan Braden Montgomery, 'The Dangers of a Nuclear Iran: The Limits of Containment', *Foreign Affairs* 90/1 (January/February 2011): 66–81.

Eggleston, Beth, 'The Afghan People: Forgotten and Frustrated', in Amin Saikal (ed.), *The Afghanistan Conflict and Australia's Role* (Melbourne: Melbourne University Press, 2011), 115–29.

Fair, C. Christine, 'Why the Pakistan Army is Here to Stay: Prospects for Civilian Governance', *International Affairs* 87/3 (2011): 571–88.

Felbab-Brown, Vanda, 'Peacekeepers among Poppies: Afghanistan, Illicit Economies and Intervention', *International Peacekeeping* 16/1 (2009): 100–14.

Garver, John W., 'Is China Playing a Dual Game in Iran?', *Washington Quarterly* 34/1 (Winter 2011): 75–88.

Ghufran, Nasreen, 'Pushtun Ethnonationalism and the Taliban Insurgency in the North West Frontier Province of Pakistan', *Asian Survey* 49/6 (2009): 1092–114.

Ginty, Roger Mac, 'Warlords and the Liberal Peace: State-Building in Afghanistan', *Conflict, Security & Development* 10/4 (September 2010): 577–98.

Gunter, Michael, 'Kurdish–Arab Tensions and Irbil–Baghdad Relations', *Terrorism Monitor* 8/12 (2010), www.jamestown.org/programs/gta/single/?tx_ttnews[tt_news] =36197&tx_ttnews[backPid]=457&no_cache=1 (accessed 17 December 2012).

Haussegger, Virginia, 'Gender and Social Justice in Afghanistan', in Amin Saikal (ed.), *The Afghanistan Conflict and Australia's Role* (Melbourne: Melbourne University Press, 2011), pp. 129–54.

Hen-Tov, Elliot, 'Understanding Iran's New Authoritarianism', *Washington Quarterly* 30/1 (Winter 2006–07): 163–79.

Herb, Michael, 'No Representation without Taxation? Rents, Development, and Democracy', *Comparative Politics* 37/3 (April 2005): 297–316.

Howell, Jude, 'The Global War on Terror, Development and Civil Society', *Journal of International Development* 18/1 (January 2006): 121–35.

Hunter, Shireen T., 'Islamic Reformist Discourse in Iran', in Shireen T. Hunter (ed.), *Reformist Voices of Islam* (New York: M.E. Sharpe, 2009), pp. 33–97.

Islam, Nasir, '*Sifarish*, Sycophants, Power and Collectivism: Administrative Culture in Pakistan', *International Review of Administrative Sciences* 70/2 (2004): 311–30.

Jahanbegloo, Ramin, 'The Two Sovereignties and the Legitimacy Crisis in Iran', *Constellations* 17/1 (2010): 22–30.

Janata, Alfred, 'Afghanistan: The Ethnic Dimension', in Ewan W. Anderson and Nancy Hatch Dupree (eds), *The Cultural Basis of Afghan Nationalism* (London: Pinter Publishers, 1990), pp. 60–70.

Jones, Seth G., 'Averting Failure in Afghanistan', *Survival* 48/1 (Spring 2006): 111–27.

Kadhim, Abbas, 'Iraq's Quest for Democracy amid Massive Corruption', Arab Reform Bulletin, Carnegie Endowment for International Peace, 3 March 2010, http://www.carnegieendowment.org/arb/?fa=show&article=40278 (accessed 11 January 2013).

Kamrava, Mehran, 'Iranian National-Security Debates: Factionalism and Lost Opportunities', *Middle East Policy* 14/2 (Summer 2007): 84–100.

Karshenas, Massoud, and Hassan Hakimian, 'Managing Oil Resources and Economic Diversification in Iran', in Homa Katouzian and Hossein Shahidi (eds), *Iran in the 21st Century* (Abingdon: Routledge, 2008), pp. 1–12.

Khan, Mohammad Mohabbat, 'Resistance to Administrative Reform in South Asian Civil Bureaucracies', in Ali Farazmand (ed.), *Administrative Reforms in Developing Nations* (Westport, CT: Greenwood, 2002), pp. 73–88.

Mackenzie, Richard, 'The United States and the Taliban', in William Maley (ed.), *Fundamentalism Reborn?: Afghanistan and the Taliban* (London: Hurst and Co., 2001), pp. 90–103.

Maley, William, 'Afghanistan in 2010', *Asian Survey* 51/1 (January/February 2011): 85–96.

——, 'Reconstruction: A Critical Assessment', in Amin Saikal (ed.), *The Afghanistan Conflict and Australia's Role* (Melbourne: Melbourne University Press, 2011), pp. 77–98.

Meijer, Roel, 'Sunni Factions and the "Political Process"', in Marcus E. Bouillon, David E. Malone and Ben Rowswell (eds), *Iraq: Preventing a New Generation of Conflict* (Boulder, CO: Lynne Rienner, 2007), pp. 89–108.

Morady, Farhand, 'Iran Ambitious for Regional Supremacy: The Great Powers, Geopolitics and Energy Resources', *Journal of the Indian Ocean Region* 7/1 (2011): 75–94.

Narang, Vipin, 'Posturing for Peace? Pakistan's Nuclear Postures and South Asian Stability', *International Security* 34/3 (Winter 2009/10): 38–78.

Nasr, Vali, 'Military Rule, Islamism and Democracy in Pakistan', *Middle East Journal* 58/2 (Spring 2004): 195–209.

Nixon, Hamish, and Richard Ponzio, 'Building Democracy in Afghanistan: The Statebuilding Agenda and International Engagement', *International Peacekeeping* 14/1 (February 2007): 26–40.

Pant, Harsh V., 'India in Afghanistan: A Test Case for a Rising Power', *Contemporary South Asia* 18/2 (June 2010): 133–53.

Pipes, Daniel, and Laurie Mylroia, 'Back Iraq: It's Time for a U.S. "Tilt"', *New Republic*, 27 April 1987.

Qadir, Kamal Said, 'Iraqi Kurdistan's Downward Spiral', *Middle East Quarterly* 14/3 (Summer 2007): 19–26.

Reynolds, Andrew, 'The Curious Case of Afghanistan', *Journal of Democracy* 17/2 (2006): 104–17.

Rizvi, Hasan Askari, 'Democracy in Pakistan', *A Future for Democracy (Panorama: Insights into Asian and European Affairs)*, Occasional Papers (Singapore: Konrad-Adenauer-Stiftung, 2011), pp. 117–36.

Roy, Meena Singh, 'Role of the Shanghai Cooperation Organisation in Afghanistan: Scope and Limitations', *Strategic Analysis* 34/4 (July 2010): 545–61.

Rubin, Barnett R., 'Crafting a Constitution for Afghanistan', *Journal of Democracy* 15/3 (2004): 5–19.

Rubin, Barnett R., and Ahmed Rashid, 'From the Great Game to Grand Bargain', *Foreign Affairs* 87/6 (November/December 2008): 30–44.

Saikal, Amin, 'Afghanistan's Ethnic Conflict', *Survival* 40/2 (Summer 1998): 115–26.

——, 'The Role of Outside Actors in Afghanistan', *Middle East Policy* 7/4 (October 2000): 50–57.

——, 'Democracy and Peace in Iran and Iraq', in Amin Saikal and Albrecht Schnabel (eds), *Democratization in the Middle East: Experiences, Struggles, Challenges* (New York: United Nations University Press, 2003), pp. 166–82.

——, 'Struggle for the Global Soul: Afghanistan, Iran and the "War" on Terror', *World Today* 60/8–9 (August/September 2004): 7–10.

———, 'The Iran Nuclear Dispute', *Australian Journal of International Affairs* 60/2 (June 2006): 193–99.

———, 'Iran's New Strategic Entity', *Australian Journal of International Affairs* 61/3 (September 2007): 296–305.

———, 'Musharraf and Pakistan's Crisis', in Rajshree Jetly (ed.), *Pakistan in Regional and Global Politics* (New Delhi: Routledge, 2009), pp. 1–19.

———, 'The Role of Sub-National Actors in Afghanistan', in Klejda Mulaj (ed.), *Violent Non-State Actors in World Politics* (London: Hurst & Co., 2010), pp. 239–56.

———, 'Afghanistan's Attitudes Towards the Region', in Aglaya Snetkov and Aris Steven (eds), *The Regional Dimension to Security in Afghanistan: Other Sides of Afghanistan* (London: Palgrave Macmillan, 2013).

Shahrani, M. Nazif, 'State Building and Social Fragmentation in Afghanistan: A Historical Perspective', in A. Banuazizi and M. Weiner (eds), *The State, Religion, and Ethnic Politics: Afghanistan, Iran, and Pakistan* (Syracuse, NY: Syracuse University Press, 1986), pp. 23–74.

———, *Afghanistan's Alternatives for Peace, Governance and Development: Transforming Subjects to Citizens and Rulers to Civil Servants*, The Afghanistan Papers No. 2 (Waterloo, Canada: CIGI & CIPS joint publication, 2009).

Shuja, Sharif, 'Pakistan: Islam, Radicalism and the Army', *International Journal on World Peace* 24/2 (June 2007): 25–35.

Sidahmed, Abdel Salam, 'Islamism, Nationalism, and Sectarianism', in Marcus E. Bouillon, David E. Malone and Ben Rowswell (eds), *Iraq: Preventing a New Generation of Conflict* (Boulder, CO: Lynne Rienner, 2007), pp. 71–88.

Simon, Steven, 'The Price of the Surge: How U.S. Strategy Is Hastening Iraq's Demise', *Foreign Affairs* 87/3 (May/June 2008): 57–76.

Small, Andrew, 'China's Caution on Afghanistan–Pakistan', *Washington Quarterly* 33/3 (June 2010): 81–97.

Stansfield, Gareth, and Liam Anderson, 'Kurds in Iraq: The Struggle Between Baghdad and Erbil', *Middle East Policy* 14/1 (Spring 2009): 134–45.

Talmadge, Caitlin, 'Closing Time: Assessing the Iranian Threat to the Strait of Hormuz', *International Security* 33/1 (Summer 2008): 82–117.

Tarzi, Amin, 'Iran's Internal Dynamics', *MES Insights* 2/5 (November 2011).

Wilder, Andrew, 'The Politics of Civil Service Reform in Pakistan', *Journal of International Affairs* 63/1 (Fall/Winter 2009): 19–37.

Wright, Joanna, 'Poppy Purge – Afghanistan's Acting Minister of Counter-Narcotics General Khodaidad', *Jane's Intelligence Review* 20/2 (February 2008): 58.

Zaman, Muhammad Qasim, 'Sectarianism in Pakistan: The Radicalization of Shi'i and Sunni Identities', *Modern Asian Studies* 32/3 (1998): 689–716.

Ziring, Lawrence, 'From Islamic Republic to Islamic State in Pakistan', *Asian Survey* 24/9 (September 1984): 931–46.

Zissis, Carin, 'Judgment Time for Musharraf', Analysis Brief, Council on Foreign Relations, 19 March 2007.

Books

Abbas, Hassan, *Pakistan's Drift into Extremism: Allah, the Army, and America's War on Terror* (New Delhi: Pentagon Press, 2005).

Abrahamian, Ervand, *Khomeinism: Essays on the Islamic Republic* (London: I.B.Tauris, 1993).

Allawi, Ali A., *The Occupation of Iraq: Winning the War, Losing the Peace* (New Haven, CT: Yale University Press, 2007).

Axworthy, Michael, *Iran: Empire of the Mind: A History from Zoroaster to the Present Day* (London: Penguin, 2008).

Bakhash, Shaul, *The Reign of the Ayatollahs: Iran and the Islamic Revolution* (London: I.B.Tauris, 1985).

Bennett Jones, Owen, *Pakistan: Eye of the Storm* (New Haven, CT: Yale University Press, 2009).

Carothers, Thomas, *Aiding Democracy Abroad: The Learning Curve* (Washington, DC: Carnegie Endowment for International Peace, 1999).

Chatterji, Joya, *The Spoils of Partition: Bengal and India, 1947–1967* (Cambridge: Cambridge University Press, 2007).

Cohen, Stephen, *The Idea of Pakistan* (Washington, DC: Brookings Institution Press, 2004).

Crews, Robert D., and Amin Tarzi (eds), *The Taliban and the Crisis of Afghanistan* (Cambridge, MA: Harvard University Press, 2008).

Davis, Eric, *Memories of State: Politics, History, and Collective Identity in Modern Iraq* (Berkeley: University of California Press, 2005).

Dawisha, Adeed, *Iraq: A Political History from Independence to Occupation* (Princeton, NJ: Princeton University Press, 2009).

Dodge, Toby, *Inventing Iraq: The Failure of Nation-Building and a History Denied* (London: Hurst & Co., 2003).

Dupree, Louis, *Afghanistan* (Princeton, NJ: Princeton University Press, 1980).

Fair, C. Christine, *The Counterterror Coalitions: Cooperation with Pakistan and India* (Santa Monica, CA: Rand Corporation, 2004).

Farber, David, *Taken Hostage: The Iran Hostage Crisis and America's First Encounter with Radical Islam* (Princeton, NJ: Princeton University Press, 2005).

Fletcher, Arnold, *Afghanistan: Highway of Conquest* (Westport, CT: Greenwood Press, 1982).

Giustozzi, Antonio, *Empires of Mud: War and Warlords in Afghanistan* (London: Hurst & Co., 2009).

Green, Jerrold D., Frederic Wehrey and Charles Wolf, Jr, *Understanding Iran* (Santa Monica, CA: RAND Corporation, 2009).

Greenberg, Karen J. (ed.), *Al Qaeda Now: Understanding Today's Terrorists* (Cambridge: Cambridge University Press, 2005).

Gunter, Michael M., *The Kurdish Predicament in Iraq* (New York: St Martin's Press, 1999).

Halper, Stefan A., and Jonathan Clarke, *America Alone: The Neo-Conservatives and the Global Order* (Cambridge: Cambridge University Press, 2005).

Hiro, Dilip, *The Longest War: The Iran–Iraq Military Conflict* (London: Grafton, 1989).

Hunter, Shireen T., *Iran After Khomeini* (New York: Praeger, 1992).

Iqbal, Afzal, *Islamization of Pakistan* (Lahore: Vanguard Books, 1986).

Jabar, Faleh, *The Shi'ite Movement in Iraq* (London: Saqi Books, 2004).

Jaffrelot, Christophe (ed.), *A History of Pakistan and Its Origins*, trans. Gillian Beaumont (London: Anthem Press, 2004).

Johnson, Chris, and Jolyon Leslie, *Afghanistan: The Mirage of Peace* (London: Zed Books, 2008).

Kapur, Ashok, *Pakistan in Crisis* (London: Routledge, 1991).

Karsh, Efraim, *The Iran–Iraq War: 1980–1988* (Oxford: Osprey Publishing, 2002).

Karsh, Efraim, and Inari Rautsi, *Saddam Hussein: A Political Biography* (New York: Macmillan, 1991).

Khan, Yasmin, *The Great Partition: The Making of India and Pakistan* (New Haven, CT: Yale University Press, 2007).

Khatami, Mohammad, *Islam, Dialogue and Civil Society* (Canberra: Australian National University, 2000).

Khomeyni, Ruhollah, *Islamic Government* (Springfield, VA: National Technical Information Service, 1979).

———, *Islam and Revolution: Writings and Declarations.*, trans. Hamid Algar (London: KPL, 1985).

Kinzer, Stephen, *All the Shah's Men: An American Coup and the Roots of Middle East Terror* (New York: John Wiley & Sons, 2003).

Lieven, Anatol, *Pakistan: A Hard Country* (London: Penguin Books, 2011).

Luzianin, S. G., *Vostochnaya Politika Vladimira Putina* (Moscow: Vostok-Zapad, 2007).

Magnus, Ralph H., and Eden Naby, *Afghanistan: Mullah, Marx and Mujahid* (Boulder, CO: Westview Press, 2002).

Maley, William, *The Afghanistan Wars* (London: Palgrave Macmillan, 2002).

———, *Rescuing Afghanistan* (Sydney: University of New South Wales Press, 2006).

Mankoff, Jeffrey, *Russian Foreign Policy: The Return of Great Power Politics* (Lanham, MD: Rowman & Littlefield, 2009).

Mirsepassi, Ali, *Democracy in Modern Iran: Islam, Culture, and Political Change* (New York: New York University Press, 2010).

Moslem, Mehdi, *Factional Politics in Post-Khomeini Iran* (Syracuse, NY: Syracuse University Press, 2002).

Musharraf, Pervez, *In the Line of Fire* (London: Simon & Schuster, 2006).

Nasr, Vali, *The Shia Revival* (New York: W. W. Norton & Company, 2006).

Norton, Augustus Richard, *Hezbollah: A Short History* (Princeton, NJ: Princeton University Press, 2007).

Ottolenghi, Emanuele, *Under a Mushroom Cloud* (London: Profile Books, 2009).

Pahlavi, Mohammad Reza Shah, *Answer to History* (Toronto: Irwin & Co., 1980).

Patrikarakos, David, *Nuclear Iran: The Birth of an Atomic State* (London: I.B.Tauris, 2012).

Rashid, Ahmed, *Taliban, Militant Islam, Oil and Fundamentalism in Central Asia* (London: I.B.Tauris, 2000).

Rubin, Barnett R., *The Fragmentation of Afghanistan: State Formation and Collapse*, 2nd edn (New Haven, CT: Yale University Press, 2002).

Saikal, Amin, *Islam and the West: Conflict or Cooperation?* (London: Palgrave, 2003).

———, *The Rise and Fall of the Shah: Iran from Autocracy to Religious Rule*, pbk edn (Princeton, NJ: Princeton University Press, 2009).

——, *Modern Afghanistan: A History of Struggle and Survival*, 2nd edn (London: I.B.Tauris, 2012).

Sanasarian, Elizabeth, *Religious Minorities in Iran* (Cambridge: Cambridge University Press, 2000).

Schofield, Victoria, *Kashmir in Conflict* (London: I.B.Tauris, 2003).

Simmons, Matthew R., *Twilight in the Desert* (Hoboken, NJ: John Wiley & Sons, 2005).

Singh, R. S. N., *The Military Factor in Pakistan* (New Delhi: Lancer, 2008).

Sluglett, Peter, *Britain in Iraq: Contriving King and Country, 1914–1932* (New York: Columbia University Press, 2007).

Smith, Anthony D., *The Nation in History: Historiographical Debates about Ethnicity and Nationalism* (Hanover, NH: University Press of New England, 2000).

Takeyh, Ray, *Hidden Iran: Paradox and Power in the Islamic Republic* (New York: Times Books, 2006).

Tan, Tai Yong, and Gyanesh Kudaisya, *The Aftermath of the Partition in South Asia* (London: Routledge, 2000).

Tomsen, Peter, *The Wars of Afghanistan: Messianic Terrorism, Tribal Conflicts, and the Failures of Great Powers* (New York: Perseus, 2011).

Tripp, Charles, *A History of Iraq* (Cambridge: Cambridge University Press, 2000).

Umar, Badruddin, *The Emergence of Bangladesh* (Oxford: Oxford University Press, 2006).

Weaver, Mary A., *Pakistan: In the Shadow of Jihad and Afghanistan* (New York: Farrar, Straus and Giroux, 2003).

Westad, Odd Arne, *The Global Cold War* (Cambridge: Cambridge University Press, 2005).

Williams, Phil, *Criminals, Militias, and Insurgents: Organized Crime in Iraq* (Carlisle, PA: Strategic Studies Institute, 2009).

Zonis, Marvin, *The Political Elite of Iran* (Princeton, NJ: Princeton University Press, 1971).

INDEX